The

Children

Who Raised Me

Shivonne Costa

This book is designed to provide accurate and authoritative information with regard to the subject matter covered. This information is given with the understanding that neither the author
nor Mommyhood: Striving for Sanity is engaged in rendering
legal, professional advice. Since the details of your situation are
fact dependent, you should additionally seek the services of a
competent professional.

Author's Website: www.mommyhoodsfs.com

ABP
Austin Brothers Publishing
www.austinbrotherspublishing.com

Published in the United States of America
ISBN: 978-0-9983071-5-2
1. Family & Relationships / Adoption & Fostering
2. Family & Relationships / Parenting / Motherhood
3. Psychology / Mental Health

An inspirational memoir about foster care, adoption, loss, and mental illness. Join the journey as this story brings *Hope* to those in the midst of dire circumstances.

Contents

To my husband, the man who has chosen to walk this long and winding road with me—I love you more than words could ever say. He is *always* with us.

To Cameron, you are stronger than you know, and your time is *now*. Be the greatness you wish to see and never ever give up.

To Taylor, the princess to my queen—you are worthy of true love, so never settle for anything less. Be your own person, and don't be afraid to *lead*.

To Isaac, my special boy—if you ever read this, know that you have *always* been loved, *always* been wanted, and will *always* be our baby.

To Wyatt, my little miracle—you filled our hearts and restored our hope. Remember that God never lets His miracles fade, so shine brightly, baby.

INTRODUCTION

Several years ago, I realized that my love for writing had begun to mirror my love for helping others. It was then that I decided to test the waters of combining the two to create a blog—*Mommyhood: Striving for Sanity*. And trust me, in our house, sanity is a daily aspiration, and not always an easy one! Sometimes we succeed, and a lot of the times we fail. A lot of the times *I fail*. Writing has not only allowed me to experience the daily struggles of being a foster and adoptive mother, to deal with my children's mental illnesses, and to process my own emotional struggles with anxiety and panic disorder...but it has let me experience these struggles through a new lens, the lens of perspective.

As I took each day's trials and began to put them into words that could make sense of our chaos, I noticed that other parents, whether adoptive, foster, or biological, could connect with each post in some way or another. I was then able to see my life through the perspective that others saw it. And in turn, I could use our struggles for a purpose, a way to help others who were hurting. My website, www.mommyhoodsfs.com, turned into more than just a place for family and friends to read our stories. It became a haven for mothers, fathers, and guardians who feel alone in their parenting journey.

Each of us needs to know that no matter how dark things may appear, there is a light at the end of the tunnel. We are social beings that find comfort in traveling our paths with another, sharing our experiences and battles with an understanding soul.

Camaraderie. It's that special relationship that helps two strangers form a bond over something that they share, some type of common interest. And that's what I've tried to create through the site. Starting out with just a blog, we now host a resources page with books to help families through specific issues. Additionally, we have a membership program that allows me to combine my day job with my passion, taking my counseling experience and using it to assist families who are raising children with mental, emotional, and behavioral needs. I do this by sending out weekly newsletters with exclusive videos or therapeutic activities to use within the home. The membership also allows parents to e-mail me freely throughout the week with more specific questions to the struggles they or their children are facing.

Above all, the website has become a central location where I can converse with people from any part of the world who are hurting, and I can share with them the Hope that has gotten me through each challenging stage of my life's journey.

And that's exactly what I pray this book is able to do for you. But in order to show you Hope, I thought it best to share with you exactly where I've been. Because Hope only looks appealing to those who are lacking it – to those who know that the daily struggle is real!

So, in order to do this, I broke down the book into five sections— one to share some history and four to share the specifics of each of my children, written to the best of my ability with the details that were given to me. The individual sections depict a new aspect of my journey as a mother, and in turn, a new aspect of my Hope. Because each of my children has had a role in raising me as a mother. And each of them is responsible for pointing me to the Hope that I've found.

My children, through their odd behaviors and unconventional mind-sets, have put me through the fire. They've held up a mirror to my innermost self, a woman that I didn't much care for. And through their struggles, they have caused me to be a parent that I never once imagined I could be—a mother that still fails but one that continues to get back up and learn to love them new each day. They've shown me my need for Jesus on such a daily level that it's not just an option to seek Him, it's a *necessity*.

Yes, my children, as broken as they may seem, have raised me.

Here is our story.

OUR STORY

Our story...a story this big makes it difficult to find the beginning. But I suppose the best place to start is by telling you a bit of who we are. Well, who we *were*. Life and children, they change who we used to be into who we are now, that's for sure. And as for what we've been through? Well, to tell you all of that in one sitting would be too overwhelming, so allow me to break things down for you.

As with every great meal, we need an appetizer, something to whet the appetite a bit and give you an idea of what the rest of the meal will entail. After your pallet has had a chance to take in our world, we'll then move onto every new course as I tell you about each of my children more in depth, really getting to the meat of it all. Some may see this style of story-telling as spoiling the ending in a way. But I see this as a means that allows you to take in the big picture before getting into the nitty-gritty of things. It's sort of like getting a God-view of the story before having to live through the tough parts with us.

But don't forget to save room for dessert, now, because every meal consisting of bitter greens needs to end with a beautiful taste of sweetness—a little something that I like to call *Hope*.

When we are young, we dream about a world of endless possibilities. We feel invincible as we look the future square in the face, preparing to make all our dreams come true. We hope for love, a family, a home. We work hard to educate ourselves, go to college, and obtain the perfect career. We pray for good health, a long life, and minimal bumps along the way.

In a sense, when we are young, we dream about a perfect world. Yet, as we get older, most of us realize that our idealized views are often a bit too far-fetched, and our optimistic glass that was always half-full...well, it sometimes dries up completely. All the feel-good clichés taste bitter when the real world tramples across our seemingly "endless possibilities."

Because as we grow up, we realize that there are, in fact, ends. There are losses. There is grief and sadness, struggle and pain. Even so, sprinkled amidst our tears are moments of love. Family and faith piece together the torn bits of our hearts, and we are able to refill our emptied glasses once again. Even so, we know that there will be more tears, more pain, but we continue to look for the moments where the sun shines through the clouds and we can lift our faces to the warmth of the light and know that through it all, it is well.

As the saying goes, *life happens*. Life. With all its ups and its downs, it continues to go on. How we move along with it, however, is a choice that each of us must make. And as for me...I choose Hope.

As a child, I grew up in the great state of Michigan. It was a charming setting that taught its children how to burrow their way through snow tunnels in the winter and how to prevent getting carried off by mosquitoes on a warm summer's night. A place where finding a Petoskey stone was the highlight of a family vacation and taking one's driver's test in an ice storm was par for the course. The entire state drives like bats emerging from hell, despite the weather or the circumstance. Out of milk for your breakfast cereal? Families in

Michigan don't sweat the small stuff. Because we all had a mother that would be back in less than two minutes from the grocery store ten miles away, just in time for us to eat and still catch the school bus, which was going to arrive, no matter that it was 27 degrees with ten inches of sleet glazing the ground.

I lived with my parents and a brother, two and a half years my junior. We were a family that loved, fought, cried, and survived. There were times we had a little money, and then there were times when we had none. It was in those moments that my dad would let us "camp" in front of the indoor wood burner, sleeping bags placed a safe distance from its brick rim in the middle of our living room. We ate tuna noodle casserole for what seemed like three years straight. And going out to eat meant that we would get a beloved Frosty from Wendy's on the way home from church.

My childhood wasn't filled with electronics or toys galore. But I knew what it was to have a family that took hard times and turned them into family memories. I had the privilege of living with a brother that would willingly toss a maxi pad under the bathroom door and a father that would walk around with random objects hanging out of his nose, simply waiting for anyone to say something so that he could break the straight face and laugh like a child. And my mom...well, she would let my dad walk around for hours with things hanging from his nose, just to spite him.

My family taught me how to be silly to the point of ridiculous, how to love one another even in awkward, hormonal times of life, and how to pray like a warrior entering battle whenever life got a little out of control. I found happiness in small things and learned quickly just how far hard work can get a person. My dad spent long, grueling hours at General Motors each day, only to arrive home and work until dark in the yard or in the garage on our car, trying to save us every penny that he could in repairs. My mom would keep our home spotless, sing in the church choir, and help me and my brother with our nightly homework. She drove us to our jobs, music lessons, sports practices, and youth groups. She clipped coupons, made the groceries stretch, and picked up odd jobs to help supplement my dad's income.

After watching the example that my parents set for me, it was easy to apply myself in school. I earned straight A's through senior high, all the while babysitting on the weekends and working two or three other jobs, playing the piano, and being engaged in sports, band, and multiple community outreach groups. And when it came time to apply for colleges, I filled out only one application. Luckily for me, I was accepted into Grove City College in Western Pennsylvania, an Ivy League-level school. Yes, all the endless possibilities were stacking up nicely, and the odds were in my favor.

My parents also showed me that loving the Lord was more important than anything else, and that His love should spill out onto those around us. I suppose that was a large reason why I went into the field of social work—that and the fact that I was intrigued by the inner workings of my own mind.

Because, despite my relationship with God and my loving family, I faced bouts of depression and anxiety throughout my childhood. Going six hours away to college gave room to more stress and increased depressive episodes. During those moments, feeling crippled by a deep sadness that I couldn't explain, I found it hard to see any possibilities at all. Defeat was all I would know until those moments passed and life would become enjoyable once again. Yet despite my own emotional turmoil, I made wonderful friends, kept my grades up, and soaked in as much knowledge as I could during my four years away at school. And when it came time to send out my employment resumé, I was just as confident that I would find a good job as I had been four years prior when I applied to college. Except that didn't happen. I sent out over one hundred resumés to social work agencies in several states. And if I heard anything back at all, I was told that there was a hiring freeze. Who had ever heard of such a thing? Certainly not this twenty-two-year-old! I mean, how could the world stop hiring people to help other people in need? The idea was utterly preposterous. But that idea was quickly followed by another notion more terrifying than the first.

I was going to be unemployed.

Never had I felt such dread as I did in those months leading up to the end of my senior year. I watched as roommates and friends received interviews, job offers, and even starting bonuses. Yet, there I was...crocheting the world's longest scarf, waiting for someone to call me, e-mail me, or just even offer me a simple interview.

And all of a sudden, my cell phone (an old flip phone that would survive a nuclear explosion) pinged to life. The moment had come for not one, but three interviews! I attended two interviews in person and participated in the third by phone, as the agency was located in Philadelphia. Lo and behold, I was offered all three jobs.

My heart was ecstatic that I probably wouldn't find myself waiting in line at the local soup kitchen while taking in felines to live with me in my cardboard box under a bridge somewhere! However, the job in Philadelphia, my *ideal job* as an adoption social worker, needed me to start work a full month before my graduation date. (I literally cried as I turned it down.) The second job turned out to pay a whopping $8/hour, which was considered poverty level, even way back in 2004. And the third job was at a Residential Treatment Facility (RTF) in a place called Zelienople. I'd assumed the woman was joking when she told me the city's name, but she wasn't.

I had no idea what working in an RTF would be like, but since they offered me an amount that would pay rent and still allow me to eat a bit each day, I took it on the spot. Two weeks later, I had secured myself an apartment and was move-in ready upon graduation. It was surreal. There I was, employed, moving into my own apartment, and paying rent like a real, live adult! And the best part was that my job was only a half hour away from Grove City, where my boyfriend of three years still had one year of schooling left.

There I was, once again, with endless possibilities! I would lie awake at night after training for the new job, wondering about future promotions, when my boyfriend and I would get engaged, which state we would live in, and what kind of house we would buy. To say I fell asleep with a smile on my face each night is an understatement.

But then, three months later, life happened again. The boy and I broke up. I hated my new job, and I had yet to make one friend in my strange-named town. Because social workers make basically no money, and because rent in a safe location is not cheap, I found myself staying home each night to eat ramen and cry. On more than one occasion, I fell asleep with a bowl of half-eaten noodles beside me while lying on my futon couch, wadded up tissues stuck to my cheek.

Well, as we all know, life goes on whether we eat ramen or filet mignon, and it cares not if we have puffy cried-out eyes when we arrive to work the next morning. Depression visited me once or twice, and then I moved on. I decided I would make the most of my career. I mean, sure, the week before I had been peed on, punched, and had a turd thrown at me by a naked nine-year-old girl, but Hope means doing life even when nude girls throw poop. And it also means buying anything other than ramen. And *sometimes* it even means making some non-conventional friendships that otherwise wouldn't transpire.

It just so happened that one of those unexpected friendships turned out to be my future husband. Oh, not right away, that's for sure! After all, he was engaged to another girl, and I was pretty sure he was the last person on the planet that was meant for me. We had absolutely nothing in common, and he had this intimidating way about him that made me instantly start sweating in weird places. Yet he was so good with the kids at work. And he could instantly turn from stern to playful in a moment's notice. I found the man...intriguing, if nothing else.

As the years went by, my friendship with the man that made me sweat took a turn. Pat and his fiancée had broken up, and I watched as our light and witty banter slowly turned into something deeper. I began to care for him in a new way, and it was terrifying. Not only is love scary enough, but telling my parents that I'd fallen for a large Italian man with bad habits and a crass personality was completely and utterly unnerving!

Did the conversation go well? Um, no. It actually went terribly. But I knew deep down what God had put inside of me, and I knew what He had put inside of the man I loved. And there was a promise of something more that continually nudged my heart closer to the man I would eventually marry.

And marry we did. Our families were able to see that the love we shared was not going away anytime soon, and after a quick conversation of me asking Pat if we should just go ahead and tie the knot, and him responding with a heartfelt "Yeah, probably," we decided to marry on August 20, 2010.

My love life was finally coming together nicely, and at work, the promotions finally started rolling in. I steadily moved up in the company where the Hubs and I both worked until I moved on to new, more challenging positions. I became employed at a funeral home where I learned how to put my grief and loss skills into practice; I got my master's degree along the way and ended up doing in-home family therapy work with children and teens.

Treating children and teens felt...natural. Easy, even. Well, anything seemed easy after having poop flung at my face and finding myself hunkered down in a six-hour restraint! But I noticed a career theme. The clients that I was given had experienced significant loss, had been through great trauma, or had difficulty attaching to others due to life tragedies. I began to narrow my career focus toward strength-based practices and trauma-informed treatments. Despite my ease working with children, I eventually began working with adults who had severe mental health diagnoses, legal troubles, and issues of trauma and addiction. It was an intimidating and unnerving transition. So I was incredibly taken aback when I fell in love with my new clients. I fell so hard for them that my heart was heavy each night as I brought home the burdens of my work.

It was so simple to look past their flaws, knowing what they had gone through. I too had an experience of molestation by a slightly older child when I was young. And although my circumstance was quite mild in comparison to those that my clients had faced, I knew the feelings of loneliness, condemnation, shame, and poor self-worth that accompanied trauma. I could relate, on a much smaller scale, to the ones that had thought about ending their lives. It became simple to see how easy it may be to turn to drugs in order to escape horrific memories.

Thankfully, the Lord is always doing a very specific work in us. And within that specific work is where we find the ability to pull from our past experiences and exhibit compassion and grace to others who are suffering. Because Hope is sometimes recognizing that our own pain is just a taste of someone else's. And it is the only thing we have left to offer after all the skills, treatments, medications, and therapies have been tried.

I can look back now and see how loving my clients had become a healing balm to my heart. I can also see how it was preparation for my future. How through each job, each patient, each story that broke my heart, I was being shaped for another great job. And its name was Motherhood.

When I was seven years old, I was blessed with the onset of puberty. As my college roommate likes to say it, I was barely out of diapers before I had to go back into them! With puberty came a lot of pain, more so than with most. And after years of having irregular cycles that left me throwing up or passed out in agony, I was diagnosed with the trifecta– the top three leading causes of infertility: endometriosis, adenomyosis, and polycystic ovarian syndrome (PCOS).

At age eighteen, my doctor suggested having my eggs harvested. I had to go home and look it up because I had no idea what he meant. At age nineteen, the same doctor asked me if I was seeing "anyone special." At age twenty, he reminded me again that I should really harvest those eggs before it was too late. By age twenty-one, I had to have laparoscopic surgery. And by twenty-two, when I graduated from college, he told me that, at best, I would have till age twenty-five to try conceiving a child. However, as we all know, just a few months later, my boyfriend and I broke up, sending me back to square one. (I'm just gonna go ahead and throw it out there; it's kind of no wonder I've battled depression and anxiety!)

So when I married Pat at the age of twenty-eight, I was basically an old dried up hag, according to my uterus. Pat knew that there was a chance I wouldn't be able to give him children, and yet he told me that it didn't matter. We both wanted kids *desperately*, but he continually reassured me that our love was enough. I tried to remain positive, yet after a year of trying to conceive while taking ovulation pills that made me throw up daily, we were a bit weary of hoping.

Having a heart for adoption and still kicking myself for not being able to take the adoption worker job in Philadelphia all those years ago, I carefully broached the subject with my husband. At first, he was leery (a.k.a. completely resistant). We did some research and then decided that there was no way on this planet that two people working in the mental health field were ever going to be able to afford adoption!

Then, I tried another approach. *What about fostering?*

Well, if adoption got a halfhearted "We'll see," you can be sure that foster care received a loud and resounding "No!" In fact, I'm pretty sure he ran out of the room after I brought it up the first time. Sure, he had some valid points. After all, we had both worked with children who had been in and out of the foster system. Remember the naked turd-flinger? Yep. Foster child. We had seen too many children who were too hurt and possibly beyond the help we could offer. How could we bring them into our home, with our dogs, with our belongings? How could we sleep well at night if we had a fire-setter or a perpetrator?

I knew he was right. *How could I ask him to do something this big?* In the end, I decided to let the subject drop. But each month, the painful realization that we would never have children in any form set in. I had spent a lifetime being an overachiever. I had never failed a test in my entire life, but each month, I stared down at the blue line on a urine test. *Failure. You're nothing but a failure as a wife. You can't even produce a child for your husband! He says you're enough, but are you really? How long will this go on before he's had enough and leaves?*

Perhaps he heard me crying in the bathroom too many times, but it was then that my husband suggested we start the process to become foster parents. If we couldn't have our own to keep, then maybe we'd be able to bless someone else's children along the way.

However, true to form, every time I've planned something in my own life, God has kind of walked in and kicked all my game pieces, sending them sprawling into a million different directions. Why? Because He knows me and my little OCD spirit. He sees how I like to plan and take charge and work hard... and He wants to use that. But He wants to use that in HIS plan, not paying any mind to the silly little ideas I have about how life will go.

We spent the next several months jumping through hoops to become foster parents. And let me tell you, if you've never gone through this process, it's *daunting*! I was on pins and needles constantly, always feeling evaluated, questioned, interrogated even. We had to attend so many trainings and fill out so many pieces of paper that I'm pretty sure we are the cause of today's forestation problems.

And at the end of it all, once we were finally approved, we were told to *wait*. But how long do foster parents really wait, *right*? There are abused kids everywhere in need of homes! Surely the call would come quickly, especially because we asked to take older children *and* agreed to take on special needs. We were practically giving them the green light for any child...and yet we waited.

In the meantime, we continued to try to make our own baby as well. There's the old expression that once the stress is off, a woman will usually get pregnant. Well, that sure wasn't happening. And it was nearly five months since we'd been approved as foster parents, and that wasn't happening either!

And then, one afternoon in February of 2012, my phone rang. There wasn't one, but *two* children in need of a temporary home. *Oh my gosh*, two children! *Finally!* After about thirty seconds worth of information from the caseworker, she asked if we would take them. "Okay, give me five minutes to phone my husband, and I'll call you back," I told her. I quickly speed-dialed Pat and filled him in. "So, should we say yes?" I asked. My excitement and nervousness rivaling one another, I just couldn't believe that I had left for work that day a non-mother and I was going to return home a mother of two! After the go-ahead from the Hubs, I called our caseworker back and told her to bring us the kids! Except...we were too late. *Too late?* She had already called another family that "didn't need five minutes to consult with a spouse." The children were already assigned to different parents— parents who don't hesitate.

That night I cried myself to sleep.

We continued on with life, though, working, cleaning, renting movies on the weekends, and doing stuff at our church. March rolled around, and we celebrated my thirtieth birthday...and I officially became old. Probably too old to parent hurting children anyways, right? That's what I told myself to feel better and wash the birthday blues away. Then God chuckled and had our caseworker call us two weeks later with another set of siblings.

Because sometimes Hope means recognizing that God is bigger than our birthdays and our ovaries.

I was at work when my phone rang. The number for Children and Youth Services (CYS), the agency responsible for managing foster children, was flashing on the screen, and I immediately felt a rush of exhilaration. And vomit. Let's suffice it to say that the moment I had been waiting for was equal parts joyful and nauseating.

The caseworker told me that there were two children, ages four and six, a girl and a boy. Their situation was one of the most complicated our county had ever seen. There had been abuse, neglect, consistent parental drug use, and legal troubles. The two children had lived together on and off over the years but had also been split up with various other siblings, relatives, and agencies. The caseworker went on for five more minutes about the complexities of the situation, and then she asked the question, "Will you take them?" I knew better than to say no, because who knew how long we would wait until we received another call? So, I told her that we'd take them.

"Good, I'll be to your house in thirty minutes." And then she hung up the phone.

What she didn't know was that I worked thirty-five minutes from my home, that my husband was also still at work, and that our house was quite literally a *disaster*. With shaky hands, I called Pat and told him to get home as soon as possible. And then I drove like a true Michigander all the way to our house, making it there in twenty minutes. I had defied the laws of rush hour for two small strangers I'd yet to meet. Once home, we spent our remaining ten minutes frantically running from room to room, cleaning random patches of house and tossing things into closets with abandon. When the knock came on our front door, we were sweaty and disheveled. *Perfect.*

Pat and I each took a deep breath and opened the door. There stood a CYS worker, accompanied by two small, wide-eyed children. They were wearing oversized clothes, had no bags with them, and the remainder of cheeseburger was still visible on their dirty faces. I will never forget that moment for as long as I live. We all stood, silent, unsure of how to proceed. And just minutes later, the caseworker was gone, and we were alone with two strangers that were now calling our home theirs.

Looking back, I realize that no one could have prepared me for that first night with the kids. No training, no handbook, no past experience. We did what we thought we should. As their new foster parents, we showed them to their rooms, gave them baths, and found them oversized T-shirts to sleep in. Promising to buy them some better-fitting clothes the following day, we said our good nights, and then *we hid* in our bedroom, unsure of what to do next!

Now, normally Pat and I would gab about our days at work, watch one of our weekly programs on TV, and grab a snack. But our work days didn't really seem to matter *at all*, and nothing on TV would've been enough to calm me in that moment. I had so much energy that I wanted to clean the entire house, but that probably would wake kids up, right? Little did I know, these children didn't actually know how to sleep. They just couldn't do it. For months, two small people would lie in bed and sing songs, talk to themselves, or pick the paint off the walls around their beds.

I realized quickly what it was like to have a newborn, only these ones were *mobile*. And they liked to knock on our door at all times of the night and ask us questions through the vent in the wall and talk in scary little whisper voices to themselves, making the hair on my neck stand straight up. It also wasn't long before we realized that sleep was not our only concern. Not by a long shot!

Cameron, our little six-year-old boy, was prone to aggression—at school and toward his sister mainly. He was in five different kindergarten classes during that first year of schooling, and he had no idea how to make friends. So he stabbed them with pencils and got suspended.

Taylor, our little four-year-old girl, was more prone to passive aggression instead. And getting into my things... and breaking them... and then smiling at me with a creepy grin as she told me she didn't do it.

Put them both together and *watch out*...let's just say that they role-played too much of what they had been exposed to in their previous homes. We learned very quickly all that they had been privy to just by watching them play. My heart broke for our two kids in those moments, yet it was a different kind of heartbreak than that of which I'd experienced with my clients at the end of a burdensome work week. And in this case, there was no coming home to unwind and let off steam.

There was no more relaxing. *Ever*. Relaxing meant that the kids would act out even more, and since they didn't sleep, that meant no sleeping either. No sleeping and no relaxing! We knew that, obviously, that couldn't continue in such a state. So once we had a decent list of issues that needed to be addressed, we took both Cameron and Taylor to see a child psychiatrist. It was there that the doctor confirmed our biggest fear—the diagnosis that I'd been assigned to study and treat for so many clients in the previous eight years - the one that made me cry at night.

"You're both in the field... you're aware of the signs and symptoms. Otherwise, you probably wouldn't be here. So you know that both of these children have Reactive Attachment Disorder, don't you?" The doctor stared at my husband and me expectantly.

All we could do was dumbly nod our heads yes. Because we *did* know it; it was obvious all along, but we were desperately hoping for something less severe—something less problematic. Something... *fixable*.

But sometimes Hope means trusting broken things to God and letting Him determine that they are, in fact, capable of being fixed.

As we all know, the struggle is *real* when it comes to parenting, especially when you add Reactive Attachment Disorder to the mix. I decided to start a blog to shed some light on the whole RAD situation going on in our house. I diligently wrote about the ups and the downs of our daily lives—the ins and the outs of dealing with children who struggle to attach to anything and everyone. Perhaps even now, you're wondering, *What in the world is RAD anyways*? Please know that this is an area of constant study. New developments are taking place in the field of attachment and differing doctors have shared various viewpoints on this topic. So, this is just the basics of what I know to be true and how it has affected our own personal lives.

RAD stands for Reactive Attachment Disorder. What this means, in short, is that when they were babies through age three, my kids' needs were not met. They weren't held a lot, nurtured enough, they were left to cry for large amounts of time, and in my son's case, he also had failure to thrive due to not being fed or given medical care. When these things occur, parts of the brain just simply fail to develop. RAD is, in a sense, a form of brain damage, as these parts of the brain only develop during the early formative years of a child's life.

Basically, the disorder affects the way my children interact with others, the way they reason things out, how they process emotions, and the overall attachments they experience with people, things, places, etc. This type of diagnosis is seen most often in adoptive or foster children. Growing up with parents of addiction who may have been present but not actually "present," being moved from home to home via the foster system, or being removed from the home due to neglect or abuse—these are some of the environmental factors that set the stage for developmental delays, the inability to properly attach to others well, and that can lead to very serious mental illnesses, even sociopathology.

Being a psychotherapist, I had worked with children suffering with this diagnosis for several years. The families, adoptive or not, were suffering right along with the child, possibly more so in some cases! I've researched ways to help parents connect with their children, manage disturbing behaviors, and learn to express emotions appropriately.

Friends, this is a *tough* disorder. There are very few techniques found to modify behavior or help families bond, and the process is *long*. There is no "quick fix," no immediate gratification. Families spend years, even decades, working hard to attach and help their children grow into adults that are capable of contributing to society and building their own relationships.

Treatment for this particular diagnosis is extremely difficult. It usually involves therapy, medication, and consistency from caregivers over large periods of time. This is done in an attempt reroute signals in the RAD child's brain, creating new pathways where old ones never developed or are, in a sense, gray matter.

How do you teach someone to feel an emotion? How do you show someone how to create a relationship with another person? How do you help someone learn right from wrong when consequences and rewards and relationships mean nothing to them? If you don't know how to answer these questions, welcome to the life of a parent with a RAD child!

Depending on the severity of the case, it can be done.

But there will be a lot of tears, screaming, throwing your hands up, quickly pulling them back down, and throwing them back up again. There will be feelings of love. There will also be feelings of hate.

In the beginning, most days you could find me in tears as I attempted to parent these two small children. I was angry at them, I was angry at myself for being angry at them, I was angry at my husband when he got angry at them, and then I was angry at him when he *didn't* get angry and I was all alone in my anger! No one else lived with it. No one else understood the struggle. No one else could see the depth of the situation. And when I tried to explain it to them, I came off sounding like the most horrible person on the planet.

Who could be mad at two little children that came from such a bad background? It wasn't *their* fault. It wasn't their choice. Why are you so hard on them? What kind of psychotherapist can't figure out how to cure her own children? What kind of mother can't keep her kids under control?

These were the questions I faced. These were the feelings I experienced each day. I felt like I was failing them, my husband, my parents, myself, and my God. And to be honest, years later, I sometimes suffer from those same feelings. I face guilt over not being more of what they need, over my lack of consistency, over my emotional ups and downs in our bad days—our RAD days. I feel helpless when I can't find a solution. I feel overly strict when I try new and creative consequences.

But let me tell you something. When there's a breakthrough, a tiny glimmer of hope, you will find me ecstatic with joy, screaming it from the rooftops, beaming with delight.

And let me tell you something else. There are more glimmers of hope today than there were last year, more than the year before, and more than the year before that.

Has God healed my children and perfected my parenting? Not by a long shot! But what He *has* done is help us grow and learn and use more wisdom in the day to day, find more teachable moments within the chaos, manage our emotions (if even just a tad) better than before, finding emotional prosthetics to learn how to walk in this life we've been given.

Sometimes Hope means praising God when someone simply remembers to flush the toilet, because Hope is in the little things.

Shortly after the kids were diagnosed, CYS came to our house and announced that the children were going to be up for adoption. Obviously, we were freaked out of our minds. I had literally just finished hyperventilating in my bedroom after another phone call from school about Cameron, and I'd just finished cleaning up a mess of my broken make-up, courtesy of Taylor.

They gave us a week to decide. And we decided to say yes. As terrifying as it was, we chose to move into this crazy life *willingly*.

Taylor was adopted that same year in October, and during her adoption, she and Cameron's biological mother gave birth to another baby—a beautiful, fat, happy baby. CYS had told us she was pregnant and asked if we would be willing to take on an infant. Originally we had said that we couldn't take a child younger than school age because of our jobs. But we did what grown-ups do, and we made a pot of coffee, sat at the kitchen table late one night, and we assembled a pro/con list. The pros had about five items listed while the cons overwhelmed us with closer to thirty. The next morning, we called the caseworker and told her that of course we'd be taking the baby.

We brought baby Isaac home five days after he was born, and he was perfection. His thighs had the kind of rolls that could feed a small country, and his laughter was infectious. The county told us that little Isaac would more than likely be available for adoption when he turned one year old, and we jumped at the opportunity without any hesitation. I can honestly say that it was the easiest decision we've ever made, because once you're so far over your head in the deep end, one more drop of water really can't hurt!

But as we all know, sometimes loving means pain. One drop of water can cause an immense amount of heartbreak, which we found out as the months went by. Cameron's adoption was finalized in February of 2013, and just as we were finding our rhythm as parents of three, the DNA testing began in the attempt to find Isaac's father.

Each time a new man was identified as a possibility, our hearts sank. And then with each phone call that confirmed a negative paternity test, overwhelming relief swept through our home. The process of waiting was exhausting at best. Some of the men looked nothing like our little guy, so we felt more at ease during those times than at others, but after test number 14, our string of luck had run out.

Isaac's father was identified in late summer of 2013. Originally, the gentleman told us that he would rather Isaac stay with us and his brother and sister, which sent our hearts soaring once again. However, as is the county's process with all children, there is a waiting period. And it was during that time that Isaac's father changed his mind.

If there is ever to be a moment in my life that will cause me more grief, God, help me... I don't know how I would survive it. Even in the process of transitioning Isaac from our home to his new one, our family faced tremendous heartache over and over again. It began with the court hearings, followed by overnight visits to his biological father. To watch the baby we had raised from birth sob without breath as the caseworker's car pulled away for each visit was gut-wrenching.

And then, on our final visit, we said our good-byes. Even now, my hands tremble as I write this, for it has been a vision that's haunted me since that day. But we will come back to that moment later in our story. What I can tell you now is that we still had one final court hearing to attend in order to end Isaac's presence in the foster system.

It was the Friday before our anniversary, and the Hubs and I felt we needed to go away for the weekend. The plan was to leave from the hearing and head out of town. We desperately needed a quiet place to mourn without little people asking questions and being affected by our own painful grief. In the courtroom, as I listened to the testimony of every person connected with the case, I could feel the panic rising in my chest. It was reminiscent to days gone by when my anxiety would spike and then the depression would follow, numbing the panic with a blanket of nothing.

The hearing was almost over, and the judge was the last to speak. In a turn that shocked us all, the judge ordered continued weekend visits for Isaac and our family, beginning the following morning, which would last for six more weeks. As the words hit my ears, I'm pretty sure they didn't register. By the look on Pat's face, I knew he and I were in the same little boat... and there we sat, afraid to make any sudden movements that would rock our small feeling of safety.

Together, we left the courthouse, stunned. Not quite ready to go home, a place that once felt like a haven but was now a battleground, we stopped for a bite to eat. Although neither of us touched our food. Instead, we sat and stared and processed. We were happy. Yes, we were elated, really. But there was also a horrible dread that settled over us when we realized that we were not through saying good- bye. That we had only just begun. Six more painful, rugged good-byes lay ahead of us...

The only thing left to do was to say "Happy Anniversary" and begrudgingly consummate our special day, despite the tears and fatigue. We canceled our trip upon returning home and braced ourselves for the next six weeks.

Because sometimes Hope means holding one another up, even when we feel that we can no longer stand.

Somehow we all survived. I'd like to say how, but it's all rather blurry. Because of the stress losing their baby brother caused, our older children had upped their behavioral antes, and what little energy we had left was divided between doling out consequences and going to work each day. I think my husband and I can agree that we were failing at both, rather miserably, I might add.

Yet in spite of the current life trauma, we had settled into a routine. Even so, as we prepared for the final return after that last visit with Isaac, I found myself in the bathroom for more of the visit than not, utterly sick to my stomach and not knowing if I could handle another farewell. We were just three weeks away from what would've been our adoption date for Isaac, and instead of having a party of celebration, my husband and I cradled our Little Love for the last time.

Later that night, I couldn't stop vomiting. Trying to keep my mind busy and off the horrors that were taking place in my heart and in my tummy, I made a to-do list for the upcoming week. At the top of that list was to make a doctor's appointment. Obviously my nerves were shot and my gastrointestinal system could no longer stand it! But as I stood over my list, pen in hand, it hit me....

I should take a pregnancy test – just to be sure.

Pat had left the house to burn off some stress, and I anxiously sat on the couch, willing him to return. It seemed like forever before he walked back through the door. And as he did, I noticed how aged and worn he appeared. He had never wanted any of this. It was all my doing. I was the reason he was in so much pain, the reason that he cried himself to sleep each night. If I hadn't felt so small in our relationship, if I had just trusted that our love would've been enough, I could have saved my husband this heartache.

And now all I wanted to do was to take away that pain... to keep it as my own and protect him from ever feeling this way again. But I couldn't. There was nothing I could say or do that would change the loss we'd endured.

So, I gave him all that I had, which happened to be two positive pregnancy tests.

He looked at me with red-rimmed eyes and sunken shoulders. I waited for his response, but there was none. Not at first, anyway. I eventually said the words out loud, hoping that he could hear them.

"I'm... I'm pregnant."

It was as if his eyes could finally adjust and his mind was able to register the news at last. Covering his face with his hands, my big, strong husband began to weep. I immediately moved to him and put my arms around his heaving shoulders. Seconds later, I noticed that his sobs had changed... was he *laughing*? Yes! Yes, he was. And my heart joined his, laughing right alongside the man that had chosen to walk this crazy road with me.

Our laughter took turns with sobbing on and off for the next little while. Once we were finally composed, we called our parents and told them the news. And a few days later, Isaac's biological father asked us if we would continue our weekend visits indefinitely. We immediately answered yes, and it was the second easiest decision we had ever made.

Because sometimes Hope means continuing to say good-bye with the prayer that one day we would no longer have to.

It was nine months later, in May of 2014, that we welcomed baby Wyatt into our lives. It had been nine months of weekend visits with Isaac, of crying each Sunday night when visits ended, and of puking. Let's just say I was glad to see the nine months come to an end and to begin my life with our little boy – one that no one could take away.

All three children loved being big sibs. Some were more helpful than others obviously, but all were renewed by Wyatt's birth. His little soul had brought back some of the joy we'd lost along the way. And it seemed that we'd all settled into a routine. I had left my job when Wyatt was born so that I could stay home and devote more time to all the children. The kids would do their chores and homework during the week, leaving the weekends free to enjoy with their baby brothers. Isaac would come to Michigan with us for vacations, and we would often get him for long weekends. Our lives weren't what we had hoped for originally, but our hearts were full.

> *Bad things do happen in the world, like war, natural disasters, disease. But out of those situations always arise stories of ordinary people doing extraordinary things.*
> —*Daryn Kagan*

It was January of 2015 when our schedule was suddenly switched to biweekly visits with Isaac. For reasons we may never know, Isaac's birth father became angry with us—he was yelling, furious, and not making sense. He had become erratic on several prior occasions, accusing us of spreading lies or turning him into the police for things that we knew nothing of. However, this time he not only changed the visit schedule, but he threatened to end them altogether.

Flashbacks of all those good-byes we had said began to play in my mind with a vengeance. We were at a loss, confused as to why this was happening. We didn't know how to fix the situation without further angering the man. Isaac began to feel like a carrot being dangled as his father tested the waters with us, reminding us that he was the one in control and daring us to challenge anything that he did or said... even if what we saw was dangerous or harmful to Isaac or his father's other children.

Our entire family lived under a constant heaviness for the next several months. Even the big kids knew that there were things going on behind the scene, things that affected their baby brother, despite the fact that we never spoke of our concerns in front of the children. That was our cross to bear, not theirs. After the countless tragedies they'd endured in their few short years, it was our job to protect them from further trauma as best as we could.

But in spite of our best efforts, in September of the same year, Isaac was taken from us for good. There was no warning, no final good-bye this time. There was just a text message informing us that visits were done and that we weren't to contact him further.

Looking back, I think I knew that the moment for him to leave was inevitable. Isaac was always incredibly bright, far ahead of others his age in his speech and understanding. He had the capacity to verbalize what was going on in his home for many months, and we knew that it was only a matter of time before his father would cut that cord out of his own self-preservation.

Isaac would plead with us to let him stay and not to take him home. He did this every week since the very first visit. And as his communication skills continued to improve, he would scream, tantrum, and yell that he hated his dad. He'd ask me with tears streaming down his face if we could run away. And I would watch as we neared his father's home each week as a deadness replaced the usual smile on his face—the face that always shone laughter and love while with us turned solemn in defeat as he faced his own helplessness.

Over the following months, we experienced a collective despair in our home, an all-encompassing loss that would show its sorrowful face in various ways. Anger, panic attacks, destruction, nightmares, bed-wetting, depression, and returning to bad habits that had previously been broken. Each of us struggled in our own way. And yet each of us learned how to pick the others up—how to discern when a family member needed a hug or to be left alone, how to tell a joke that brought a smile when the others were lost in silent memories.

I don't know what the future holds. But I know that in the present, we are learning an awful lot about healing and the power of prayer and about respecting the grieving process while refusing to live captive to it. But most of all we are learning about loving fearlessly.

Because sometimes Hope is believing that your story is not done yet.

CAMERON

I certainly hope I didn't spoil your appetite, because the next course is going to be one that will make you feel all the feels. My oldest son's story is one of polarity, and it seems that for every joy, there is an equal and opposite devastation. At the same time, it seems that for every failure, there is also a growth that keeps moving him forward. In fact, as you read this, you may very well feel the urge to drive to my house and smack him upside the head, only to get back in your car the next day because you realize that he needs the world's biggest hug.

Welcome to my life!

Pat and I stood there, sweating with anticipation and fear of the unknown as we willed ourselves to open the door. In walked a caseworker with two small children. The boy, I will never forget, had the roundest little face and the most nervous eyes I had ever seen. He was wearing sweats that were at least four sizes too big and an old, stained coat. I stepped forward cautiously because he looked like he scared easily. Bending down to his level slowly, I stuck out my right hand and said, "Hi. I'm Shivonne." He looked at me, unsure of what I wanted him to do with my extended limb. I pulled back and gave him some space.

In a small, timid voice, he answered, "I'm Cameron. Um, do you beat kids here?"

It was a question that I hadn't even considered would be the first that I'd hear when this day had finally arrived. In that moment, I became fully aware that we were jumping in with both feet. There was no turning back. I didn't have to know his story to realize that "complicated" didn't begin to describe his relationship status with his former guardians. A little taken aback but wanting more than anything to put his mind at ease, I said, "Nope. We don't beat anyone here. The adults don't beat the kids, they don't beat each other, the kids don't beat the adults, and they don't beat the other kids or the animals. Sound good?"

Cameron nodded his chubby head in agreement. His sister had a considerably greater amount of confidence than her brother, but I'll leave that encounter for later. You'll need a little more time to warm up to her spitfire spirit! After the caseworker left, we showed the children our home. *Their home.* We had only prepared one room because we didn't really count on getting two children at one time. But since we live in the world's oldest farmhouse, we definitely have the space. Sure, our floors slope, and sometimes the lights refuse to turn on when you flip the switches, but space is something we have in spades!

Quickly converting the futon couch into a bed in our upstairs office, we dressed it with warm sheets and the fuzziest blankets we could find. Cameron took in the room but didn't touch a thing. We had a few toys that we divided between both children's rooms before deciding to give them some time alone to acclimate to their new surroundings.

Pat and I quietly went downstairs and stood in our kitchen. We kind of just stood there for a long time because we had literally no idea what we should do next! Both donning grins that read equal parts "Yay!" and "Holy crap," we contemplated the following day, which was a Friday. I mean, I had to go to work... *oh, my gosh! I had to go to work! How was I going to go to work when there were these children in my house?*

Thankfully, Pat's job was flexible, and he shifted his hours around to accommodate our new little ones. After quickly informing our families of our new situation, we crept (as well as creaky floorboards allow) back up the stairs to where the kids were adjusting. Both Cameron and Taylor were huddled together in Taylor's new room, half-heartedly playing with a few toy dolls. Even then, it was obvious they didn't get along splendidly, but they were all the other one had in that moment.

"Um, is anyone hungry?" I asked.

"No, we had McDonalds on our way here."

"Well... do you guys need baths? Or do you shower, maybe?" I tried.

"I like baths," Cameron answered, which his sister quickly followed in agreement.

"Okay... um, here's where the bathroom is. Uh, let me show you how to turn the water on, and I'll get you some towels."

It then occurred to me that the children may have no idea how to bathe themselves. I quickly rewound my own memories, trying to think back to what age I was when I could independently wash myself, but I drew a blank.

"Wait, do you usually bathe yourselves or do you get help?" Even as I asked the question, it felt awkward to be a stranger just inviting myself into their naked time!

"I need help," Taylor said instantly.

"I can do it myself," replied Cameron.

So I filled the tub with water and helped Taylor with her bath while Cameron played in the other room with Pat. When it came time for bath number 2, I told Cameron the tub was ready for him. He went inside and closed the door. We didn't have any clothes for the kids in their sizes, and they hadn't brought anything with them, so I went to find them long shirts to sleep in. I didn't get far when I heard a voice from the bathroom.

"Um... hey? I think I need some help."

I stood outside the door and asked if he would rather have Pat help him, but he asked if I could come in instead. I poked my head inside the bathroom to see a pale little boy, standing buck naked, hands carefully covering his goods.

"Cameron, would you like to wrap up in the towel maybe?" I suggested.

"No, I'm fine."

Okay. So... now what was I supposed to do? I had helped little boys bathe before when I used to babysit back in high school, but he was six. Was I supposed to just tell him what to do or did he need hand over hand help?

He turned to get into the tub, and that's when I noticed the bruises. Up and down his thighs, his lower back, and across his bottom were bruises, courtesy of a belt strap, according to CYS and Cameron. He winced as he lowered himself into the warm water, and he quickly pulled the washcloth over his lap. I was thankful when Pat knocked on the door and asked if he could come in. Cameron gave his consent, and we exchanged knowing glances as my husband noticed the marks on Cameron's legs. "So, Cameron, do you normally wash yourself or does someone help you?" I asked. "I can wash myself..."

But then he sat there as if he wasn't sure how he was supposed to start. I gave him another washcloth so he could keep the one in his lap where it was. I wet the cloth down in the water and lathered it with soap. Carefully transferring the rag onto his hand, I explained to him how to wash his body.

"All right, it's always best to start at the top and work your way down... after all, you don't wanna wash your butt and then your face, you know?"

He grinned, and I felt an instant rush of relief. Okay! We have a connection! I continued telling him where to wash, making sure he got behind things and in between things... things that I'm guessing he hadn't been doing since he looked very confused when I'd told him that each toe should be washed individually.

Finally, bath time was done, snacks were given, and children were tucked into beds that had been lonely for far too long. Sadly for us, tucked in doesn't mean that they were to go to sleep any time soon.

Around midnight, Cameron finally drifted off, leaving me to fight sleep in his sister's room until she eventually closed her eyes... for a mere *four hours*. But we'd figure it out, right? I guess we'd have to. There was no other choice.

We had a good two weeks, really we did. And then the attachment issues set in. And the behaviors escalated. (I mean *really* escalated.) After several months, we found ourselves trying to love kids that we'd only just met, that struggled to love us back, and that made us want to play in traffic (at 5:00 p.m.... on the interstate). As an informed therapist and God-fearing woman, I tried desperately to curb my seemingly bipolar swings that ranged from loving children to hating children on a daily basis. But no matter how hard I tried, I found myself falling short.

In fact, within a period of just twenty-four hours, I'd grounded the children to their rooms four times, locked myself in my own room twice, threatened to take away all their toys and give them to the neighborhood kids (PS we don't even have neighbor kids), and I all but vowed to disassemble their beds and reassemble them in the yard if they touch that poison ivy one more time 'cause *God knows you're not coming into my house with that stuff!*

Six months in, we were still not sure what the heck we were supposed to be doing with these little people. Six months since our house was taken over by a small army of two – of teaching them rules and then watching them break those rules seconds later – of practicing indoor voices by screaming at full-volume anytime the bigger one touched the smaller one's baby doll. Six months of behaviors that, for the sake of the children's privacy, I will not go into... but let me assure you, there were some odd and uncomfortable ones (courtesy of their previous upbringing). Those first weeks seemed like so long ago....

In that time, the kids weren't the only ones learning new rules. No, sir! We spent the better part of each day trying to get to know the strangers that were now living across the hall from us—strangers that called us Shivonne and Pat in lieu of Mom and Dad as they waited to see if they would be sent back to the crazy depravity that was their previous life.

Yes, those weeks and months were an adjustment period for all of us. Learning that children really like to see adults naked, and therefore, adults should lock all doors at all times was a fun rule to learn! Wondering if I was going to be stabbed in my sleep or if our house was going to be set on fire was also pretty interesting. After all, these kiddos came with a past—a past of things done to them and a past of things they'd done. And sadly, the list was long on both ends. Our caseworker had told us to treat the kids as if they were our own. *But how?* If they were my own children, hugging and kissing on them would seem normal, yet if I were to hug and kiss on a child off the streets, I'd likely be arrested. The same thing goes with discipline. However, these kids were much closer to kids off the street than ones that I'd raised and loved since they were born. So affection was something that felt awkward and, in all honesty, needed to be done very carefully in our home, or it was rewarded by more uncomfortable behaviors.

Upon looking back, I can honestly say that the learning curve for fostering older kids is huge. We're talking *tremendous*, here! I thought that I'd have everything figured out after six months, that we'd be a normal family, all cuddled up on the couch together eating popcorn and watching whatever latest Pixar movie was out on DVD. Everything would be *happily ever after*. Instead, after six months, I found myself wondering, *Am I the only parent who fakes sleep when their kids enter their room each morning?*

Yes, that first half of a year was full of learning. Cameron had finally been enrolled in our local school district, and it was the longest he'd ever been in one school. He had graduated into the first grade after what seemed to be an extremely lengthy summer at home with his sister and a babysitter who was no longer willing to watch our children by summer's end. Not that I could blame her; they had snuck out and wandered off several times, broke things in her home, and gave the poor woman's grandchildren an impromptu anatomy lesson. By the time first grade rolled around, trust me... we were all ready for that school bus to pull up!

However, it seemed that Cameron was struggling to make friends. Not only was he neglecting to learn his classmates' names, he was neglecting his classmates altogether. The fact that he was continuously being held back from recess due to not being able to stay quiet when he's supposed to be listening or because he hadn't finished his assignments probably didn't help matters either. Sure, he'd been suspended twice for violence and kicked off the bus several times for inappropriate behavior and bullying, but thankfully, we are now on a first-name basis with the school's dean of students, and she is a very, *very* compassionate woman. She understands that we didn't cause the problems Cameron was facing and recognized that we would do whatever it took to fix the issues.

Anyways, to help him make friends and to improve his self-esteem, we decided to sign Cameron up for a sport. Only, what do you do with a little boy who is directionally challenged and runs like a duck? *Soccer.* As I read the flier, I knew it was the only true option. "No experience necessary," "Only $35 for the entire season," "Non-competitive," and if I remembered correctly, when we went to see my nephew's soccer game last year, wasn't he catching butterflies and doing the "Thriller" dance on the other end of the field? Yes, soccer was the definite way to go.

I signed Cameron up as soon as I could (a few weeks past the registration date, so I literally knew nothing about his team, where the field was, or who the coaches were... best mom ever, right?). However, it didn't exactly occur to us that he wouldn't know what soccer is... or that he is *completely* uncoordinated (like, pitifully so). It was then that my husband and I realized that this could utterly backfire and make him feel even worse about himself.

If only there were a sport or team-building activity that would allow him to dig holes, play with bugs, and look at tractors for hours at a time. Then my kid would kick some first grade can! But until we were able to enroll him in John Deere school, we were going to give soccer a try and hope for the best. I was the mom out there every Saturday supporting our team (whatever our name was), death-gripping her travel mug, chanting, *"Please* run the right way, please run the right way," and screaming like a maniac if my kid made contact with the ball.

Unfortunately, Cameron did far more crying on the field than running. There was a lot of wandering about and sitting down on the field as well. In fact, the poor kid was almost stampeded to death when the ball quickly changed direction and my son was too busy plucking grass to notice. But we finished the season, he got a participation trophy (which meant more to him than anything in the world), and then he pleaded with us not to make him ever play soccer again. We more than happily agreed.

It was only two weeks after Cameron and Taylor came to stay with us that words like "permanency" and "adoption" started flying about. Why the rush, you may ask? Because that was certainly the question running through our minds! So, here's a little back story about their case.

Cameron and Taylor share a biological mother with two older boys, their half-brothers (eleven and thirteen). The Children and Youth Services (CYS) agency got involved with the family when neighbors began calling, saying that there were small children walking from house to house asking for food for them and their baby brother, Cameron. Their mom was found unconscious from yet another drug-binge, and Cameron was left in his car seat at four months old, very small and very malnourished. He was diagnosed with "failure to thrive." After numerous attempts to help the kids' mom get clean and learn better parenting skills, the shuffling process began.

CYS located family members to shuffle the boys off to for a few weeks, maybe even months, at a time. And when that family could no longer handle a sick baby and disobedient boys, they were shuffled again. The three were also shuffled in and out of mom's care, giving her every chance in the world to make things right. But she didn't. She couldn't.

You see, their mom had her own history full of abuse and hardships. She was no more capable of making a positive choice than were her young children. With as much wrong as she's done in her life, it's easy to forget that she too was once a small child that never got what she needed and a whole lot of what she didn't.

Then one day, CYS realized that Cameron and the boys' mom was pregnant yet again, and a short time later, Taylor was born. She was allowed to stay with her mother for a while before the shuffling began again. Each new complaint moved the new baby and her toddler brother to new homes, back to mom, and so on and so forth. After some rather problematic behavior from the older boys toward their younger siblings, behaviors that were actually taught to the boys by their mother, the kids were entered into the foster system.

Cameron and Taylor were placed with Cameron's aunt, who shared the children with their birth mom and Cameron's birth dad. The older two boys were placed in separate foster homes and headed down a path toward juvenile detention. *Shuffle, shuffle, shuffle.* This went on for four years, from house to house, from town to town, from mother to mother.

Finally, after being unable to manage Cameron's increasingly aggressive behavior, his aunt sent him to live with his dad. And, according to Cameron, that's when the marks and the bruises happened.

That's when our story began.

There are no words to fully express the conflicting emotions that pour in and out of a person when they're suddenly asked to adopt two children they barely know. After all, our emotional journey had already been one full of ups and downs as we waited to be able to conceive a child, waited for fertility pills to work their magic, waited to be called as foster parents, waited for court rulings. All it seemed we did was wait! And then suddenly, without warning, we're put on the spot.

"Agree to adopt the children within the next few days or we'll remove them and put them with a family looking to give them a permanent home."

It was then that I realized how much the child welfare system likes its ultimatums! Honestly, the first feeling I encountered was indignation. It had only been two weeks, for crying out loud! *How* dare you come into my home and demand that I give you a life-changing answer in a matter of days! I spend more time contemplating what style to get with my next haircut!

Indignation was followed by fear. *Oh my gosh, if we say no, we'll never see these two kids again... what will happen to them? What will happen to us? Would the agency blacklist us from getting future children placed in our home? But what if we say yes? We'll finally be a family, and these little ones could finally have a safe place to call home. Am I ready to be a mother? Am I capable of meeting their particular needs and dealing with their particular issues 24-7 for the rest of their lives? Can't we just keep fostering them and "see how it goes"?*

By the way, I am fully aware of how unfeeling or even cruel these questions may seem. But please keep in mind that after only two weeks, I had a better relationship with my dentist, and to be quite honest, I still hadn't made up my mind about him either – which led me to my next round of feelings....

Guilt, peer pressure, and overconfidence. *Only a horrible person would even question not taking these two kids permanently...am I a horrible person? How can I be a Christian and a social worker if I won't even open myself up to being a forever mother to these children? Not to mention, what will people think of us if we turn them away? Our family, our friends, our church, the agency? Wait, what kind of person even wonders that? Okay, I seriously AM a horrible person! Why am I doubting if I can do this in the first place? Of course I can! I'm a Christian and a social worker! If I can't do it, who can, right? Right. Okay. We'll do this. Yes. We will!*

But even though our decision was made, visits and court hearings with the biological family were to continue until the adoption was finalized. For Cameron, that would mean ten more months of calling two women *Mom*, of wondering if he would be taken away *again*. For us, that meant ten more months of peeing all over the house, peeling paint off the walls, climbing out onto his roof, breaking our belongings, and still not knowing if he could ever trust or love us. Ten more months of his biological mom telling him she'd get him back, which scared him and elated him all at the same time. He spent almost a year wondering why his sister was getting to be adopted first, wondering if that meant we loved her and not him, convinced that we were going to leave him the first chance we got. Sadly, it was virtually impossible to explain to a six-year-old that parental rights had already been terminated on his sister, but that they were still in that process for his case.

It was a long ten months.

Visits with his birth mother were twice a week, and it became apparent that we were in for a stressful night and at least day or two following each of those visits. Cameron had gotten in trouble one particularly loud evening after visiting with his family. This was after he'd blatantly lied to my face about an incident that had happened at school.

Now, my husband and I had a pretty good working relationship with both the school and the bus company by this point. When the children first came to us, we enrolled Cameron into kindergarten for the last six weeks of school, just in time for him to stab a little girl with a pencil in the hand. I didn't even know they suspended kids in kindergarten, being a first-time mother and all, but I certainly wasn't going to argue their point! After all, the poor girl *did* have to go to the emergency room and yet still graciously accepted Cameron's homemade apology letter... that we made him write... because that's what parents of stabbers do, apparently.

But this call home wasn't about another punch thrown or a headlock given on the bus (thank goodness, because our poor, sweet bus driver already has an overflowing file cabinet of apology letters from the Costa home). In fact, the incident was something so very minor – something so not worthy of a lie and the fit that followed. But a fit is what we got.

There was yelling and stomping and "you don't believe me's!" being thrown around left and right. And then there was a simple act of revenge as Cameron emptied out my bottle of shampoo. Even though this was par for the course, my things getting broken or simply thrown out when the children were angry, it still had the power to raise my blood pressure to stroke level.

Ever so calmly, I went up to his bedroom and addressed the situation with him. I told him I loved him but that it hurts my feelings that he doesn't even feel the need to apologize for lying to me. I also informed him that he missed snack while he was busy dumping out the shampoo and that he can try again for snack tomorrow.

Oh, you would've thought I'd murdered his dog and made him watch! This one comment brought on such gut- wrenching sobs that it sounded like a fire alarm blaring in the next room, even through the closed door. I figured he'd wear himself out and fall asleep... and after almost forty minutes of inconsolable scream-weeping, he pulled himself together (well, sort of), came to my room, and apologized. I hugged him and thanked him for making such a good choice. I told him I loved him once more and then sent him off to bed.

He left my room and returned minutes later to ask if he could move to a new foster home. (I hadn't expected that to hurt as much as it did.) When I asked him why he wanted to move, as calmly as I could muster the question, he responded that he just doesn't like being here and it makes him too sad.

Finally, a little honesty.

I told him I understood, but that all parents would send him to bed for lying and emptying the shampoo out. Besides that, this wasn't just a foster home; this was his home... the home where he is going to stay forever once we adopted him because we love him and would be heartbroken if he left. Tears ran down his face as he said, "I just think I want to live somewhere else, okay?" I told him we were all tired and that we would talk about it in the morning. Then I cried into my pillow for the hundredth time since the children had come. (Although I'm pretty sure it's not *technically* a pity-party if there's no cake involved.)

I was raised in a Christian home and accepted Jesus into my life when I was four years old. Growing up, I had Christian parents, grandparents, aunts, uncles, cousins, and friends. Our family attended a church where we learned values and practiced Christian traditions. We prayed and read our Bibles daily, attended youth groups, bake sales, Bible studies, choir practices, missions trips, and church camps.

I went on to major in psychology and minor in Christian studies for four years at a faith-based college. There I took classes on theology and religion, and I began to work out my salvation in new ways, learning why I believed what I believed.

And yet *nothing* has challenged my apologetics more than having children!

Who is God?

What's a prayer and why do we have to say it? What's a Bible and why do we have to read it? What is church and why do we have to go to it? What's heaven and why do people want to go there? Does God kill people to take them to heaven?

Ew, why are people drinking God's blood and eating his body at church? Why do we have to sing to God? Why do people get "bathtized"?

If I cut open my heart, will I see Jesus?

What's a cross? Why did Jesus die? Did you see him die?

Were you sad?

Why didn't my old family teach me these things? Are they going to go to heaven or "down there"?

I found that by answering any one question, a million new ones followed. And each question's answer required my kids to have some sort of base knowledge about God and Christianity, a base that they didn't have. I was often met with blank stares or confused expressions, no matter how child-friendly I made my answers. *How was it that I was able to communicate the Word of God to people in foreign countries better than I can to children living in my own home, speaking the same language?*

Months of hard questions and messy answers led me to realize that I needed to try a new approach. Luckily for me, my kids were four and six with the combined working memory of a gnat, so all my previous ramblings and tripped- over words were already forgotten.

"Okay, guys, let's start over. Ready? In the beginning, God created the heavens and the earth..." And after explaining the words "created," "heaven," and "earth" for a half hour, we were finally ready to move on to verse 2 of the Bible. Verse 2! I recognized the long path we still had to walk and that my children had very short legs. So, I figured it was probably best to *show them* Jesus instead of just telling them about Him.

And for months, I tried really hard. I mean really, really hard! Not because loving Jesus is difficult. That's the easy part, honestly. But living Jesus when you have four small eyes watching, mimicking your every move? That's the part that's hard. I tried, I failed, and I tried again.

After seven months of parent-led bedtime prayers, the children finally felt ready to say their own one evening. This completely warmed my heart because I'd been explaining to them since they came to live with us that it's easy to pray. You just talk to Jesus the way that you would talk to anyone else. Remember to thank him for the things he's done for you, ask him to help you with something you need help with, and then tell him that you love him.

And here's how our beginners' prayer went...

Tay: "Dear God, thank you for this day... your turn, Cameron."

Me: "Taylor, why don't you say something else to Jesus."

Tay: "Dear God, thank you for this day. Thank you for giving me lots of money to buy pictures and curtains."

Cam: "What are curtains?"

Me: "They're drapes... don't interrupt your sister, please." Tay: "Dear God, thank you for this day. Thank you for yummy food and new clothes that aren't from the dollar store and for pencils... and nail polish."

Me: "That's very specific. Thank you... now, Taylor, do you want to ask Jesus to help you with anything?"

Tay: "Dear God, thank you for this day..."

Me: "Taylor, you don't have to start over each time you add something to your prayer, okay?"

Tay: "Um... help me to have fun."

Me: "All righty then. Cameron, do you want to take a turn?"

Cam: "Dear God, thank you for this day... um, what do I say now?"

Me: "Why don't you tell God what you're thankful for?" Cam: "Thanks for my stuff... now what?"

Me: "How very *non*specific of you. Would you like to ask Jesus anything?"

Cam: "Can I have a tractor, God?"

Me: "Cameron, this is not a letter to Santa Claus."

Cam: "Okay! Dear God, help me to be good at school tomorrow and..."

Tay: "Help me at school too, God!" Cam: "Taylor! Stop!"

Me: "Hey! We are praying to our Lord, now knock it off !"

Cam: "Be with my family and help me to have good dreams...what else do I say?"

Me: "I have an idea. I'll start this sentence, and you finish it...Jesus, help me to be brave when..."

Tay: "I'm under water."

Cam: "Taylor!"

Me: "Okay, guys, *enough*! Taylor, stop interrupting your brother. Go ahead, Cam."

Cam: "Help me to be brave under water too, God. And help Pat and Shivonne not to argue about the tablecloth." (Sidenote: At this point, Cameron had not yet felt comfortable calling us mom and dad... and yes, our family argues about tablecloths.)

Tay: "And help Mama not to smack Daddy's bottom anymore when he makes a mess..." (said through peeking eyes and a mischievous smile.)

Me: "All right, all right. Now remember to tell Jesus how much you love him."

Tay: "Dear God, please love me."

Me: "He loves you even when you don't ask him to. Pretty cool, huh?"

Cam: "Yup. Can I have a tractor though, for real?"

Me: "No, go to bed." (Whiny, tired cry inserted here.)

Me: "Taylor, why are you crying?"

Tay: "Because I forgot to thank Jesus for *strawberries!*"

Me:"Honey,then thank him for the strawberries already!"

Tay: "Dear God, thank you for this day." (Oh. My Word.) "And thank you for strawberries. Amen."

It really could've gone worse. Let's just hope Christ found what was lost in translation...

However, it wasn't just issues of God and the Bible that were causing some confusion. Relationships were also up for large debate, particularly with my son. Before coming to our home, he had never lived with anyone who was married, or for that matter, in a non-abusive relationship. So this was all very new for him!

Cameron came home from school one day and announced that he was now married.

"My congratulations to you and the missus," I told him. "Do I know your wife?"

"Yep, it's Riley," he replied.

"Ah, sweet girl... but can she tie her shoes? That's the real question."

"She can! I seen her do it!" He answered.

"Cam, I have to say, I'm very disappointed in you." I did my best to look at him disappointedly.

He gave a big sigh. "Ugh, because I'm too young to get married, right?"

"No, Cameron. Because I wasn't invited to the wedding! Your own *mother*."

He looked relieved. "That's all right, you can come to my next wedding!"

"Um, how many are you planning on having there, kiddo?"

"A lot!" He seemed far too excited about becoming a young Mickey Rooney.

"Well, at least you have a plan... where are you two going to live, now that you're man and wife?" I asked.

"I'm gonna live in my room..." Cam said, with a look of confusion.

"Where's she going to live then?" I pressed.

"Oh, maybe she can live in the backyard?" He looked at me hopefully.

"You really know how to treat a lady." "Yup, I do."

"You'll be getting a job now, I suppose. But you're not allowed to be a first grade dropout. I simply won't allow it," I informed him.

"Can I still do cub scouts if my grades get good?" He's got a wife sleeping in the backyard, and the kid's worried about cub scouts.

"Sorry...no girls allowed at cub scouts. It's the rules," I said.

Taylor decided she'd been silent for far too long. "I have a wife and his name is Aiden!"

"Taylor! Stop copying me!" Cam bellowed.

"Taylor, stop copying Cameron," I repeated. "And Aiden can't be your wife, just your husband."

"You don't even know what a husband is, Taylor!" Cameron insisted.

"Yuh-huh! It means I get to sleep in the same bed and get changed in the same room!"

"Well, there's just a wee bit more to it than that, Taylor," I interjected.

"I know! I also get to lick his tongue..." she answered matter-of-factly.

"That's it. I'm sending a note to both of your teachers, and you're getting your marriages annulled in the morning!" I announced.

Taylor's smile vanished, and her face turned quizzical. "What's nulled?"

"It means no licking Aiden... ever," I replied. "So, we can't lick our friends, just ourselves..."

"Taylor Lynn...just keep your tongue in your mouth!" "Fine!" she sighed with exasperation.

Good Lord, help me.

Taylor's adoption finally took place, and on that same day, she and Cameron's biological brother, Isaac, was born. He was now a fun-filled addition to the family, and Cameron fell in love with him instantly. For a short time, we noticed that behaviors were starting to improve. Sadly, it was a very short time. Within weeks, we were back to the stealing and the tantrums and the lying... oh, the lying!

What to do with a child who lies perpetually? They should really teach a class on these things. After months and months, I'd been hoping to see some sort of dent being made in that respect, yet it seemed that their skills had only intensified. In fact, if lying were an occupation, both of my kids could drop out of school right now and make more money than professional athletes (all of them combined). I suppose I should encourage them down a path of used car salesmen... or politics.

I know that constant lying is part of their disorder. And nothing worked to change that behavior, especially for Cameron. Take away his toys? Eh, he didn't care. After all, he has attachment issues, and that includes with his belongings. Ground him? Not a problem. But this kid could sit and stare at a wall or write sentences like it's nobody's business. Reward charts, early bedtimes, loss of special snacks or activities, heart to heart chats—none of it worked.

At one point, I actually dreaded telling anyone that I have extensive schooling and job experience working in behavior modification, because obviously, all my training and experience had been in vain when it comes to my own children. They refused to be *modified*!

However, despite all the lies, my mother had this great idea for Pat and me to do the *Twelve Days of Christmas* with the kids. It was that time of year, after all, and it allowed us to get the kids pumped up for Christmas as we'd put a small gift in a holiday bag and hang it on their bedroom doorknobs each morning. But great ideas don't always go as smoothly as planned in our home. We made it to day 2. *Day 2, folks.*

On this particular day, their Christmas bags contained a reindeer antler headband, all furry and decorated with jingly bells. The vision I had of them in their matching antlers was that of a future Christmas card. Just as I was putting on the finishing touches of mascara that morning, that I heard a door quietly creak open. The sound of tiny hands as they brushed against tiny bells was followed by a whispered, "Awesome!" It was Cameron. He was the first one awake that morning and was obviously excited to see the antlers.

Counting down the minutes until it was time to leave for work, I quickly finished getting ready. I could hear him pitter-pattering around in the hallway outside of the bathroom, followed by quick footsteps back to his room and the thud of his door closing. Moments later, Taylor walked into the bathroom, tears and wails and hysterics flying, as she held broken antlers in her little hands. She told me that they were in her bag that way. And since I was the one that had gently placed them in the bag only a half hour earlier, I knew that this wasn't true. Just as I was getting ready to confront her about this, I noticed something... they were *Cameron's* brown antlers instead of Taylor's white ones.

I knew exactly what had happened. I could actually see it play out in my mind—gift bag on the door, super impulsive child, Taylor still sleeping (none the wiser), the ole switcheroo. So, I called Cameron into the bathroom.

"Cam, the broken antlers that your sister has... they're yours, aren't they?" It was a statement, not a question.

"No, they're not! I swear!"

"Honey, yes, they are. I gave you the brown ones, and Taylor the white ones."

"Nah-uh! Santa must have switched them!"

"Nice try, Cam, but you know that those are from Dad and me, not from Santa... be honest. Did you break them and then switch them with Taylor's?" Give him every opportunity to be honest. That's what all the books said.

"No! She's lying!" he said defiantly as tears streaked his cheeks.

"No, Cameron, you're the one who's not telling the truth.

Did you break them on accident?" I prodded gently. "She broke mine. I didn't break hers!"

"At this point, buddy, you're just hurting my feelings... it's time to be honest. Did you snap them while trying to get them out of the bag? Or did the bag shut in the door, and you realized they were broken so you gave them to Taylor while she was still sleeping? Because I know both antlers were in one piece moments before you found them."

"You're a liar! I hate you and this dumb house!" He then stormed out of the bathroom and slammed the door.

Ah, just another wonderful morning in the Costa home! After giving Taylor the rightful antlers, I peeked back into Cameron's room. He was hiding under his bed and there were broken toys scattered across his floor. He screamed that everyone in our house hates him and that he wanted to go to another foster home where they don't lie.

The poor kid. Not knowing if he's staying or going, feeling jealous that his sister is adopted while he's still in limbo, wanting to be accepted for who he is, yet finding it impossible to distinguish who he is from his unacceptable behavior. He was longing to be back in an old life where lying and stealing and outbursts of anger were allowed, but he was seeing that there's something better about being good, yet not knowing how to be good.

"Cameron, you can wish that all you want, but the fact is you're *here*. And in this house, we tell the truth... *always*. You can act mad at me, but the person you're really mad at is yourself. You're upset that you broke your new toy, and you're upset that you got caught cheating your sister out of hers... but I think you're even more upset that you have something inside of your heart that keeps making you lie."

There were tears, but less defiant ones. "Buddy, you need to spend some time up here thinking about what's going on inside of you. Pray and ask Jesus to help you stop lying, because until you do, you're going to be a very unhappy little boy, and you're always going to feel disappointed with yourself. I love you... even when you're being a snot-face." He shot me a slight grin before remembering he was mad at me.

"I'm not going to buy you anything at Santa's Workshop today," he quietly challenged, looking up at me over eyelids, trying to see if he'd hurt me with his statement.

"Cam, it's my money you're using to buy the gifts anyways. But if that's how you want to be, then you have more to pray about than I realized. I'd start right away if I were you." And with that final statement, I left for work.

Later that day I returned home to Cameron holding out three presents to me, all in shiny, metallic-looking bags... all of which he accidentally spilled the beans about within the first hour of my arrival. (So, maybe he shouldn't be a politician after all.) But I've continually hoped and prayed that something, *anything*, was sinking in—that a small, tiny nugget of conscience was perhaps taking root. Lying, it was all they knew for a long time. And perhaps nine months hadn't been long enough to change years of bad habits, despite how desperately I wanted to "fix them" and make life more about sled-riding and snowman-building than uncovering lies and fixing broken toys. And that prayer will always continue.

It was also around our first Christmas together that Cameron began testing the waters with my name—Mom. He didn't make eye contact with me the first several times he said it, but his body language screamed with the need to feel my approval after he called me mom for the first time. Meeting his simple gesture with an equally understated act of approval, I gently hip-checked my new son and gave him a sideways grin. He peered up at me with the first genuine smile I'd seen from him in months. He understood.

That Christmas, our anxiety-ridden kiddo came out of his shell, ever so slightly, but it happened. He talked with all the new family members he met at Christmas parties; he made new friends with kids and cousins (that, in and of itself, was an outright miracle given the lack of social graces these two children have), and he became super affectionate toward my husband and me. There was a distinct change from the them to the us in our family dynamic. And Cameron was finally able to embrace us.

It was also around the same time that Cameron's birth parents finally terminated their rights. Pat and I were beyond relieved when this happened but amazed that it had taken this long to complete the process. But perhaps knowing that he wasn't going to return to an unsafe home is what spurred the new connection with our family.

Scared to jinx it all, I simply acknowledged and returned his affections as I praised his friendliness toward others. We returned home from the holidays in Michigan and the mom-calling increased as Cam prepared for his final visit with his birth mother.

It's almost funny how something I had awaited for so long came and went as nonchalantly as brushing one's teeth. I wanted to be called mom, and then it happened.

I wanted there to be a final visit, and there was. Don't misunderstand, I certainly don't minimize these events or trivialize them in any way; it simply felt as though this was the only possible outcome. These kids were meant to be in the family they were born to. Yet, due to things completely out of their control, that was no longer an option.

And that's why I'm amazed when people tell me they don't believe in a loving God. Yes, these kids had to face horrific tragedies at an early age. But that is due to our own free will that God granted to us out of love. However, it's that same loving God that knew to provide a back-up plan for these little lives. Our children weren't destined for us originally, but out of love, we have been prepared by God to be their second chapter in life, and hopefully, all the chapters that are to follow.

I may have struggled to make the adoption decision out of fear and uncertainty, but Cameron found a way through fear and uncertainty, and he made his way into our family. He showed *me* what he needed, not to talk it out for the millionth time, not to get worked up over a final good-bye, not even to count down days until that adoption hearing. He needed to be able to finally call me mom, which worked out perfectly, since that's all I really needed too.

As we awaited his adoption date, I thought it would be fun and necessary to spend some quality time with Cameron one weekend, just the two of us. After giving him the opportunity to pick our activity (naturally he chose the pet store), I quickly realized we were either going to be coming home with tears or a guinea pig. I chose tears; although, the guinea pig was awfully cute and Cameron's tears were awfully convincing! Even though the day itself was productive and filled with memorable moments, it was these conversations between the two of us that will remain in my mind for years to come.

"Mom, am I gonna get married some day?" "Yeah, probably, Cam."

He did a big sigh. "I don't even know how I'm gonna find a girl with the last name Costa..."

"Well, bud, that's not how it works. When you get married, the girl changes her last name to Costa, like yours will be... you don't have to find a girl with that name already. That would make for slim pickin's."

Relief and a new look of questioning came over his face. "Oh good... but how do I find a girl to marry? Do I just open up doors and say 'Hi, my name is Cameron, do you want to marry me?'"

Reminding myself that all the previous families he'd lived with were unmarried and that the first wedding we attended created a great deal of confusion for the poor kid, I tried to stifle my laughter.

"Uh, no, that would be weird. You meet girls and ask them on dates... after you've graduated from college, of course."

"What's a date," he asked.

"A date is when you ask a girl to go to dinner or a movie or to hang out, and then you spend lots of time talking... and you pay for her meal."

"Hey, that's not fair!" He sounded indignant.

"It's dating. It's not supposed to be fair," I explained.

"Who do I ask on dates?"

"Well, when you're much older, you will find a nice Christian girl that loves her family, has a good sense of humor, cares about animals as much as you do, someone that helps others, and someone who you think is pretty, and you'll ask her on a date."

Cameron gave me the most bashful grin ever grinned. "She'll be pretty..." he said softly.

My heart warmed. "Yes, she will be pretty." I smiled back at him in the rearview mirror. "And then after you've taken her on many, many dates, you'll fall in love, ask her to marry you, have a wedding, and then get a house together." That last statement was met with an even larger sigh.

"Ugh, that's a lot of work. I think I'll just get a llama." (Fast-forward to an hour later.)

"Mom, when I was living with my old dad, he would do bad stuff in his room with his girlfriend. They moved the bed all over and broke it. It was nasty!"

"Well, Cam, not everyone is quite as expressive to one another as to break the bed, but that's what married people are supposed to do."

"No way! I'm not doing that when I get married!" "Then you won't be having any babies, bud. That's how mommies get pregnant." Silence.

"Are you serious?" His mouth hung open as he whispered the question.

"Sorry to say, but yes. There has to be a certain amount of bedroom time for a baby to come about."

"Well, now I'm *definitely* getting a llama!"

It will be my greatest joy to remind him of this conversation when he is sixteen years old, hormone-ridden, and looking for the future Mrs. Costa.

I'd like to say life with Cameron has been all funny conversations about marriage and learning how to pray, but that's just not the case. In those ten months before his adoption, we observed a number of Oscar-worthy performances from a dramatic little boy that tried to convince us that someone *else* was peeing in his pajamas at night, wadding up the sheets and soiled jammies, and hiding them around his room (including in his drawers with his clean clothes). This happened *weekly*.

We also had quite a fun time when Cameron lost *both sets* of keys to our new family car. You know, the keys that are a few hundred dollars to replace? We spent four days tearing the house apart, only to find the cheaper set without the automatic starter on it. It was weeks before the other one mysteriously appeared back in the key jar.

And then there was one very special week when Cameron and Taylor made a make-shift ladder, climbed to the top of the storage closet, and smuggled non-washable paint up to their rooms while I was using the bathroom. They then painted various parts of the walls, floors, and furniture. Only when they realized that the paint wouldn't come off, they moved their furniture around the room to cover up the marks... except when they did this, they scratched up the walls and left a hole in the plaster.

Later that week, they took bubbles upstairs and blew them all over Taylor's bedroom (leaving a slippery, soapy mess *everywhere*), another mysterious hole showed up in Taylor's wall, Cameron pulled out the laminate flooring and then jacked them up trying to put the panels back into place, Taylor created a climbing mechanism to get to the top of the medicine cabinet and then proceeded to cover herself in Dora Band-Aids (then lied about it *while* still covered in Band-Aids... it's a good thing she's pretty), she locked the bathroom doors from the inside and we couldn't get into the bathroom (leading to Cameron trying to use the once-missing car keys to open the door), Cameron drenched himself in a mud puddle directly before getting into my car after I had just told him not to, followed by him stealing a drink from subway and then lying to me about it. But let's not forget the weekend prior when the kids called 911, and then Cameron stole from Pat's mother—the only person left that was willing to babysit them!

Not that I was completely surprised by these behaviors. I mean, the first Mother's Day I spent with my children involved a lovely plant, hitting, kicking, screaming, and fecal smearing. And that was just before church! When I started finding my underwear missing and noticed largely inappropriate pictures being taken with the toy cell phones the kids were using, I started to get concerned that there were not enough adult eyes that could watch the children's eight limbs at all times! Even after I managed to get my showers down to seven minutes and I refused to use the restroom unless it was absolutely necessary, they *still* managed to outmaneuver me.

When they were told to play together, we could count on disaster as much as we could count on the sun rising the following morning. But even when sent to their own rooms to play, safety was never guaranteed. I can distinctly remember walking up the stairs and smelling something burning in Cameron's room. I rounded the corner and saw him holding a paper plate to his lightbulb, with the lamp shade lying on his bed, as smoke sizzled up toward the ceiling! When I grabbed the plate away and asked what he was doing, he simply shrugged his shoulders and told me that he was just trying to see what would happen. *Um, we'd all die, dude. Seriously!*

But one of my "favorite" days ever occurred in late July. It was insanely hot and we live in an old farmhouse that lacks all kinds of air-conditioning, making the upstairs feel like the center of a volcano. And in that July heat, for a week straight, all I could smell was stale urine as soon as I began ascending the stairs. I had checked sheets, drawers, closets, and rugs. I couldn't find it, no matter how diligently I tried. I even asked the kids if they could please just tell me where the smell was coming from so that I could stop gagging constantly.

"Mom, we promise, we didn't pee on anything!"

Famous last words, right? But my nose couldn't be convinced otherwise, and my nose is never wrong. Finally, one day I just decided to clean their rooms thoroughly. After all, my blessed mother-in-law was watching them and the baby for the afternoon so that I could get some much needed time to myself—time that I should've been relaxing, but instead I chose to use trying to rid the house of old pee.

I cleaned *everything*. And did I find one drop of urine anywhere? Nope. My biggest fear was that someone had peed down the vents in the floor. That was the only solution left. So, after finishing the floors, I dumped the dirt into Cameron's garbage can and lifted the bucket to take it downstairs to empty, and that's when the sloshing began.

So many things happened at one time. The recognition that the garbage can was incredibly heavy, the smell that wafted up through the cardboard and papers he'd used to cover his indiscretion, and the fact that my instant repulsion caused me to drop the can... all over myself.

The only thing left to do once realization washed over me like urine from a can was to throw up all over the place. And so I did. All the way to the shower. It didn't matter that it was one hundred degrees outside, I took the hottest shower imaginable as I tried to cleanse myself of someone else's week-old urine. Once the water began to run cold, I got out and had to clean up my mess along with Cameron's. I scrubbed and scrubbed like a crazy person.

But I still smelled pee! I stood up slowly and glared down the hallway toward Taylor's bedroom. There's no way, I thought. Only I knew that there absolutely was a way. I also knew that I was going to be wiser when I carefully picked up her garbage can. Fool me once, right?

Sure enough, there was another garbage can filled with pee.

(I'm pretty sure my screams were heard around the world, causing irregular weather patterns in foreign countries.)

I got into my car and drove to my mother-in-law's home, definitely in search of blood once I got there. When I burst through the door, it was as if both kids knew that their lives were going to end.

"Why does your room smell like urine, Cameron?" "Because I peed in my garbage can?"

"Did you or didn't you, child?" "Yes, I did."

"How long ago, Cameron, did you pee in your garbage can?"

"Um, five or six days ago?"

Gag! "And how many times did you do this?" "A few?"

"And now for the important question, Cameron... Why did you pee in your garbage can?"

"I wanted to see what it would do..."

"What it would do? Did the pee come out of your penis the same way it does when you're aiming at the toilet, Cameron?" Each time I spoke his name, he shrunk further and further into his seat.

"Yes."

"Then why did you keep doing it, Cameron!" "It was closer than the toilet..."

"The toilet is five feet from your room! Do you realize how gross it is to have someone else's old pee dumped on you in the middle of the summer? Do you?"

"I'm sorry?"

"Taylor... why is there pee in your garbage?" Silence.

"Taylor! Why is there pee in your garbage!" "I'm thinking."

"No, the time to think was before peeing in the garbage... now is the time for explaining. Why!" "Because I wanted to?"

It was obvious in that moment that I was raising a bunch of loons that answer questions with questions, and I realized I was not getting anywhere. I, therefore, informed them that there was going to be a lot of reading and writing in their futures and a lot less playing and swimming— scratch that, they can't swim, because they cut a massive hole in the bottom of the swimming pool earlier in the week... *my bad*. And I certainly wasn't going to send them to their rooms. God forbid they pee on something again or peel more paint off their walls because they're angry over being caught.

PS, sometimes Hope means believing that God has not given you more than you can handle, despite the very obvious evidence proving otherwise.

Eventually, as it always does for a few days or so, life calmed down. And during one of the calm moments, just a few weeks after his seventh birthday, the long-awaited, much-anticipated moment had arrived. Cameron David Costa was finally adopted into our family as of 9:30 a.m. on February 28, 2013. Leading up to the day was such an emotionally distressing time for Cameron and our family, anxiety being this little boy's kryptonite. At the adoption hearing, Cam was nervous, bashful, and very concerned about all the people at the courthouse that day.

Afterwards, we went out for a celebratory lunch to a hibachi restaurant, which was an interesting adventure in and of itself with the kids. Baby Isaac was thoroughly enthralled by the Asian man tossing the knives around, Taylor was focused on when her food would be done, and Cameron, although mesmerized by the flames on the hibachi, was far more interested in the mechanics of the table and the man's obvious skills with cutlery. We realized rather quickly that we would have to hide all of our knives for at least the next six months just in case anyone got any "creative" ideas.

Later that night, I overheard Cameron talking in his room, although to whom I wasn't sure. I cautiously peeked around his door without him realizing I was there. That's when I saw that Cameron was not talking to himself but that he was talking to his stuffed animals. I stood there watching as my son introduced himself to his teddy bears as Cameron David Costa. He let the name hang in the air before explaining to his bears that he kept his first name because he liked it but changed the other two names to "something better." Then it hit me as I stood quietly in his doorway.

We are his something better.

It was so sweet to watch him feel settled in his new name—a name that would hopefully begin to wash away the stigma, negative memories, and fear associated with his previous name. When Cameron realized that he was being watched, his shyness returned. I asked what he was up to, and he said, "Nothin'... I'm just practicing my new name for school tomorrow."

Anne, an adopted child herself to Merilla and Matthew at Green Gables, said it best: "What's in a name? A rose by any other name would smell as sweet... but I have a hard time believing that a rose would smell the same if it were called a thistle or a skunk cabbage." Cameron will always be Cameron... sweet, quirky, helpful, mischievous (especially the last one). But my prayer is and always will be that because of this name change, he would find a turning point for his life —one that would cause him to see himself in a new way.

Cameron, you are no longer the thistle that others have deemed you, nor are you the skunk cabbage as you view yourself. You are part of our family, and you will not be seen as a weed that needs to be plucked. Cameron, you are our rose. It's time to bloom, son.

When you're seven years old, the world is an exciting new adventure just waiting to be explored. When you're seven years old and you've been severely abused by the ones who were supposed to take care of you, the world can be extremely dark and terrifying. You learn to be distrustful, defensive, and fearful of everyone and everything around you. Hurt or be hurt. Hate or be hated.

In late May of 2013, my seven-year-old stopped being the fearful boy that he was only a year before. It was then that he took a huge step of courage in speaking about his abuse allegations regarding his birth family. There were many court hearings and lots of meetings with lawyers, District Attorneys, and judges. In the end, Cameron decided not to follow through with a trial, as it would've been a very long and arduous process. But he made this mama incredibly proud that he wanted to stand up for what is right.

Fighting social injustice—who said you need DNA to have your kid take after you?

Since his courageous moment, please don't think that our child outgrew his impulsive ways. Oh, that would be an understatement. I distinctively remember swimming in a weird foamy chemical smell (once we'd finally patched the hole in the swimming pool that the kids had made), only to find that Cameron had found the key to the garage and that he'd emptied a can of wasp spray into the pool's water. Or when after having a C-section and enduring four days of labor, Cameron decided to take the opportunity while I was upstairs nursing young Wyatt to go outside, grab Pat's ax from atop the woodpile, bring it inside, and use it to chop open a can of white paint so that he could paint his clubhouse.

Two years later, I still have white paint splatters on the floor and each piece of my furniture.

But when we were in the process of Isaac being returned to his birth dad, that's when we all noticed a change. Cameron became withdrawn and more inwardly violent. He would bang his head or punch himself in the face over simple homework assignments, and he'd bite his arms until they were raw if another child called him a name or he was sent to his room for acting up. The attachment that we'd worked so hard to build with him slowly began to crumble. Faced with the loss of yet another family member, he just couldn't bear to feel it.

During the year following Isaac's move, these are things you'd hear coming from my husband's and my lips multiple times an hour if you were at my home any given day of the week:

"Cameron, *why* did you flush your sister's hair ties down the toilet?"

"Cameron! Stop walking across the porch railing! You're gonna fall!"

"Cameron, you can't threaten to run away *every day*...it's definitely losing its momentum, my friend."

"Is it yours? Then stop touching it. Now... stop touching it *now*."

"Cameron, keep your hands to yourself or I'll do it for you."

"Cameron, clean your room." (x 100) "Teeth are for biting food, not people!"

"How the heck did you break your lamp *and* the toilet?"

"Cameron, stop riding your bike in front of the lawnmower and cars!"

"Seriously! Wipe your butt!"

"Cameron, take your meds... Cameron, take your meds... Cameron! Take. Your. Meds!"

"Stop. Stop. Stop. Stop! I said STOP!"

At school, he started getting in trouble again for not listening, hitting other students, and getting out of his seat repeatedly on the bus. At home, he increased his hitting (himself and others), lying, stealing, binge-eating, breaking things, and biting. My toothless child, who came to us with a mouth full of caps and blank spaces, had *finally* grown several teeth over the summer. Although I was thrilled his teeth were finally coming in, I had no idea that he would use them as a *weapon*. Not only did he break skin on his sister's shoulder, but he attempted to bite my mother-in- law multiple times while she was trying to help him calm down during one of his fits!

Our quickly-growing son had also taken to very large tantrums whenever he wasn't given his way. And with each correction I offered, this is what I got in return: "Not only are you the worst *foster* mom in the world, you're the worst real mom, too! I hate you! You're mean and a jerk and I'm going to kill myself !" That last statement is one that we have revisited often in the time that's passed.

It's in those days that I'd remember how broken my children were. Because it's easy to get caught up in the regular moments—days when I'd get to be a "normal mom" dealing with "normal kid" problems, like fighting over whose day it is to feed the dogs or who has to turn the light out because they were the last one in a room. There's a part of me that smiles each time my kids don't empty their pockets before their clothes go through the wash. And although I may bark at them for it, I don't mind stepping on thousands of Legos, silly bands, and barrettes as I walk from room to room. These are the things that kids do. They leave stuff out to be stepped on, send entire Kleenex boxes through the wash, and argue over light switches. And it makes me feel amazing inside.

Then there are days when their broken pieces come a little bit unglued and their cracks begin to show. On those days, I do not feel like a normal mom dealing with normal kid problems. On those days, I'm reminded that parts of them are still broken and that they're prone to shattering more easily than a "normal kid."

It's often the small things that cause them to chip— their new, shiny beings that we worked so hard to polish up with pleases and thank-you's, therapy sessions and reward charts, prayers and petitions. We put them in nice clothes and comb their hair until it glistens. We clip toenails and remind them to stand up straight. They look the part. My kids look all new. They looked so good that sometimes I'd forget that when I raise my voice, my daughter will be unable to meet my eyes with hers and will hunch over with fear. And my son can seem so friendly that you'd never expect him to pull out his own teeth when a child at school makes fun of the silver caps covering his less-than pearly whites, the result of being bottle-fed soda throughout his baby years. It's on those days that the small lines of their glued together parts are most evident.

In third grade, Cameron had been suspended twice. Honestly, I had thought we were past that stage. After multiple suspensions at the end of kindergarten and throughout first grade, we were pleasantly surprised to have no incidents in second grade. *What a relief*, I'd thought. *Problem solved!* But I was wrong.

Because, you see, in his third grade class, there was a boy that reminded him of a step-brother that he had to leave behind when he came to our home. A boy that was slightly older than him, whom he tried to emulate, despite the boy's reportedly bad behavior. All the long talks about being a leader and not a follower flew out the window in a desperate attempt to fit in, look cool, and appear tough in front of this boy and his new classmates.

And then one day my son stole a sweatshirt. He stole a sweatshirt and made up an elaborate story of how he earned the shirt by participating in a fundraiser. He stole the shirt, made up a story, and then *wore it to school the next day*. The poor boy who originally owned the item was in his class. (At least my kid is still somewhat stupid when it comes to his crimes.) After some more lying and lots of tears, followed by a suspension and a full weekend sitting at the table for a rousing rendition of "Read, Write, or Draw," I spent the better part of the next four weeks applying more glue to the lines and painting over the chips that had started to show once again.

It wasn't long after that I'd received another phone call from the school because my son had made "terroristic threats." *For the love of all that is good and holy....* As if on cue, my kid started his routine cover-up. Lie, blah blah blah, and then lie some more. After wanting to bang our heads off the walls, my husband and I were finally able to get the whole story. Cameron was caught cheating on a worksheet (it has to be noted, the worksheet was for fun, not even for a grade). But he wasn't caught by the teacher. No, he was caught by the sweet little girl whose paper he was not-so-sneakily copying. Naturally, she threatened to tell. And naturally, my son threatened to kill her entire family. *I'm not even kidding.*

How was I to explain to a little girl's parents that my son is not, in fact, a sociopath, but that he was trained to lie, cheat, and steal at all costs in order to survive with his first family? How do I get a freaked out mom to understand that her child wasn't the only one threatened—that my child was also threatened by his first family and their ever-changing paramours? And if he chose to tell his fears to the nice people in his life, the workers supposed to protect him, if he were believed at all, he'd be sent to live with yet another family, leaving all his belongings behind, changing schools *again*, only to find that they didn't want him either? How could I show her that I'm so, so sorry and that I don't condone my son's words, without it seeming like I'm making excuses for him?

Because I won't make excuses. I can't let him think that it's okay to do wrong because of previous wrongs done to him. And I won't let him turn others into victims and perpetuate a cycle of violence, theft, and lies.

Yet there I sat, grounding and re-gluing him at the same time, wondering when my broken kid would just get the chance to be normal. No labels, nothing to live up to, no one to please, no one to fear—just be able to live without the cracks and chips.

It was then that Cameron broke into my thoughts to show me something he'd written during his long sit at the table. It was his autobiography, something they'd just learned about in school that week. It was only one page, double-spaced and written in large letters, but I could see that it was his best handwriting.

It read something like this: Once upon a time, I lived with a bad family. I was scared and had belt marks on me. And then one day I moved to a new family with a Mom and a Dad that are nice to me.

They don't let me do bad things and teach me to be good. I love my new life very much. The End.

While it may not be the end, it just may be a beginning.

And in that moment, one small crack healed.

When Cameron first arrived to our home, we were given very little information about his physical health. The county had told us that he had just ended a three-month cycle on steroids "due to a problem with his liver or kidneys or something." They weren't sure what the name of the condition was, but they assured us they'd get back to us.

Alas, they never did find us that information, but they told us that his puffiness would go down. Oh, and that we were to watch for a rash on his belly and for swollen legs. I had absolutely no idea why, but that's what we were to watch for. After a while, we went on with our lives and found our routine, giving no more thought to the random disorder he may or may not have had when he'd arrived.

That routine led us to clothes shopping for school, which was starting the following week. For the record, clothes shopping with two RAD children is worse than bikini shopping when you're on your period and you've just eaten a box of donuts. And that's the truth, right there.

Halfway through our trip, Cameron began throwing fits. He was fighting about trying pants on because his belly had gotten quite chubby recently, but that was the entire reason we needed to try them on! I was tired of him complaining that his pants made him hurt. Finally, my son threw a pair of pants across the store and started yelling at me, tried to swing at my head, and then fell to the floor in a fit of sobs.

Parenting Cameron has helped me get over my fear of causing a scene in public, by the way. There was just no more room for embarrassment in my life at that point. However, something was obviously wrong. His face was beat red, and he was sweating profusely.

Baby Wyatt was three months old and needed to nurse, so he was crying hysterically in his carrier. Taylor was calling my name from the dressing room eighty-nine times in a row because she wanted to show me the shirt she had tried on. And I sat on the ground of a department store staring at my son who looked like he was going to die.

I quickly grabbed the other two and made it to the front of the store before Cameron just fell over. He could no longer hold himself up, and his face that had been red moments before was ashy—eyes sunken in, lips blue. He was awake but not coherent. A beautiful stranger helped me get my kids and belongings into our van as I called my husband and told him we were going to the hospital. We were forty-five minutes away.

Two minutes into our trip we hit construction, and a nail that was left in the road flattened our van's tire. We were now forty-three minutes from the hospital but unable to move any further. I maneuvered our brand-new minivan into a gas station before the tire was completely deflated. Flustered and panicked about my sick child and wailing, hungry infant, I discovered that I had no idea where the spare tire for the van was located. I checked all the usual places, but no tire. Perhaps it's because we purchased the van *while I was in labor*, but I literally had no idea how I was going to change the tire when I couldn't even find it!

I called my husband and in-laws, but there was no answer. So I ran inside the shop to buy Cameron a Gatorade and quickly nursed Wyatt before proceeding to beg stranger after stranger to help me find and change my tire. I was still sore from my C-section, carrying a newborn, and my son was falling over on the sidewalk as my daughter complained that Cameron got more Gatorade than she did. And each person walked by without responding to my plea.

There are not words to describe how royally ticked off at humanity I was in that moment! My husband finally returned my call but was working two hours away, and AAA couldn't get to us for at least six hours. Familiar anxiety washed over me as it always seems to do when I feel utterly helpless. Trying to hold the dread at bay, I did all I could to solve the situation. *I could call a tow truck, but how would I get the kids and myself to the hospital? I could call an ambulance, but surely they wouldn't allow all of us to ride along, would they?*

As an answer to prayer, my brother-in-law showed up after my husband had let him know our predicament. He found our tire (who knew that they stored it underneath the van!) and replaced it for us. By the time we got to our local hospital, they had us immediately turn around and go back the way we came from to Children's Hospital of Pittsburgh. That was where we stayed for the next several nights.

Cameron slept in a hospital bed on the nephrology floor, I slept on a foam cot, and Wyatt rested in a roll-away crib. As it turns out, Cameron was diagnosed with a relapse of Nephrotic Syndrome and was additionally labeled with Minimal Change Disease. This condition means that the filters in his kidneys are too large, and they allow protein to leak from his body through his urine. When this happens, he rapidly gains weight, mostly from retained water, his blood pressure gets incredibly low, and his kidneys start to become toxic; hence, the steroids he was on before he came to live with us.

The doctor informed us that a relapse is not uncommon, but that there usually is just one. For some reason, Cameron's body chose this particular circumstance to practice being an overachiever, because in the next two years, he had seven relapses. He spent the better part of those two years on steroids, creating even more undesired side effects. Sadly, he even relapsed twice while on a preventative medication. A condition that was once viewed as more inconvenient than anything had now become something of great concern. The nephrologist could not explain why Cameron continued to relapse. He couldn't say why the first medication didn't work. However, one thing that he could tell us was that we had a very difficult choice to make.

There was one other preventative medication to try—an immunosuppressant med that has a list of side effects taller than my son. This medication would slowly destroy Cameron's kidneys, allowing him to only be on it for a few years of his life. However, the level of toxicity that the protein in his body is creating would kill his kidneys even quicker than the medication. The doctor also alerted us to the fact that if this medication didn't work, we would have to look at chemotherapy, dialysis, or a possible kidney transplant.

That's it. Those were our only options. Needless to say, my son, who already struggles with being different, now has to take medications that will kill his kidneys in order to keep them working longer than if he didn't take them at all. And a boy that already faces depression now worries about dying.

Sometimes being a parent means making someone else's hard choices. Choices that we would never choose to make if there were a better option. Even as I gave the nephrologist our answer to go ahead with the medication, I was shaking inside. Because I knew that once he took that first dose, the clock would start ticking. And each time they have to check his blood to make sure the levels are where they should be, that fear would well up inside of me.

Then right before the start of fourth grade, it all just became too much for the poor kid. In a moment of impulse and anger, Cameron devised a detailed suicide note, complete with funeral plans, and then he took off out of the house. I had been in the middle of cooking dinner, Wyatt had just woken from his nap and was crying through the baby monitor, and Taylor was sobbing that Cameron was "really serious this time." I grabbed my shoes and ran out of the house, but Cameron was nowhere to be seen on our forty acres. I yelled his name repeatedly, but the only response I received was Taylor screaming from inside the house.

"Mom! The stove is on fire!" she wailed.

I ran back inside and put out the small fire, only singeing some arm hair in the process but completely scorching the chicken. We opened all the windows, and I immediately called my mother-in-law to come assist me with the others while I went to find Cameron.

Returning to the yard, I screamed bloody murder for him to respond. After what seemed like an eternity, he walked out of the woods. He nonchalantly staggered toward me, taking his time as if it was just any other day. Equally relieved and completely enraged, I willed myself to breathe. It took him a good ten minutes to walk back down the hill to me, and in those ten minutes, I chose to look at his suicide note. My heart sank as I read about his self-hatred. In those ten minutes, I realized that the time for compassion, if ever there was one so obvious, was now.

By the time he reached me, I was emotionally undone. I pulled him into my arms and held him as he began to cry. He expressed that he was angry with his life and with how he acts and that he also gets angry when people call him out on those actions. He stated that he hates taking steroids and gaining weight from them, that he hates his capped teeth and his toenails that curl under, that he hates it when Taylor gets attention, because he wants it all. And then he told me that he didn't think that I really loved him.

The words were hard to hear after spending so many years trying so hard to connect with my children. The word failure began to ring in my ear once again. It was a word that I was already so familiar with. But I decided that I wasn't going to accept it this time. I'd already been there, already done that. I told my son that I *did* love him. I apologized for all the things I've ever done and said while upset or grieving the loss of his brother that led him to feel that way. But I also called him out on his own self-loathing. We talked about not letting those negative thoughts take root in our minds and hearts. We talked about the feeling of failure and how both he and I were going to have to choose to succeed instead—choose to love and move forward each and every day.

However, we did call his therapist. We developed a safety plan for the evening and were, thankfully, able to stay out of the hospital—a place we'd been too often already.

Because sometimes Hope means trusting that we will all choose *life* for the next twenty-four hours.

Yes. For twenty-four hours, we were safe. But five weeks later, I found a knife in my son's room. Let me just go ahead and tell you that finding a knife in your nine-year-old's room does something to a mama. I mean, the range of emotions, the action plans, the list of suspected reasons, the list of assumed consequences... Folks, it was a long four hours from the time I found that knife to the time he stepped off that school bus!

It all started the week prior. Pat and I had been waiting to tell our kids that we'd lost all visitation with their younger brother, Isaac. We had been able to keep weekly visits going for about a year, which the dad then moved to biweekly visits before abruptly ending all contact. My husband and I were beyond devastated, and we'd decided it was best to wait to tell the kids, just in case Isaac's father changed his mind.

He didn't.

Therefore, we had to break the news to our kids on a Friday, on the day we were supposed to have our regular weekend visit with our little guy. Since both of my kids' RAD symptoms had been holding their own near the "normal" mark for a good few weeks, I had no idea what I expected would happen when they heard the news.

Tears? Anger? Screaming? Depression? Panic? These are the things that I myself had experienced during those several week, and I'd assumed my kids would follow suit. However, I had completely forgotten about the other possibility. The RAD possibility.

Cameron, always the one to explode or react, kept quiet about the entire situation. When he first heard the news, he let out a long, exasperated sigh, and then he never spoke of it again. Instead, he would occasionally come up to me, put an arm around my shoulder, and ask, "You doin' okay, Mom?" It was such a sweet sentiment, but I found it sad that he felt he had to be the strong one at nine years old, especially since my husband and I had done our best to stay brave-faced and stable(ish) through the entire process.

When Taylor would bring up a question about Isaac, Cameron would instantly yell at her. *Finally*, I thought, *he's gonna tell her to shut up because it's upsetting him*. But no. Instead, he would say, "Taylor, stop it! Can't you see you're going to make Mom cry?"

I knew there was more behind his words, but he wasn't ready to verbalize them yet, and I didn't want to push either of them until they were ready. I knew firsthand how important it is for these two kids to come to things in their own time. I was prepared for the acting out to start at any moment.

So I obviously wasn't shocked to receive a call from the guidance counselor. The three usual words were thrown out: impulsive, intrusive, invasive. Yep, that's my boy, right there in a nutshell! He has the social skills of a needy puppy, but without all the cute, wrinkly skin and floppy ears.

What I *didn't* expect to find, however, was the knife. I never would've even considered looking for one had I not walked past his room and seen mounds of garbage all over his mattress and floor. Disgusted and grumbling to myself about getting my tubes tied, I immediately looked under his bed. Of course, the garbage continued. What shocked me most wasn't the amount of garbage, but it's content. There were used Band-Aids, gauze, antiseptic wipes, athletic tape, and tissues strewn everywhere. *What in the world*? I couldn't fathom what he had been doing with all the supplies from his first aid kit.

Normally, I wouldn't think twice if I saw his sunglasses case lying out. But that motherly nag started in as I gave it a second glance. There it was, tucked partially under his bedding, as if he had been trying to hide it. I picked up the case and slowly opened the lid. And there was a pocketknife, secured next to his bed, next to the gauze and the bandages and the wipes and tape and the tissues...

I quickly scanned his room and went through each drawer. My heart was in my throat as I moved through his room like a woman on a mission. I went to the final toy bin, and hidden in the bottom of the container was a frame housing Cameron's favorite picture of himself. It was a black and white photo of him sitting in the wheel of a giant John Deere tractor. We had professional pictures taken and specifically chose that picture for his room.

Why? Why would he shove this beautiful picture into the bottom of a bin, out of sight?

The sinking realization struck me like an anvil. Knowing that he had threatened to kill himself just five weeks earlier, and seeing the mess that was his room, my mind went to the place that no mother wants to go. I sat on the floor of his ransacked room and felt all the feelings. Anger. Rage. Grief. Fear. An urge to run to the school and yell at him. An urge to run to the school and hug him, to tell him that it would all be okay—to examine his body for signs of self-harm—to just sit with my son and let him tell me what in the world was going on, to tell me why he couldn't let himself grieve the loss of his brother, to tell him that I didn't want him to hurt himself.

But I didn't run to the school. I sat in my home, and I worried. And then I prayed. And then, I hate to say it, but I worried some more. When the school bus arrived, my son walked through the front door, smile on his face, acting like he didn't have a care in the world.

The tension in my eyes must've been obvious because he immediately questioned what was wrong. I told him that we needed to talk, but that we were going to wait for Dad to come home in a little bit. Cameron stared at me with big eyes.

"Am I in trouble?" he questioned, nervously.

"Well, we just want to talk with you about some things we're concerned about, okay?"

"Whatever it is, I'm just going to tell the truth, I promise. I'm not even gonna try to lie. That'll just make everything worse," he said, matter-of-factly.

From a year ago when every sentence out of his mouth held at *least* one lie, I was impressed with his reasoning and hoped he was being honest with me even then. Moments later, my husband arrived home. I pulled the items in question out and laid them on the table. I had barely started my well-planned speech when Cameron cut me off.

"I stole the knife from Grandma's house. I found it in her garage, and I took it."

I was taken aback by his quick admission. But I pressed further, asking him what he had in mind when he took the knife.

"I just wanted to be able to open stuff. I knew you wouldn't let me keep it, so I didn't tell you and I hid it."

I then asked him if he had damaged anything with the knife or if he had damaged himself in any way. My heart was pounding, and I felt sweaty as my lips formed the words.

"No way, you can check my body! And I didn't break anything either... I just opened my new package of underwear with it! Plus, I thought if there was ever a fire, I could cut the screen and get out quicker. Or if a robber broke in, I could save us all."

Oh, my heart...! I assured our son that he really needs to work on being the child here and that he doesn't have to be the protector of the adults or anyone else. That's our job, and we planned to continue to do good work in that area. I then pressed him about the bandages and wipes.

"Mom, my athlete's foot is so gross, and I don't want it to spread, so I was trying to bandage my toes apart. But I tried to clean my feet with the wipes, and then I needed the tape to get the bandages to stay, and the gauze to wrap around my toes."

For heaven's sake... this is why we have the foot spray! Finally, I asked him about the picture. "But, Cam, why did you hide your favorite picture of yourself in the bottom of your bin, honey?"

"Mom, that's a summer background. I put it away so I could decorate my room for fall. Didn't you see the pumpkins and potpourri on my stand? I still like my picture. I just wanted to redecorate."

Okay, seriously? I spent *four hours* with my heart going to hell and back in a fit of panic, only to find that my son was hiding a knife so that he could open underwear packages and protect his family if need be, that he was playing doctor to his foot fungus, and that he has a knack for *seasonal decorating*?

I told him that he was going to have a consequence (to be determined later) because of the stealing and the knife and the disastrous room, and then I sent him upstairs to clean. However, as soon as he was out of ear shot, I *cracked up*! Because I'd thought we were headed down a terrible RAD road, and all along, he was just playing with pumpkins and his toes!

The Hubs and I decided we would go easy on him because he was so honest with us, and because... well, because he was feeling the loss of his baby brother, whether he realized it yet or not.

Only Cameron couldn't wait. He wanted to know his punishment *that night*.

"Mom, can you just spank me, please?"

"Um, do you want me to spank you? Because I really don't want to, and I don't think this is a situation that would call for it, buddy."

"But Mom... I stole a knife! That's *really, really bad*."

"You're right. It *is* really bad. But I believe that you weren't trying to hurt anyone or yourself. And we talked about why that was an incredibly *stupid* decision, but that doesn't make you bad. It makes you a boy—a nine-year-old boy... who has a flare for fall décor."

"Well, will you at least ground me? Take away the tablet... wait. I'm already grounded from the tablet. Wanna just take it away even longer? Or I could stay in my room and not go outside? Or you could make me play with Taylor!"

I had to stifle a giggle at that last one.

"Cam. I appreciate your enthusiasm to make this right, really I do. But once again, let Dad and I be the adults, okay? We will choose the consequence and let you know. Until then, finish cleaning your room, and be prepared to help clean the house tomorrow with us."

His eyes began to water and his chin quivered. "Mom. I'm *really* sorry."

"I know you are, honey. Thank you."

I don't know how all this happened. I am not a great mother. I certainly haven't always handled my own grief and emotions properly amidst all this chaos. However, my son managed to tell the truth, show empathy, display protection, follow directives, admit to wrongdoing, apologize, and ask for a way to make it all right... while not hurting himself or others *all in one week.*

You guys, the gravity of this situation was not lost on me. Nor was the humility that I felt in the midst of it all. Over the years, Cameron has taught me how to love differently than I ever thought possible. He showed me that love needs to be *intentional and without condition*. I didn't know that I was capable of this particular kind of love until he walked into my life, demanding it from me in the most unlovable of ways. For the longest time, I wondered if I would survive these kids that we saved. And now, I marvel at the realization that they may just have saved me instead.

TAYLOR

Well, I sure hope you've enjoyed the first two courses, because this next one has a bit of a kick to it. Although, don't be thrown off by her size. After all, ghost peppers are tiny, yet they pack a mean punch! Friends, if there's one thing I've learned through all this parenting stuff, it's that unexpected things come in small packages. And at age four, wearing twenty-four-month clothing, she was one small package! In this section of the book, allow me to introduce you to our little fireball, our daughter, Taylor.

That first moment she walked in our door was defining for both her and me. It was in those first three minutes that I had a firm grasp on who this pint-sized creature was and how we were going to relate. Unlike her brother, there was no meekness attached to her small frame. There she stood, twenty-five pounds, bangs cut bluntly across her forehead, and a hand on her hip that jutted out with an attitude that matched.

"Hi, my name is Shivonne, and this is Pat. What's your name?" I asked sweetly.

"Hi. Um, I'm Taylor, and guess what? You're gonna have to buy me all new stuff because they sent me here with nothin'."

Bossy. Brass. Intimidating. Am I actually terrified of a four-year-old? I thought these things to myself as I forced my smile to remain firm and unflinching. *We are so gonna butt heads, I can see it now,* I remember thinking. But as those thoughts rang through my mind, new words began to form. *Gumption. Fearless. Survivor.* Yet even as I wrapped my head around all I'd learned of this little girl in a few brief minutes, I knew one thing for sure. We were going to have our hands full!

Funnily enough, Taylor *loves* this story! Since we don't have stories to tell our kids about what it was like when I was pregnant with them or how I felt the first moment their swaddled little bodies were placed in my arms, I can tell them the story of how we first met. And my girl, she just adores the fiery personality that comes out as I talk about her younger self. Although she does recognize that if she were to go into someone's home now and demanded things from them, she'd be in a world of trouble. In fact, she always follows this story up with one specific observation: "It's a good thing you raised me right, Mom, or I might have *always* been rude!"

But that first night, I had no idea what to do with this child! She marched up our stairs, making a significant stomp for such a small creature. Immediately, she found the room that she wanted and claimed it. Her older brother, obviously more passive, followed behind her and took what was left.

Every now and again, I could see moments of insecurity in her large blue eyes, but once she caught me staring, she seemed to will it away with sheer determination. Although Taylor insisted she needed help in the bathroom, it was obvious that this girl had been caring for herself for quite some time. Unlike Cameron, she could soap and lather her hair like a pro, and she held the washcloth like she'd been washing herself straight from the womb. For Taylor, it wasn't so much that she needed the help; it was that she desperately wanted attention... *all of it.*

If I were talking to Cameron, Taylor would climb into my lap, hold my cheeks in her hands, and put her face directly in front of mine. "I love you, Mommy! You're the best mommy I've ever had!" Normally that would have been endearing, except she'd only been in our home for four hours, so it actually was far more off-putting than anything else!

During those short hours on that first evening, it was obvious that she was used to being the favored child—the one that was always held, coddled, and taught basic life skills. And it was equally obvious that Cameron had been given less attention for most of his young life. He would immediately stop talking when she interrupted, defeated before he even began; whereas Taylor seemingly gave no thought to the apparent dichotomy, as it had been the norm for so long. It was almost as if I could see a volcano start to bubble just below Cameron's surface and the jealousy that was physically palpable.

That night, I was exhausted. Taylor, however, was not. And whereas Cameron preferred to lay silently in his bed alone, his sister begged for me to lie in her bed with her until she fell asleep. The problem was, she just wouldn't sleep! We had been lying there for hours, and that child talked my ear off about anything and everything. "What's your favorite animal? Do you like to eat spaghetti? It's my favorite. When are you going to get me new clothes? Can I go with you to work tomorrow? What do you do there? Can we get a pony?" Finally, around 12:30 a.m., my eyes could handle no more. I allowed them to close and prayed that she didn't do anything weird to me if I dozed off.

Minutes later, I felt little fingers tracing my face—around my eyes, over my cheeks, across my lips, and finally landing up my nose. My eyes popped open and she quickly removed her finger, closing her own eyes tightly. And just when I thought she was close to sleep, eyes still shut, she began to whisper in a sing-songy voice a made-up tune about strawberries and ponies.

I told her she didn't have to sleep, but that I did. So I made my way to my room and collapsed on the bed next to my snoring husband. (We were six hours in, and he was *already* getting more sleep than me... just sayin'.) Four measly hours later, Taylor woke us up by talking to us through the vent that connected our two rooms. Now, coming from a sound sleep and waking up to creepy little girl whispers coming through your vent, especially when you're used to that room being vacant, well, let me tell you... it's the most terrifying thing in the world. We're talking *The Shining* type of scary!

And this was the nightly routine for the next several months. Taylor would sing weird songs, whisper creepily through the night, and sleep for a maximum of four hours. Then, she'd be fully awake and energetic for the entire day with no nap. We were later informed that this is a common side effect of children who were born with drugs in their systems, but that information didn't help us much.

Eventually, we resorted to melatonin. We had no idea how to survive on such little sleep, nor did we know how she was doing it! My head constantly felt fuzzy, and I had no strength to deal with the weird behaviors the kids brought with them. Honestly, our only choice was to knock her out cold. And that very first night of the melatonin she said to us, "Finally! They sent my sleepy medicine over!"

Wishing someone from CYS had filled us in on that tiny tidbit of information at the beginning, we gave her the smallest dose we could. She swallowed the little pill like a champ and was out cold twenty minutes later. This is how we started getting a full seven to eight hours of sleep each night.

Because sometimes Hope comes in small doses from a melatonin bottle.

When Taylor came to live with us, we were quickly aware of two things: (1) She had amazing survival skills. This girl knew how to wash her own hair, clean her own bottom after doing her business, fold laundry better than my husband, and manipulate any situation to get her needs met. (2) And Taylor knew nothing else. Sadly and literally.

If we asked Taylor to state her favorite color, her response was, "What's a color?" If we asked Taylor to choose a number between one and ten to see who would go first in a game, she guessed "X." And forget taking the poor kid to the park! Instead of running around with all the other kids, she stared them down with a cold glassiness in her eyes, refusing to engage or play with anyone other than an adult or a baby.

We realized in those first five months that our daughter was a pint-sized surviving machine, but how in the world would she survive her first day of school at Head Start? Immediately, I'd imagined getting called into the preschool principal's office to be lectured on the dangers of letting my child bite, hit, pinch, and hauntingly stare at other kids. Not only that, *she was so far behind educationally*! How would she ever catch up? Would she feel embarrassed and discouraged? Would she refuse to go back after the very first day?

Most parents spend time teaching their kids shapes and the ABCs instead of teaching them how to iron clothes and wash dishes. If this was home economics, Taylor would be the shining star of the class. But since four-year-olds don't exactly take home ec., we were stuck with preschool and learning how to raise our hands and not run with scissors. After what seemed like too many weeks, it was finally Taylor's first day of school. To celebrate the occasion, the teacher wanted each student's parents to come and stay in the classroom with the kids all day to help them adjust. After all, it is a big deal to go from being at home all day to five hours of school, rules, and new foods! So, I took the day off work to meet with Cameron's teacher for a conference and to be with Taylor in her classroom (since I really can't picture my large Italian husband perched on the edge of a kiddy chair for five hours without something catastrophic happening).

Surprisingly enough, it was seriously one of the best days I'd had with the kids since they'd been in our home. I was still extremely tired, but the only thing I had to do in that moment was to be present for them—no work, no cleaning, no papers to fill out—just straight attentiveness to the kids.

The other benefit that I found was socializing with other parents. I mean, did you know that all kids are crazy? It's not just mine! In fact on that first day, Taylor, who is usually lazy as a sloth, was the best cleaner-upper in the class *and* she asked to take a nap! There must've been magic in the water at school (or benefits of having her mom home and attentive to her all day) because this was a brand-new child, and I was loving it. Especially when the teacher had the kids and their mommies make kissing hands.

The very sweet and animated preschool instructor read a story about a nervous raccoon that had to go to school and was terrified of missing his mom while gone. The mama raccoon then kissed the palm of her baby's hand and told him that her love would never wash off. If he were to get scared at school, he could place the kiss on his cheek or his heart, and he would know his mother loves and misses him.

Aw, right? So, us mommies and kiddies traced our hands on construction paper, cut them out, drew a heart on each one, and then kissed the paper hands. Taylor was to keep my big hand at school and I keep her little hand with me at work. This way she could pull it out if she missed me.

Now, my kid has attachment issues, and I figured there was no way in this world that she'd ever give one more thought to my cut-out hand. However, about a half hour later, my work phone rang and I had to slip out of the classroom to answer it. Taylor was busy with another little girl and I figured I wouldn't be all that long on the phone, so I left without telling her where I was.

However, when I returned to the classroom just minutes later, I was greeted by the teacher and my little girl, face stained with tears, holding my kissing hand to her cheek and choking on her sobs. This is the first time my heart broke and rejoiced at the same time. I never wanted her to feel sad, but I so desperately wanted to feel real love from this baby of mine. I picked her up and hugged her tightly. And then I thanked her for missing me.

The next day, she had her first day of school—the first official day where the parents *weren't* invited. I had anticipated consoling a crying child as she slumped off the school bus at the end of the day. But instead, Taylor's first day of school was a success! In fact, she'd immediately informed me that she thought she might just keep going every day, as if this were an option of sorts. Nevertheless, I was glad she was on board, so I told her it was a good choice to keep going.

Once home, I'd asked her all of the normal school questions: *What did you do today? What did you eat for lunch? Did you make any friends? What were their names?* It was the answer to the last question that left me wondering if we needed to get her hearing checked. Taylor announced that she had made three best friends and that their names are "Lucash, Zuke, and Leven." Now, unless her classroom is filled with hobbits, this seemed highly unlikely to me. But since they were her "best friends," I wasn't going to judge... even if they were short with large, furry feet.

And hence we began the fun world of Taylor's new social life.

Shortly after we'd agreed to adopt Taylor and Cameron, we knew that they were going to need some help socializing them because school was just not cutting it. Cameron was stabbing people and Taylor was bossing everyone around, including the teacher. Their "friends" appeared to be scared of them when we saw them at the park, and when we asked kids to come play with ours, they usually left in tears.

This is why we decided that hobbies would be good for them both—sports, in particular. Things that would have them working with other kids toward a common goal, encourage team building, positive peer interaction, and for God's sake, a little coordination! Never in my life had I seen a more noodly, awkward, clumsy lot! Due to Taylor's unique size (a.k.a. ridiculous tininess), we figured she'd be a shoo-in for gymnastics. And once we taught her how to pronounce her new sport, she brightened considerably.

Friends, it took her six months to learn how to do a forward roll. I'd thought every kid knew how to somersault! But it was as hard for her as learning to count to 10 (which actually took longer than six months). However, that determination, and the fact that I refused to let her quit, led to her finally accomplishing not only a roll but a cartwheel within that first year. Blessedly, once she figured out how her body worked, she began to progress like crazy.

Four years later, my daughter is in an advanced class with all the bigger girls at the studio. She shows her walkovers and handstands to anyone who will watch, and she practices handsprings and aerials religiously. Our little noodle-armed child who cried when we wouldn't carry her for the long walk *down our driveway* now has muscle definition, balance, coordination, and she even runs like an athlete instead of a farm animal.

More than that, I watched as an overconfident little girl realized that she wasn't the queen bee at something. She had to learn what hard work meant and what perseverance could lead to. Her confidence had shattered quite abruptly those first few months. But then again, I think it needed to. We were slowly getting both kids onto a level playing field. Neither was going to be given privilege over the other. No one was the golden child. Actually, they were both quite equally tarnished! However, the pleasure for me was to see her broken and reshaped more and more each day, both in and out of the gym.

Not that this process was quick... and not that we didn't have our work still cut out for us!

Maggots. There were *maggots* in Taylor's room. I didn't know that it was possible to feel so many emotions at one time, but there I was, facing all the emotions. First off, I hate all things that have the wrong number of legs. If it has no legs or more than four legs, you can count on me hating it with all the hate I can muster. And maggots are the *grossest* kind of no-legged creatures. They're all white and wriggly, and they seem to multiply at a rate that defies all mathematical logic.

Furthermore, why the heck were they in my house? I don't know how, but I managed to carry the Shop-Vac to her room without passing out. However, the dry heaves continued the entire time I sucked up each little worm, closely inspecting every inch of her room until I was quite certain that I'd gotten them all, including the source of the problem.

We have a rule in our home: No having food of any kind in our rooms, because, once again, we live in an old farmhouse that is prone to experiencing lots of things with no legs or too many of them to count. This rule had not been successful in keeping the children from sneaking all kinds of edibles into their rooms and hiding them around for safekeeping. And the Day of the Maggots was no different.

Hidden underneath books on her shelf was a half-eaten by her, half-eaten by worms, week-old Happy Meal from McDonalds. Equally grossed out by the worms and the fact that the sandwich was still actually intact after a full week, I disposed of the infested mess.

Upon her arrival home from school, I'd very calmly and rationally confronted Taylor about the hidden food in her room. Naturally, she denied the entire thing. When I told her that I remembered buying her the Happy Meal, she told me that I was lying. And then when I became frustrated, she told me that I put the Happy Meal in her room to get her into trouble.

I was half-tempted to take the Shop-Vac full of maggots and dump it on her pretty little head, but the other half of me resorted to a chant-like state, reminding myself to remain calm and remember that she has trauma issues.

Realistically, though, there is only so much that chanting does for a person, you know? Because shortly after the maggots, there was the *continual* stealing of my make-up, hair supplies, medicated facial wash, and basic toiletries. I had no idea what she was doing with my tampons, but I knew that they were no longer there for me when I needed them! And to take a woman's precious hair products and empty them down the drain, when said woman has curly hair issues, is just cruel and unusual, at best!

Entire bottles of foundation would be smeared across her face as I could see she'd used my lipstick as eye shadow. But Taylor would stand there and defend herself to the death.

"Nope. It wasn't me. I swear! It was Cameron!"

"Taylor, you're *wearing* the make-up right now, as we speak."

"No, I'm not! This is what my face looks like." "Uh, no it's not."

"Well then... I guess someone *else* got into your make-up and put it on me when I was sleeping."

"Really? That's how you're going to play this?" "I'm not playing, and I'm not lying!"

This was a conversation that we had daily... for about three years. I would hide my things, but she'd find more to get into. I'd lock things up, and she'd find the keys or break the lock. I would lock the bathroom door upstairs, so she would pee on the floor and claim she "couldn't make it" to the bathroom downstairs, despite the fact that she had just gone to the bathroom ten minutes prior. It was a never-ending battle of wills and lies. And it was insanely expensive! But the more consequences I gave her, the more she broke my things. And the more I cracked down on the lying, the more she would then break the things that I had bought her. Consequently, I would take all of her belongings away for a time, and she'd peel the paint and plaster off her walls, leaving beautiful holes to decorate her room. She didn't care that she lost her stuff... after all, she'd lost all of her things numerous times in her life. And since she struggled with attaching to people, how was attaching to physical objects really any different?

We tried reward charts, but those usually stopped working by the end of the week, especially since both kids struggled to earn rewards, even when we made the standards as low as humanly possible. The self-sabotage was intense, as were the tantrums that followed. And once the child found scissors, life as we knew it was all over. It didn't matter that she was short, the girl could climb like a mountain goat and get anything from anywhere. Those legs that would be too tired to walk up the driveway? Yeah, gymnastics ruined that for us, because now she can balance and climb to precarious heights in her goal to obtain whatever she desired, and for a long time, that was scissors!

Taylor began cutting holes in her clothes, cutting the feet off her footsy pajamas, and she cut her own hair... several times. I can only imagine what her teachers and the parent helpers in her classroom thought when she'd come in to school some days. Utterly obsessed with wearing dirty clothes, she would pull them out of the hamper and layer them under other outfits in the mornings, and then she'd get to school and strip down to smelly, stained clothes that were freshly cut up, with uneven bangs and chunks cut up the sides of her head.

She looked like she belonged on the cover of a *Feed the Children* brochure.

No matter how many adorable outfits I bought her, still with the dirty clothes! She wanted to wear what she wanted to wear, and that headstrong personality was not going to be broken until she was ready. When I look back on that battle, I know that I should have listened to Elsa and "let it go," but it was a battle of wills between her and me. It was something I felt I had to win in order to show her that she didn't make the rules. But in the meantime, it served as just another way to put off dealing with the real issues that were going on inside of her little mind.

For Taylor, keeping me angry about clothing and make-up was a defense mechanism. It kept me from talking to her about the things that she hid away, deep inside. Whereas Cameron would open up in a pool of tears, Taylor would clam up and turn into a statue when her past was mentioned. Sure, she could talk about her cousin and what each house she lived in was like, because those things weren't scary to her. Yet if I mentioned some of her behaviors that led us to believe she'd been exposed to disturbing circumstances, she'd shut down and then break my things once again.

You see, that little girl was the only female in a family of boys. And her mom was a woman of necessity, so she found herself a new man every time she needed a place to stay or an exchange for whatever substance she was currently craving. She exposed her vulnerable daughter to life situations and people that make my stomach tighten into knots. And after years of being in our home, Taylor finally started trusting us, and that's when all the stories began to pour out of her like a faucet.

Suddenly, her random headaches, belly aches, leg pains, and other various wounds that could not be seen or medically accounted for began to make sense. Inside of my feisty little girl was a child who felt dirty and confused. She hated her memories but felt equally guilty for telling secrets that her birth mom had told her to keep. Constantly torn between loyalty and anger, it was easier for Taylor to shut down than to deal with the feelings from all she'd been through.

She was just a baby... three years old. And it's easy for me to become angry and to want revenge against the adults in her life that should have been protecting her but didn't. It's easy for me to wish the same things on them so that they could know what they've put my daughter through, so that they could know what they've robbed her of in this life. But I, too, struggle with an emotional battle. My humanity runs full speed in one direction, while my spirituality tells me to take a breath. I know that my heavenly Father loves the adults that have hurt my children. Oh, I know that doesn't seem fair. Not in the slightest. However, God's love was never meant to be fair; it was meant to be holy. And that's why He can love us at our worst, despite the fact that we nail Him to a cross daily with our sins. And is my sin less than theirs? Is yours?

I think that's why grace is so important in this world. I know that if it weren't for grace, I would be a goner. And I know that if weren't for that same grace, I would've already taken care of business with the people that hurt my children. So, while I continue to fight for justice, I choose to say no to vengeance. Instead of what is due them, I hope to break the cycle of violence and stand on the side of grace.

Because sometimes Hope means knowing that God is in control of justice, even when I am not.

One lovely evening, that very child with whom I have battled so much did the unthinkable. She stole my grandmother's ring from the memory box that hangs on our living room wall. The box houses some of the material items that once belonged to my grandmother—things that I cherish so much from a woman that was very dear to me and everyone who knew her.

But there was no denying it... the ring was gone. Why, you might ask? Because Pat and I had a meeting with a life insurance man in our kitchen one night; thus, Taylor wasn't being given our undivided attention.

Now, I didn't notice that the ring was missing right away. Nor did I notice the scratches on the glass window of our living room... or the misspelled word carved in big letters on the hood of my car. No, I noticed these things the following day.

Always in such a rush these days, I raced to my car while the sun was still barely visible over the trees. I drove to work and proceeded through my day without a thought. That was until one of my clients asked me if I had intended to carve the word "Hell" in big letters across the hood of my car.

What! I ran outside and stared at my car, but I saw nothing... until I moved just a little to the side and the light caught the carving perfectly. There, scrawled in chicken scratch writing, was the word *Hell*.

My mind immediately went to Cameron. He was, after all, the only one that could spell a lick of anything at that time, and that would be just like him to write a bad word on my car! It took every ounce of patience I could muster not to drive to his school and enroll him in a work-release program until his debt had been paid.

However, when I arrived at home, Cameron came to greet me from playing in the yard, only to say, "Mom! What happened to your car?"

"Gee, Cameron, I don't know... what did happen to my car?"

"Did one of your clients do that?" He looked genuinely surprised, and I started to question my accusations.

"No, none of my clients did this. When Dad and I were meeting with the insurance man last night, you and Taylor were playing in the yard. Did you write on my car, thinking it would wipe off?"

"Mom, no! I didn't write on your car... wait. Maybe Taylor did it with your grandma's ring?"

Oh. My. Gosh. I ran inside the house and headed straight to the memory box. Sure enough, the ring was gone.

"Taylor!" I screamed her name so loudly that it's a wonder she came toward the direction of the sound. A person with any sense at all would've just packed their bags and ran in the opposite direction until they met the ocean, and then they would start swimming. It was a sound that should've let her know that she was about to meet her Maker.

But nope. My daughter lacked sense like she lacked the ability to spell. She nonchalantly came into the living room and gave me an innocent look as she replied, "Yes?"

"Where is my grandmother's ring, Taylor!" "In my room."

She wasn't even denying taking it! I didn't take the time to look in the mirror, but my face must've been at least twelve shades of purple and my fists balled so hard that my fingers hurt.

"What is it doing in your room, child?" "I wanted to try it on..."

"Go get it... *now.*"

While she was going to fetch the ring, Cameron cautiously entered the living room from outside. Perhaps he had planned some final words to say before I dismembered his sister. Either that or he was just excited that she was finally getting into as much trouble as he usually had! Moments later, Taylor returned holding the ring out to me. I carefully placed it back in the memory box and turned my attention back to the devious child in front of me.

"Taylor. Did you carve the word Hell into the hood of my car with my grandmother's ring?"

"Uh, no! It must've been Cameron..."

This set off a battle of the siblings as the two argued back and forth. My husband, staying clear of the situation from the other room offered a hand, but I didn't need a hand... I needed a guillotine!

Over an hour later, we finally got to the bottom of the situation. Taylor, to her credit, was correct. She hadn't written the word "Hell" onto the hood of my car with my grandmother's ring. She had attempted to write the word "Hello" with a *rock*, but she forgot how to spell it and gave up. She carved up the living room window with the ring.

"So, there!" she said, pointedly. As if that showed us who was right and who was wrong! I just stood limply in place, because there really were no words to be said in that moment. Telling her that she was wrong wouldn't have mattered to her in the slightest. She had done it on purpose because she was angry. Plain and simple. I sent her to her room, just so I didn't have to look at her face for one more second.

My kids, they spent a lot of time in their rooms for a couple of years. It was to save their lives, basically, but I like to think that it was good parenting skills on my part. After all, it was giving them time to think about what they'd done... except they usually just used it as time to think of new ways to destroy the house.

Later that night, after I had cried lots of frustrated tears and my husband stared at me with absolutely no more solutions, other than to lock up everything that I own (because seriously, how do you lock up a car? *Come on*, honey, you're better than this, I wanted to tell him), I decided to have a heart-to-heart with Taylor. *Maybe*, I rationalized, *if she knew how much she had hurt me by doing this, we would have a breakthrough in our relationship!*

I went to her room and knelt down by the bed. Calmly she sat, staring at me with blank eyes. "Taylor, can we talk, please? I just think that there are some things we need to get out in the open. I mean... do you like the way our relationship is?"

"Not really. We are always angry at each other."

"Yeah, that's exactly what I've noticed too. Why do you think that is?"

"Hmm... I don't know," the four-year-old responded. "Is it because you're mean to me?"

Breathe... "Well, I'm just taking a stab in the dark here, but do you think I'm often angry with you because you seem to break my things an awful lot?"

"Well, it might be that too."

"Honey, I *really* want our relationship to be better than this. I need to know that I can trust you and that you're not going to break my things when you're angry. Could you do me a favor? If you feel upset by something, could you just try talking to me about it instead? You know, so we could work out the problem without either of us having to get upset or in trouble?"

"Yes, Mommy. I'm sorry I took your grandma's ring and ruined your car."

"Thank you. I appreciate it. Give me a hug, you goon!"

Taylor giggled and hugged me hard. My eyes were glistening with tears, feeling like we'd really made some progress in that moment. I felt such relief that she was able to respond to a conversation without having a list of consequences or not seeming to care about my feelings at all. "Okay, girly, go brush your teeth, and I'll be back to tuck you in."

Ten minutes later, I went into the bathroom to shut off the light that had been left on for the trillionth time. It was then that I noticed a pile of make-up emptied into the sink and smeared all over the counter, drawers, and mirror. And that was the first time I felt truly betrayed by a child. It was an emotion that my husband and I were forced to experience many times over the next several years—feeling as though we'd done good parenting work, only to be thrown in the opposite direction moments later.

Needless to say, Taylor did not get a tuck-in that night.

It's interesting just how much little ones keep you on your toes—emotionally, that is. I know that kids "say the darndest things," but since when do they know how to make backhanded compliments? Are they teaching it in school these days or do my kids just have a knack for this? It had seemed like for months, Cameron and Taylor were both mesmerized as they watched me put on my make-up before I left for work each morning. There were plenty of questions like "What's that?" to go around, and a good helping of "Can I wear some?" It was early on that my guard was completely down, and I assumed that compliments from children were all sugary sweet and heartfelt.

One morning, Taylor had informed me that I looked so pretty with my make-up on. I beamed and thought, *Aw, what a sweetie pie she is!* She paused (do four-year-olds pause for effect?) before adding, "But you look really ugly without it."

Yikes! Where did that one come from! And then later that same evening when I served Sloppy Joes and cheesy broccoli, both kids looked at me like I'd placed a pile of dog food in front of them. Apparently the children had been served filet mignon and lobster at their prior homes.

"What is that?" Cameron asked. I explained that it was a Sloppy Joe and it's what we were having for dinner. Taylor took a tentative bite after staring her sandwich down for about ten minutes.

"You know," she said, "you are not a very good cook today, but I bet tomorrow you'll be better." I thanked her for the encouragement and then promptly reminded her that I'd seen her eat a booger just the day before. And so she finished her sandwich, mumbling to herself, "The booger tasted better..." But the hits, they just kept coming! The very next night, Taylor informed me that she hated calling me "mommy." Okay, I get it. She was still having visits with her birth mom, and she was constantly being doted on during visitations.

Maybe she was just missing her birth family, and that's why calling me "mommy" was so difficult for her?

I think it stung so much, mostly because she'd been super affectionate the previous few weeks (affection that didn't lead to her breaking any of my things), barely talking about her biological family and calling me mommy fairly regularly. Pat and I didn't start encouraging the kids to call us mommy and daddy until we were well on our way with the adoption process, but it'd been a struggle to make the switch to these new titles for them, nevertheless.

When I asked her why she hated calling me mommy, she wouldn't look me in the eye. She told me that maybe when she gets big she would call me mommy, but that she didn't want to now. I assured her that was fine and that she could call me a different name if she wanted... mama, perhaps? She thought about it for a second and gave me a "maybe" followed by an "okay." Although she didn't sound very convinced at that time. Taylor went the rest of the evening being completely unaffectionate, and she didn't even ask for a tuck-in at bedtime, something that would normally induce an all-out tantrum if missed.

After several months of doing nothing but pouring myself out for my two kids, I realized that my "Super Mom" efforts were in vain. Not only was I not a Super Mom, but I wasn't even wanted as a regular mom. I'm the rule-maker, the woman that makes dinner, and the one who tells them to brush their teeth longer than three seconds. I'm the person who spends so much of her time trying to heal their rejected hearts that she ends up feeling rejected herself. These were feelings that overcame me after bedtime each night—when there were finally a few minutes to process all the pent-up emotions I faced while raising another woman's children.

Honestly, when I dreamed of having kids, I never imagined having to win them over, working relentlessly just to have them like me, let alone love me. Despite the upcoming adoptions, both kids were still having two visits per week with their birth mom and two older half-brothers. Had something been said at one of the visits? I knew that their birth mom was still demanding that they call her "Mommy," which I could understand, even though rights had been terminated. Maybe she became resentful or even challenged the children's loyalty to her by asking them not to call us by our new titles.

But I had to wonder, how were we to ever going to bond with these kids if there was such a constant and strong reminder that we were not, in fact, their parents? Would we ever feel more than frazzled or frustrated? Would we ever do more than tolerate our days? Would we ever make it through a twenty-four-hour stretch without yelling or tears? As I laid my head down each night, I said a simple prayer, "Lord, please help my kids love me. And please help me love my kids."

The evening eventually came when Taylor faced her final visit with her biological mother. Her adoption was coming up the following week, and she was given one last encounter to say her good-byes. We expected a great fallout. We expected tears, tantrums, misbehavior, or, at the very least, a rift between siblings (as Cameron was still required to have visits for the time being). However, what we didn't expect was calmness.

Naturally, I decided to roll with it because I couldn't see the point in ruining a good thing by attacking it with questions! And then, just when my heart thought it could rest for a moment, she dropped the bomb.

Taylor was in the middle of talking about her visit when she referred to her biological mother, not as "Mommy" as she always has, but as "Mama." This was the name that she'd been calling me for the previous few months, since she already had several Mommies in her life. Once she expressed that she didn't like calling me mommy, we had several conversations before she did decide to settle on Mama—a special name that was unattached to any other women in her life.

That one word took the wind out of me, and it actually took me several seconds to realize that she'd been asking me a question and that I needed to respond. I pulled myself together and had her repeat her question before I quickly answered. Moving on to wash dishes, I kept myself busy to hold the tears at bay. But once the dishes were done and put away, I still felt a nervous energy pulsing through me as the emotions still hadn't found a proper outlet. Then it hit me: Puzzles. Yes, that would do the trick! Let's do an alphabet puzzle. That way, even if my kids never actually attached to me, at least they wouldn't be stupid.

We spent the next hour doing alphabet puzzles, number puzzles, and color puzzles. They learned, they had fun, and then they got ready for bed. We read our story, did our prayers, and had a tuck in, complete with hug and kiss, and I told her good night. I ducked into my room and was just slipping into my pajamas, allowing myself a moment to process the earlier string of emotions that, at last, I had time to process. This is when another unexpected event happened. Taylor's tiny, little Minnie Mouse voice called out from the next room:

"You're my bestest... I love you as much as the sky." A silent smile joined silent tears.

"And I love *you* as much as the ocean," I said back.

"I love your ocean too."

"Good night, Tay." "

Good night, Mama."

Because sometimes hope means recognizing that one word is all that's needed to start healing a relationship.

It was October 23, 2012, and a momentous day indeed. It was the first time we would say an official yes to parenting as we joined with family and the judge to celebrate Taylor's adoption day. After seven months and a million daily doubts, we had finally arrived at the much-anticipated moment. All dressed in our nicest clothes, we walked into the courthouse for what seemed like the hundredth time.

Although this time was different. This time we were going in without facing abusers, without being questioned on the stand, without having to shield our little ones from angry glares and nasty memories. On this day, we were walking through those big oak doors with smiles, ready to make a new memory in the same room that had been so scary for so very long. In that half hour, we vowed to love and protect our daughter—to treat her as our own flesh and blood. It resembled a marriage ceremony in a way, which really was no surprise, since foster care had felt a lot like a really, really long blind date. As we smiled for our picture with the judge, we knew that life was never going to be the same again.

And that feeling terrified me to the core, because what I had known before—fostering, being a temporary parent, not being able to fully bond—it hadn't felt complete. But at least it *was known*. The fear of what was unknown was earth-shaking, and that's putting it mildly! I had already seen what the short ones in my life were capable of, what baggage they brought to the table, and we'd said *yes* despite it all. My life? No, my life was definitely not going to ever be the same again. And maybe that's exactly what I needed.

We walked from the courtroom feeling light, riding on a fluffy surreal cloud. And as we were met by a stream of congratulations, handshakes, and gifts, we were also notified that Taylor and Cameron's baby brother had been born and that we would be bringing him home in a few short days.

No. Life would definitely never be the same again.

And it most certainly wasn't! Taylor was incredibly happy to be officially part of our family. She was, in fact, so happy that she had me write a letter to her teacher expressing that Taylor had been adopted and now bore the Costa last name. When questioned why she didn't want to tell her teacher the good news on her own, she informed me that because she lies so much, the teacher stopped believing anything she said, and she really wanted her to know that she was telling the truth this time!

It was a note I was more than happy to write.

Although she was elated with her new life changes, she struggled each time that Cameron had a visit with their birth family. She couldn't understand why he was allowed to still go but she was not. Meanwhile, Cameron didn't even want to keep going and continually asked why he couldn't just get adopted like Taylor. He felt upset that everyone at the visits usually had focused on Taylor, and once baby Isaac was born, Cameron faded into the background of his birth family's life completely.

But as we always seemed to do, we settled into a routine. Yes, a significantly more exhausting routine, but nevertheless there was a system that was working for the most part. Pat's job allowed him to work in the evenings once I'd return home from working day shifts. We would swap kisses and pass off children with all of their homework and important information for the day. I would get them fed and to their therapy appointments, soccer practices, and gymnastics events. It would be late into the evening when Pat and I would finally rejoin one another in the solace of our mostly quiet home, until Isaac would finally drift off and we were able to rest, officially off duty for a few hours.

But those moments of rest didn't last long, because before we knew it, morning would come and all of the kids would awaken, ready to do battle. With whom? Well, that just depended on the day. However, since Isaac was born, Taylor was in a constant battle with me over not treating the flimsy newborn as her own personal baby doll. If you took your eyes off her for just a few seconds, she'd have Isaac in her lap (him weighing half of what she weighed, if not more!), her bending his limbs the wrong way or pinching his nose closed.

It didn't seem to matter that we told her *over and over and over again* that she could hurt her baby brother by doing those things. Her own impulses were just too great, and she would look for any opportunity to shove food into his mouth while I was cleaning up dishes and Isaac rocked in his swing, just a few feet away from my place at the sink. I'm pretty sure she didn't believe me—that she honestly thought she could parent Isaac and knew better than I did. That was generally the case, though, as my kids were largely untrusting, which is still a struggle to this day. In fact, when I finally became pregnant with Wyatt and we broke the news to them, the kids actually thought we were lying for the first several months! As if I would go to such lengths as daily puking and getting fat, just to pull one over on them. However, as is the case with all children who have experienced early childhood trauma, trust is scary and requires far too much vulnerability. If someone spent years, or even just months, telling you that you're unlovable, that your physical body is theirs to do whatever with, and that your needs meant nothing, it wouldn't matter if that person also apologized or said, "I love you," each day. Because it wouldn't take long before your brain would realize that people were not to be trusted. That safety was not a guarantee in life, that love was not real.

Therefore, trust has never been easy for my children. That's why they hold on to every last word we say as the Gospel truth. God forbid we make plans with someone and those plans fall through because the other person got sick or had car trouble, because to my children, that meant that we had lied to them, proving once and for all that we are untrustworthy. Even still, knowing what I do about trauma and the brain, it still didn't make living with the daily effects any simpler.

Besides not being able to trust us, which was honestly a very mutual feeling after a while, I would hate bringing my children in public. Not because they were terrible. Actually, a lot of the time they would hold it together well enough while we were out, saving their real selves for once we returned home. So not only did my kids think we were liars, I was pretty sure our family and friends were beginning to think the same thing.

"I think you're just being paranoid..."

"*All* kids do that..."

"Have you tried time-outs?"

"I've seen your kids, and they're not nearly as bad as you make them sound..."

"It's just because you're new to parenting. Soon you'll laugh and realize this was all normal..."

Normal? Oh, my gosh, really? Because if that's the case, why in the world were people still having sex? It's a wonder that word hasn't spread like wildfire: Beware! Children are rotten! Use abstinence! Although, I was still pretty convinced that normal kids didn't pee on their carpet or harm the family pets on a weekly basis. But how was I to make those around me see that I wasn't making it all up? That parenting these children felt more like raising Tasmanian devils than humans?

Those regular cycles of actually liking and disliking the short people living in my home were akin to those associated with menstruation... except that children don't make me bloat and PMS doesn't make me homicidal. So, when my parents came out from Michigan to help us manage life (oh, and to celebrate the Thanksgiving holiday), it gave me a bit of time to pull back and yell less... less. It was then that my father had a novel idea.

He suggested that I try to be calm with the children.

Is this man out of his precious mind? I thought. *He'd been with my rascals all weekend and saw how taxing they are!* But he reminded me that being reactionary makes me feel worse instead of getting my point across to unruly kids. I mean, duh... that's Therapy 101. However, because I'd been so used to living on the crazy farm, I'd lost all common sense entirely. That's why I decided to try my dad's plan.

That evening, I calmly told the children to clean up their rooms. I had to *calmly* tell them about forty times, but I did it *calmly* nevertheless. Then, I *calmly* informed Taylor that she could refuse to get her potties out before bed, but that I would then wake her every ten minutes throughout the night until she peed for me. Finally, I *calmly* reminded the kids that their constant squabbling over insignificant matters breaks Jesus' heart and that we now have three children, so that means we have a spare—just in case one of them would happen to, say, disappear in the middle of the night and never be heard from again.

Both Cameron and Taylor looked at me with slight grins. They were *pretty* sure I was kidding, but they weren't positive. So they figured they'd better behave.

Sometimes Hope means listening to your dad's advice, even if it only works for an evening.

That first Christmas with the kids was nothing short of a miracle. Let it be said that these children broke no less than ten holiday bulbs, stole each other's letters to Santa from the elf mailbox in the kitchen, and would sneak out of bed in the middle of the night to gorge themselves on holiday sweets. Naturally, they'd lie about it. But when Taylor came out the next morning with a half-chewed Tootsie Roll stuck in her hair, I felt fairly confident calling her out.

But for us, December wasn't just about our first Christmas; it was also the first birthday party that we were able to plan for one of our kids (did I say *we*? Because all I remember was a *me* doing all that planning... just sayin'). Taylor was born two days following Christmas, so our house resembled an explosion of boxes and bows, toys and clothes. All I could say at the end of that week was that I'd seriously be okay if I never saw wrapping paper or tape again for the rest of my life.

However, what I *did* decide was this: had I birthed Taylor myself, I would've done things differently. Well, I would've done a lot of things differently, like not using drugs while pregnant. But I most *definitely* wouldn't have chosen to get pregnant in March so that I'd never have to deal with the stress of planning a child's fifth birthday party *two days after Christmas*!

Christmases will never be the same again, birthdays will always get overshadowed, and parties will have to be canceled due to freak blizzards that leave your driveway unsurpassable or by the nasty flu bug that threatens to contaminate each person who eats a piece of birthday cake that was blown on by a five-year-old with spittle issues.

Be that as it may, I have to say, not only did we survive that party, but we kinda *rocked* it! The house finally look clean for the first time in ten months and the kids loved the makeover theme Taylor had chosen... even the boys! We had Mexican pirates, fairy cowboys, and princesses with enough make-up on to satisfy the entire cast of *The Jersey Shore*. I didn't expect to see little boys falling down the staircase wearing my high heels, but no one got hurt, nothing got broken, and the birthday girl had a good time (relatively speaking, that is. After all, RAD children tend to get exactly what they want and then cry because it was a letdown in some way... but we made it work).

I'm sure that I will forever curse the "March Madness" that overtook one woman five years ago, but she did give me my only daughter, which was more than I can say for my own uterus, so I suppose a thank-you is in order. However, I plan to send her a strongly-worded postcard mid-February from this point forward, just in case Valentine's Day gets the best of her!

My version of a fairy tale has changed drastically since I was young. Getting old does that to a girl. I used to dream of a handsome prince to marry, sweet little children in trendy clothes to run around our spacious yet cozy home, and rainbow-dowsed happiness to fill my every moment. But now, all I dream about is getting a few extra minutes of sleep, not having to talk to anyone ever, and peeing without someone shouting at me through the door.

However, that was my reality. There seemed to be a daily routine in my home that the children had started. It began when my car pulled into the driveway after work and ended when the last child had fallen asleep. This routine was called "Utterly Ridiculous and Continuous Question Asking." On most days, I would sit in my car for a few minutes before mustering up the courage to go inside my own home, knowing that I would face a mountain of mundane questions, followed by a sea of endless prattling. As I'd put my hand on the doorknob and slowly turn the handle, I could hear Cameron start yelling questions to me as Taylor shouted louder to be heard over him.

In fact, the first questions had already been fully uttered before I'd even finished opening the door! Day after day, I reminded the kids that I hadn't even come into the house yet, taken my shoes off, gone to the bathroom, or even said "Hello" before they were attacking me like a piece of meat fallen into piranha-infested waters.

And do you want to know the most ridiculous part of it all? I'm convinced that these children didn't actually want answers to their questions. No, after years of observation, I realized that they were just talking to hear their own voices. I know this because the questions that they asked me every day were ones that had blatantly obvious answers, or ones that I'd already answered a thousand times before.

"Mom, did you wear that coat to work?" (Tay)

"Nope, I thought I'd sneak into the house wearing it, just to throw you off." (Me)

"Mom, did you see my homework?" (Cam)

"Since I was at work all day and haven't even walked through the door yet, I obviously haven't seen your homework." (Me)

"Did you do your hair today?" (Tay)

"Yes." (Me)

"And your make-up?" (Tay)

"Taylor, look at my face... do you see make-up?"

(Me) "Yes..." (Tay)

"Then did I do my make-up today, Taylor?" (Me)

"Yes." (Tay)

"Are you making dinner right now? What are we having? Can I have a snack?" (Cam)

"Can I do your hair, Mom? And will you play dress up with me? You never play with me... can you put barrettes in my hair? And a headband?" (Tay)

"And when are you going to help me with my homework project? Did you finish washing my clothes? Can I call my friend?" (Cam)

"Mom, will you help me put my puzzle away and teach me how to play the piano? And when are you going to buy me boots like yours? Do I get to stay up late tonight? Can I have a pony?"

This was usually when I'd get a far-off look in my eyes as I would let myself envision what it must be like to be deaf. Sure, it's a disability... to some. But one person's garbage is another person's treasure, right?

Fridays were always the toughest. I was exhausted from the week and the chores had been piling up since the previous weekend. I just didn't have the strength to deal with the questions. That's why I found myself parked along the road one particularly tiring Friday. I was just so sleepy, and there was a small turnaround that looked so lonely, and I just wanted to shut my eyes, only for a few moments. No one to talk to, no questions to answer.

That's why I turned off my car, in order to save the little gasoline I had left, curled my legs up underneath me, and I buried my face snugly into my oversized sweater. The thirteen-degree weather quickly cooled down the car, and I had to wrap my coat around me like a blanket to keep from freezing. Moments later I could see my foggy breath as I inhaled and exhaled, wetting my sweater where my nose and mouth were buried. I closed my eyes, and despite the cold, I felt a wave of sleep making my head lower heavily onto the center console.

For twenty minutes I slept, curled up and shivering as the air grew colder and colder inside my vehicle. And then a thought hit me. *I'm literally risking frostbite in order to avoid talking to my children.* This thought was quickly followed by another one, *I wonder if they let people take naps in the library?*

Eventually, I made the choice to go home and not to the library. I answered all the inane questions that could ever possibly have been asked. But had I stayed in my car just a little while longer, perhaps now I wouldn't regret asking Taylor if we needed to have her tested. With confused eyes, she looked at me dumbfounded and asked, "Why, Mama?"

"Because, Taylor, if I ask you to pick up your pile of belongings from the middle of the floor and you walk over to the pile and pick up only one thing, it must mean that you need to be tested for something because no one is that lazy!"

I know, I know. I'm a terrible mother, and I let my exhaustion get the best of me. However, my daughter was not deterred. She simply answered, "But, Mom, I am that lazy!"

And knowing is half the battle.

The announcement that I had been dreading for the year prior finally came. I always knew that it would, but I assumed it would be when one of my children was angry with me or after they got in trouble for doing something they shouldn't have done. However, I wasn't prepared for the words to arrive, without warning, in the middle of pleasant days and positive behavior. And I certainly wasn't prepared to hear it from my five-year-old, who lives more in the moment than any other person I've ever known.

"I miss my mommy." The words hung in the air as she looked at me with more true emotion than I was used to seeing from her. What was I to say? What in the world is the correct response to that? A simple "I'm sorry" wasn't going to cut it, and I didn't want to show her the hurt that had just crept into my heart. And yet there she was, waiting for me to say something. *Anything.*

A mere twelve hours prior, my husband and I had found her sleeping with a picture of her biological mother and brothers. It was tucked under her pillow, just the corner tab protruding out from under the fabric sham. I stared at the picture for such a long time. I noticed that she looked so much older now than she did in the photo. She still had the same shorts, but I was pretty sure they wouldn't fit her by the time summer really hit. Her bangs were bluntly cut, and she squinted against the sun as she looked to the camera. It was strange, but even her eyes looked different somehow. And as I tucked her in that night, I felt two pangs of sadness. One was for myself and the other was for her.

The following morning is when she let the bomb drop with words that caused me to choke on my heart—that heart that was still getting used to the idea of being this little girl's one and only. *I miss my mommy.* In an instant, I felt dethroned. The position that was supposed to be mine was taken away and given to a woman who had seemingly done little to deserve the title. It was a feeling so bitter that I could sense my heart hardening to keep the pain at bay.

Maybe it's because I was rushing to get ready for work or because the words caught me off guard while I steadied myself enough to apply my mascara, but the heaviness of her statement followed me throughout the day like a rain cloud. By the end of the day, I felt drenched by the weight of her words.

Cameron informed his sister that she was free to move out if she didn't like it here, only to realize that his only playmate would then be gone, so he graciously reneged his statement and allowed her to stay. But Taylor had already leapt at the idea and informed me that she would ask the judge to move her back "home". There was heartbreaking disappointment in her eyes when I explained to her that was no longer an option—she'd already been adopted.

"I guess I waited too long," she whispered as tiny tears made their way down her cheeks. I immediately searched my mind, trying to remember the speech that I'd prepared long ago—the one that allowed me to answer all the hard questions and set little minds at ease. The things I wanted and needed to stress to her were these:

1.   That she was *chosen*. No other little girls were chosen to be our daughter. We chose her.

2.   That her birth mom was unable to take care of her but that she will always love her.

3.   That she'll understand more when she's older. But for now, she just needed to know that I love her.

She's had multiple mommies... but I've only ever had one daughter —and I'm glad it's her.

As I sat on her *Dora the Explorer* bedspread, I gave my three-point speech in a way that could've earned me an Emmy (if Emmys were given to people that sometimes trip over their words and say "um" way more than necessary). In return, she told me the things she missed about the first four years of her life, things that only a child would think of—certain baby dolls, toys in her grandma's backyard, playing with her cousin. And then, all on her own, she came up with reasons why it's better to live here, with me.

"I have clean clothes instead of having to wear dirty ones over and over. I have my own bed and room with toys in it. I have *lots* of shoes. And you teach me to be good... I don't have to understand things now, but I will when I get taller, right?"

She'd hit the nail on the head, she did. Sadly, she is very short. So, I fear it's going to be a while before she fully understands. However, my little girl seemed satisfied with our conversation, and that's all that mattered in the end, really. Afterward, I even allowed her to use baby talk and act like a toddler. It seemed like she needed a moment to be small with me and let me experience the Taylor that I missed out on for four years. Maybe if I could find a way to give her some of what she should've received back then, she wouldn't miss her old life quite as much.

The thing about the past is that it's often hard to let go of. It holds onto us with white knuckles and tries to keep us there with weighted memories. The past feeds our souls with lies, telling us that we'll never be happier than we were back then, that no one will ever love us again, that we should fear the future and all its unknowns.

I know there are plenty of things in my life that I've said good-bye to, things that were bad for me. Yet, strangely enough, when I find myself reflecting on the past and its large history, I still miss many of those somethings and someones that were so unhealthy. I suppose that's human nature. One day, when Taylor is taller, she'll understand that, too. And hopefully, with any amount of grace, she will break free

from the past that follows her, and she'll learn to smile into the future with her head held high—no tears to be found.

Taylor has a special bond with her baby brother, Isaac. From the moment he was born, she did all that she could to entertain him. That included doing all the things that we'd told her *not* to do, but she was not to be deterred. She loved him and despite her accidentally hurting him on a daily basis, he seemed quite smitten with her as well.

My daughter quickly became obsessed with all things baby-related. She *had* to have the baby dolls you could feed with bottles that looked as if they were really emptying. She had to have baby dolls whose eyes shut when she laid them in their cribs. And she had to have baby doll diapers... an entire pack that she went through in about two days. Obviously her baby doll had dysentery.

The day that Isaac discovered his private parts was an especially momentous day in our home. Not because he found his weenie and was compelled to grab at it every two seconds, but because of Taylor's insight into what Isaac must've been thinking when he discovered his new nubbin. "Mama, does Isaac know it's inappropriate to touch his privates," she'd asked me during a particularly weenie-grabbing diaper change.

"No," I responded. "He's just finding all of his new body parts, just like when he found his toes and couldn't stop biting on them, remember?"

"Well, it's a good thing he can't bite his weenie," she said seriously, followed by perhaps the funniest thing she's ever said. "He's probably like 'Hey, why is there a nose on my butt?'"

She had no idea that it was hysterical; however, she continued to follow her brother around, treating him like her very own baby for eleven months (at which point, he quite literally weighed more than she did). But despite how close she was with him, her reaction to the news that Isaac was leaving us shocked me on numerous levels. Reeling from my own disbelief and heartache, I had a son that was despicably angry and a daughter who sat there like nothing had happened at all.

She finally cut into our emotional disaster and questioned why we were all so upset? Looking at her with uncomprehending eyes, I reexplained that her beloved brother was going to be leaving our home permanently. This was yet another moment that her type of RAD shone brightest.

"But why are you crying? He's still here right now... why wouldn't you cry later, when he leaves?"

In her own way, that was the most honest response she could offer. My daughter, who struggled to feel emotions at all, was doing her best to understand our feelings, but she just couldn't rationalize our tears during a moment that the pain wasn't actually happening. As hard as she tried, she could not comprehend crying when, to her, nothing had changed.

Over the next several weeks while we cherished our last few moments with Isaac, Taylor watched us all intently. She would stare at the tears coming from our eyes and then go to her room and try to make herself cry. Making a strange weepy sound that eventually turned into singing, we realized that she just couldn't feel this loss... not yet, at least.

But on that final day when CYS drove Isaac away from our home, she curled up into my arms and wept. It was only for a few moments, but it was the appearance of true emotion. Surprisingly enough, she let the rest of us have the time we needed to grieve while she played in her bedroom. And, after a sufficient time had passed, she asked my husband if he would take off her training wheels so she could practice riding her big girl bike.

Not knowing what else to do with that day, feeling too drained to think about our loss for one more second, we removed Taylor's training wheels and watched as she finally learned to ride her bike all on her own. She was so happy and I was so sad that part of me felt anger toward her. I knew in my mind that she was processing this event the same way she'd processed all of the other losses in her life— by simply moving forward. Yet, my heart convinced me that she was calloused and unloving, incapable of feeling anything truly real.

When we received the news that Isaac was going to be coming back for weekend visits, she smiled and seemed about as happy as if we'd told her we were having spaghetti for dinner. And when we'd be in the middle of saying good-bye to him each Sunday evening, our hearts would be crushed, yet Taylor would be pestering us to play a game with her or watch a movie. Still, I knew that she was trying to feel, or better yet, she was trying to avoid feeling. But there the anger would rise up again. Because despite all that I knew about psychology, in my eyes, she was robbing me of my grief by being insensitive and selfish.

It made me pull away from her more and more with each passing week. After a year, we were just people that lived together. One of us cooked and cleaned while the other one looked for attention by breaking even more of the first one's things, lying continuously, and picking fights with her big brother. As I look at it now, it was the only way she could deal with losing Isaac, and it was the only way she could deal with losing yet another mom.

I wish I could say that I was the great support my daughter needed during those many months. But the fact of the matter was, we were all a devastated mess. Every last one of us in our home had been on a constant emotional merry-go-round. Not one of us was able to deal with losing Isaac—not when we had been so close to adoption, not after we'd worked so hard to build connections and attach to little strangers. The compilation of the previous eighteen months was just more than we could handle. And in that time, and for many months to follow, I found myself hating.

We were so far from attached that when our family therapist suggested simply touching our children more, my stomach churned and bile rose to my throat. I didn't want to touch either of the kids. There I was, crying myself to sleep each night, and there they were, destroying everything we owned, getting into trouble at school, and fighting with each other during all of their waking moments. I didn't want to attach to them anymore. I didn't *want* to love them. I just wanted to survive them and then be left to my empty heart once they finally moved out.

It had become obvious that the depression I'd faced before had returned, and this time it brought a friend. Panic attacks began to plague me periodically, often in the middle of the night. I would awaken drenched in sweat, heart racing, incapable of catching a breath. I'd run to the window in the dead of winter and throw it open, pressing my face against the frozen screen in an attempt to bring air – to bring relief. A few hours later, the children would wake me up with their fighting, and all I could do was cry out to God in the middle of it all.

Even still, I always loved people. It came naturally to me. It's how I ended up in my current career. The sicker the client, the more in love I fell, the more empathy I felt, the harder I worked for them. But hatred... hatred was new. The weight of it sat heavy upon my chest, creating such a burden that the hatred began to spread. Not only could I hate my children for breaking my car and stealing my grandmother's ring, but I'm pretty sure that with enough effort, I could pin them with global warming as well.

If this were a dating situation, me and my kids, we would've broken up long ago. Instead, it resembled a poorly arranged marriage to a set of strangers that I couldn't divorce. I was given a longer time getting to try out my new mattress than I did these children before having to make the decision to keep them. And there I was... stuck. Stuck and hating the children living in my home, the ones I had vowed to love.

However, hate doesn't stop with the kids. No. Any self- respecting mother who hates her own children will naturally find it pretty simple to hate herself as well. And why stop there when I could bring my spouse down with me? Pretty soon, we were a family of haters, each trying to survive and look "normal enough" to the rest of the world. Sometimes the effort would get too great, and I'd throw my hands up to the sky and say, "Do You hate me, too?"

"God, why won't they change?" I screamed this to the creator of the universe so many times a day that I'd actually stopped even trying to hear an answer. Until one day, a firm and loving voice broke through my hate.

"Why won't *you* change?" God asked.

I didn't have an answer. Because sometimes Hope feels absent. And in that moment, all we're left with is the decision of whether we will choose it or not.

Although hatred is a scary place to live, it seemed like I was going to be forced to pay rent for as much time as I spent there. I had already exhausted a year and a half trying as hard as I could to do all the hard things, and then the only one in the family that I truly felt I couldn't live without was ripped from my arms. Grief isn't an excuse to hate, but it was my apparent ending point for trying to love. I simply didn't have any more effort to give, and hating was just plain easier.

For beings that were created in the image of Love, hatred is something that doesn't feel natural; it isn't natural. Sure, it's easier than loving at times, but it doesn't sit well with us because it's the opposite of our heart's make-up. It grabs you and holds you hostage, tying you up and putting blinders on your eyes. And then, hatred does the worst thing of all—once you're securely held down by its grasp and weakened by its immense power, hatred begins to brainwash you.

I allowed my pain to brainwash me into thinking that all that remained in me was evil and that all that remained in my kids was evil. I knew that I needed to love, but I just couldn't figure out how.

How do I make myself love? Repulsed by my children, and ultimately repulsed by my own response to them, I felt like a failure all over again. The body of Christ said to love them. "*How*?" I would ask.

"By just doing it," they would say.

"But *how*?" I would ask again. And there was no answer, no manual, no instruction guide. How do I love kids that I don't love, how do I love kids that don't know how to love back, and how do I walk in love toward a world that is constantly bashing me over the head for my struggle to love?

Even to this day, at times I play whack-a-mole with my hate. It rears its nasty, molish face, and I try to beat it back with a club. But if I'm not quick enough, if I get too busy looking elsewhere, then the moles start to multiply. Pretty soon I'm that angry, crazed woman swinging a club wildly, hitting anything that comes into her path.

When I became pregnant with Wyatt, it was easy to blame it all on the hormones, you know? But deep down, I knew that what I was feeling was too far beyond a chemical in my body. I knew that it was an anchor in my heart. And I realized that it would eventually pull me down to a place from where I would no longer be able to return.

Trust me, I know how hard it is to read about someone hating children. I get how ugly and unsettling it is. And even as I hated, trying my hardest to love, Taylor would follow me from room to room, mimicking my every word, hair flip, and expression. She was the shadow that wouldn't go away, even when the sun had departed. I couldn't turn around without tripping over this child, which would make me yell at her to get away.

One evening, as usual, she was attached to my heels... except all I could hear was this horrible click-clacking as she walked. I turned around, ready to explode once again, and there stood my small daughter with a round pillow under her shirt, hair in a messy bun, and wearing a pair of my old high heels.

"What in the world are you doing?" I'd asked her. "I'm being you, Mama!"

It hit me in that moment that, in the end, who else was she to imitate? Her drug-addict birth mother? No, this child was following me around because her trauma didn't allow for her to deal with feelings and reactions very well. All she had to mimic was this new mom who just wanted to be able to do the dishes without stumbling over her.

And in that moment, my heart filled with compassion for her—the beginning of true love. I couldn't explain the change in me if I tried, but it was there nevertheless.

Sadly, within the hour, Taylor was back to breaking my things, but of course, not without the help of her bother. (It seemed that the only time the two children came together on anything was to wreak havoc!) Typical children have some sort of end point—a line they won't cross, a move they won't make. Trauma kids, however, they fly right past that line as if it means nothing at all.

I asked my daughter why she ruined my hair supplies again. Her answer? "Because I wanted to." I asked her if she thought about how that would make me feel, trying to retain any amount of the compassion that had passed through me earlier that day. "Very angry."

Good... she knows the right answer. Yet, when asked why she did it anyways? She responded with, "Because I didn't care."

I felt constantly torn between honest worries that my children were either demon-possessed or sociopaths. I don't know that "human" described them accurately, so I felt forced to look outside the box. I don't remember pods in the backyard the day they came, nor do shining

UFO lights ring a bell. What I did know? I was terribly and fearfully unhappy. Therapy, medicine, church, prayer, positive reinforcement, negative reinforcement, behavior charts, time-outs, incentives— nothing was making a dent. That was, until, I finally had Wyatt and my maternity leave kicked in.

This happened just in time for the kids to be done with school for the year and for them to be at home, with me, alone, for three straight months. You guys, I'm just being real here, but I was more terrified of spending alone time with my children than I had been to deliver Wyatt after a four-day labor. When I say this fear caused me to tremble, that's not a joke. I was freaked out!

But wouldn't you know it, the kids loved having me home? They continued to act like lunatics quite often, but there was a renewed ability to connect with children that were previously acting rather unlovable. I had a very strict set of rules, a summer schedule we followed, and something fun that we would all do together each day, even if it was just to prepare a meal, make up a dance, or go for a walk.

When I was working, I noticed that over the previous summer, the kids had lost all their educational skills (and there wasn't that much there to begin with!). Consequently, while I was home with them, I wanted to make sure that each day there was learning, reading, and practicing new skills. I often used those moments that the kids were held hostage on car rides as an opportunity to quiz them on various math or spelling facts.

Me: "Remember to listen up because if you don't know the answer to your question, your sibling can try to get the point. Okay, Cam, what is the number ahead of 62?"

My kids struggle with their numbers and have to start over counting from 1 whenever they're asked what comes next in a sequence—hence this learning lesson.

Cam: "Um... (wicked long pause) ...63?"

Me: "Yes. Good. Taylor, what is one number ahead of 15?"

Tay: "16?"

Me: "Very good. Cam, what is one number behind 35?" Cam: (Counting in his head.)

Me: "Cam, stop counting. Think about what number comes before the number 5."

Cam: "8?"

Me: "Nope, not 8. What number comes right before number 5?"

Cam: (Counting again.) "4?"

Me: "Yep, so what comes right before 35?" Cam: "72?"

Me: (Wow... that's... not even kinda close.) "No, bud, if 4 comes right before 5, and we're in the 30s, the answer would be thirty...?"

Cam: "38?"

Tay: "I know! Is it 34?"

Me: "Yes, Tay, it's 34. Do you get it, Cam?" Cam: "Huh?"

Me: "Cam, do you see how we got the answer 34?"

Cam: "34 what?"

Me: (Really?) "Really?"

Cam: "Really what, Mom?"

Me: (Big sigh.) "Taylor, what number comes after 99?"

Tay: "Hmm... that's hard because I can't count to 100 yet."

Me: "Tay, you just said the answer." Tay: "Is it 99?"

Me: "No, what comes *after* 99?"

Tay: (Thinking...) "Is it 99?"

Me: "Taylor, the *answer* isn't 99. The question is what comes *after* 99?"

Tay: (Staring blankly.)

Me: "Remember when you count by tens...."

Tay: (Excitedly interrupting...) "10, 20, 30, 40, 50, 60, 70, 80, 90, 100!"

Me: "Yes! Exactly, so if you are looking for the next number after 99, it would be...?"

Tay: (Nothing... just... nothing.)

Me: "Tay?"

Tay: "99?"

Me: (Oh. My. Gosh.) "It's not 99, I promise.The number after 99 simply cannot also be 99. If you were counting in the 90s, it would go 91, 92, 93, 94, 95, 96, 97, 98, 99...?"

Tay: "Well, it's not 99..."

Me: *Dear Jesus, please help me not to crash this van. We have an innocent baby on board.* "Cam! Wanna come in for the steal, man? What comes after 99?"

Cam: "Huh?"

Me: "What. Comes. After. 99?"

Tay: (Whispers loudly to Cameron.) "It's not 99!"

Cam: "Duh, it's 100, Taylor!"

Me: "Good! Here's an easy one, Cam. If 100 comes *after* 99, what comes *before* 100?"

Cam: (Silence.)

Me: "Cam!" Cam: (Nothing.)

Me: "Cameron!"

Cam: "Huh?"

Me: "Answer the question, dude!"

Cam: "I wasn't listening..."

Me: "What comes before 100?"

Cam: "Um... well... 24?"

Me: "Cameron, you just told me that the number that comes after 99 is 100... so the number that comes before 100 has to be..."

Cam: "Well, it's probably 23 then."

Me: "Actually, it's probably not even close to 23. Taylor, it's all you, and you got this one, girl What number comes before 100?"

Tay: "Well, it's *not* 99..."

Me: (Turns up music *loudly*.)

We'd only been doing the same exercises for the entire summer and all; it's not like numbers are important though. We just won't use them, and that's that. Problem solved! But despite the lack of ability to hear correctly that day or do math, I'd decided to do a cooking activity with them as our "something fun." We chose to make homemade pizzas. And it was every bit the disaster that math had turned out to be.

Me: "Now, carefully smooth the sauce around on the dough and try to keep it from getting onto the pan."

Tay: (Takes a heaping spoonful and smears it across the pan.)

Me: "Yeah, great job, Tay... way to listen."

Tay: "What? You said to make sure to get it all over the pan!"

Cam: "Nah-uh, she said to *not* get it on the pan, Taylor!"

Tay: "Cameron! Shut up!"

Me: "Hey! Knock it off or leave the kitchen. I said to try to not get it on the pan, Taylor. It's just going to be burnt sauce now."

Tay: "Well, I didn't *hear* you."

Me: "You haven't *heard* me all day. *Listen*. Okay, guys, now sprinkle your cheese around your pizza and try to *not* get it on the pan."

Tay: "Okay." (She said pointedly.)

Me: "Good job. Now put on your peppers and onions. Maybe even make a cool pattern with them for something fun."

Tay: "Where's the cheese?"

Me: (Looking at her questioningly.) "The cheese? The stuff under your peppers and onions?"

Tay: "No, Mom, the cheese."

Me: "Yes, Taylor, the cheese is under your peppers and onions."

Tay: "No! The *cheese!*"

Me: "For the love of all that his holy, what are you talking about, child?"

Tay: "Ugh, you never listen!"

Me: (Really? Hello, Kettle, meet Pot.) "I hear you saying you want the cheese, Taylor, and I'm telling you the cheese is on your pizza... I'm not sure what else to say about this..."

Tay: (Huge sigh.) "Cameron, tell Mom I want the cheese!"

Cam: "Mom, she wants the cheese."

Me: (Staring blankly at both of them.) "Someone... just please... oh my gosh... I just can't..."

Tay: "*Never mind.* I just wanted the kind you sprinkle!"

Me: "Oh, the Parmesan cheese?"

Tay: "Yes!"

Me: "You mean the stuff sitting *directly in front of you*?"

Tay: "Yes..."

Me: "Well, at least we know that basically none of your senses are working, and it's not just your ears."

Forgiveness. What sometimes appears to be such a simple concept is often one of the most difficult things to do. I found it ironic that the one devotion toward the end of summer I did with the kids was on such a huge topic, yet it had the shortest memory verse. Psalm 130:4 "But you offer forgiveness." The text talked about how God offers forgiveness to us when we've done something wrong, but it was hard to look at the verse as anything other than a command to us. To me.

But *you* offer forgiveness. You offer it when it's hard. You offer it when it's painful. You offer it when it's undeserved. My mind instantly jumped back to writing that still sat, scrawled across the hood of my car. Small whispers filled my heart. *You offer forgiveness.* And as I pictured Cameron saying very inappropriate things to his sister when he thought no one could hear and then *lying repeatedly* when confronted, I was struck between the eyes with the words *You offer forgiveness.*

Phrases like "kids will be kids" didn't do much to aid my forgiveness toward these two for a long time, let me tell you! I held grudges like nobody's business, and my children were fully aware of it. I took each action as a personal attack (as sometimes they were), and I let unforgiveness set as firm as cement in my heart toward them. So, when I opened those pages and saw the topic, I cringed.

How in the world was I supposed to be the one to teach them forgiveness when they'd seen me be bitter and vengeful so many times?

You offer forgiveness...

We worked on memorizing the four-word verse, which both Cameron and Taylor immediately forgot, proving once again that summer vacation is far too long. We then read the story that went along with the verse about a girl who had stolen $5 from her sister. She felt so guilty about what she did that she wasn't able to sleep until she confessed her sin to God and her sister and asked for forgiveness from them both.

I wasn't born yesterday, so I was fully aware of the stolen glances my children were giving to each other as I read. *Guilt.* It was there as plain as the growing noses on their faces. I stopped reading for a moment and looked between the two of them.

"Is there something the two of you would like to tell me?" I asked calmly. Simultaneous head nods occurred—only Taylor nodded her head yes while Cameron nodded his no. *Hmm...* "Is there something that you're both feeling guilty about, but that you don't want to tell me?" Again with the nodding discrepancy.

"Taylor, is there something you and Cameron did together that you want to get off your heart, but you don't want Cameron to be mad at you?" It was nowhere close to a long shot, but she stared at me like I was psychic with all my magical mind-reading powers going on and all.

"Yes," she spoke slowly. "Well, that and I don't want to get grounded and have to miss Artsy Doodle today." I turned my gaze toward Cameron.

"What about you? Anything you're feeling right now?" I asked.

"Well, there *might* be something... but maybe you could promise that we won't get in trouble if we tell you?" he ventured.

Ah, the thin line us parents walk presented itself. Teach our children the value of confession or teach them that there is a consequence for every action and risk them lying to cover up their mistakes. I tried to balance the tight rope carefully and attempted to do both. "Well, here's the thing. Depending on what it is will depend on if there needs to be a consequence or not." (I mean, it's not like they haven't done some pretty outrageous and dangerous things before!) "If I were to break the law, there would still be a consequence despite me apologizing to the police officer, right?" I continued. They both nodded their heads in agreement and looked at each other one last time.

It was Taylor who cracked first. "Well... sometimes we sneak candy when you're upstairs with the baby, even when you've told us not to."

Phew, okay, that's not horrible! Forgive. I can do this one!

"Thank you for telling me," I said. "I forgive you."

Cameron seemed to immediately grow braver. "And we ate most of Dad's pack of gum. You remember that day when you asked us about it and we told you Dad said we could have some and that you could call him and check? Yeah, he didn't tell us that, and we were really glad you didn't call him." I felt a little tension in the back of my neck, so I casually rolled my shoulders to shrug it away.

All right. Lying sucks, but at least they're being honest now, right? "Okay, thank you. I forgive you."

Taylor sat up straighter and jumped in again. "And sometimes we give the dogs the food we don't like from our plates when you leave the room, even the stuff we know the dogs aren't allowed to eat because it makes them sick. You forgive me, right?"

That explains the random piles of dog vomit I've had to clean up over the last few weeks. Tension... there was more tension. It crept down my spine and made my tummy constrict, ever so slightly.

To the untrained eye, however, I was rocking my forgiveness on the outside. "You do realize that you could hurt the dogs by doing this, and that we have these rules for a reason, right?" I said with an amazingly calm composure.

"Yes," they agreed in unison.

"Okay... I forgive you, but do not let it happen again, do you understand?"

Apparently in the sharing mood now, Cameron confidently informed me that, while playing outside some time ago, they found an old pop bottle with leftover pop in it. He said that they kept it (along with stolen snacks) in the old refrigerator (that they were told repeatedly not to play with) out on the junk pile. They would sneak into the fridge and drink pop and eat snacks when they wanted some; this was over the course of a couple months from what I gathered. Mental images frantically ran through my mind of Punky and Cherry playing hide-and-seek in that ever famous eighties episode that ended with Cherry being found unconscious after getting stuck in an old refrigerator (if you're a girl and you're in your thirties, you know what I'm talking about!).

"You did *what*?" I asked the two kids sitting in front of me. Their confidence vanished immediately, and they gazed at each other with looks that said, See what you did? You woke the dragon, and now we're in trouble! Tension—it seemed to leave my stomach and was making my eye twitch, ever so slightly. "Do you guys have any idea how dangerous it is to play in an old refrigerator? That's why I've told you so many times not to go near it because it is unsafe. And did you even think about what would happen by leaving food out in the yard? We have *coyotes*! Not to mention raccoons and crazy-attacking hornets that are drawn to these things! Ugh, and you have no idea whose pop that even was or how long it had been outside! Would you pick up someone's chewed gum from a parking lot and eat it? *Of course not! Because it's gross!*" Tension... crazy eyes... heightened blood pressure....

But you offer forgiveness.

Ah, crap.

Weak, nervous voices asked the question of the hour. "Do you forgive us?" I contemplated their request for a moment. Such a thin line. I wanted them to know that forgiveness doesn't give them permission to intentionally continue doing things they know are wrong. And I didn't want them to think that there are no consequences for disobedience. But I also didn't want them to think they can't tell me things they've done wrong due to fear of getting in trouble.

And quite frankly, did I even want to forgive them? I mean, who knew how long this fun game of confessions would continue if I kept granting them forgiveness! How many times were they expecting me to do this?

My guess was seventy times seven.

"Okay. *I forgive you.* Both of you," I said eventually. *I mean, you're idiots, but I forgive you*... ugh, tension! They looked relieved. I sat, waiting for any other confessions to come flying at me, but my kids seemed to realize that this game had run its course and that they'd better quit while they were ahead.

"Do you guys feel any better now that you've told me what you've done and that I forgave you?" I asked.

"Um, can we still go to Artsy Doodle?" Taylor tried. You can't blame the girl for checking.

"Yes... you can still go to Artsy Doodle."

She brightened and said, "Then yes! I feel a lot better. I already asked Jesus to forgive me for being sneaky... but now you forgived me too, so I feel good. And I'll try not to be sneaky anymore, okay?"

My grin was tight under this burden of forgiveness, but I knew that it was my job to teach them that valuable lesson—my job to right the wrongs I'd shown them by my actions months ago. "Well... good. I'm glad you feel better then."

Both kids cleared their books from the table and decided on going outside for a while to play. I wasn't going to argue! A little alone time is never something a mama turns down in August—certainly not when the "I'm boreds" and the "Ugh, it's too hot to play outsides" were in full swing.

And as Taylor walked past, she looked up at me, patted my back, and said, "Good job, Mom," before walking off.

Thanks, kiddo.

If you, O Lord, kept a record of sins, who could stand? But with you there is forgiveness, therefore you are feared. I wait for the Lord, my soul waits, and in his word I put my hope. (Psalm 130:3–5)

"Mommy, what is sex?"

I don't know about you, but when I envisioned this question making its way to our house, I didn't anticipate the words *Mommy* and *sex* to be in the same question. Seven years *old* has to be too early for this, right? Although, it's not like I live with my head in the sand. I knew the time was drawing near when someone in my house would pop the inevitable sex question. I had just hoped it would be once they were done with bed-wetting and all.

Ready or not, the question was out there with nary a warning nor hint of its coming. It was the end of Taylor's first grade year, and the unusually warm weather had pushed us outside one day after they'd returned from school. There I stood, unsuspectingly pushing the baby in his swing, Taylor on the swing next to us, Cameron playing in the dirt at our feet. And there it was.

"Mommy, what is sex?" Taylor's Minnie Mouse voice echoed out. Cameron's head popped up, and he immediately stood to attention, quickly forgetting whatever muddy contraption he'd been constructing just moments before. I think the baby even choked on his thumb.

I gasped out a few *ums* and *hmms* and *wells*... enough to write a book on how not to answer the sex question with your children. Finally, I formed words that created a sentence.

"So where did you hear that word, Taylor?" "All the kids at school say it."

Stupid public school with its stupid sex-talking first graders...

"And... um, what do the kids at school say about it?" "They say that people do sex all the time."

Phew... if she's still calling it "doing sex," she can't know that much, right?

"And what else do they say about it?"

"Um... they say that you have to take your clothes off."

Sweet Jesus.

This is where Cameron, in all of his third grade knowledge, piped in.

"Nah-uh, Taylor. You don't have to take all your clothes off, just your pants."

Taylor looked at him with annoyance and back to me, the queen of great answers.

"Mom, you don't really have to take your pants off to do sex, do you?"

Okay. Moment of truth. Tell my young children the anatomically-correct version of sex or make up a crazy story about people doing sex with their pants on and babies magically appearing in cribs nine months later.

"So here's the thing... people... adults... when they're married... they want to have babies, you see? And when they want to have babies, they do a thing called sex."

I looked at them to see if this was enough to answer their questions, to see if I really had to go on or not. They stared back at me with confused eyes, eager for clarification.

Rats.

"Um, okay. And when the mom and dad have sex, that's how the mom gets pregnant and can have a baby. Do you get it?"

"Mom," Taylor interjected again. "Do they take their pants off ?"

Good grief.

"Yes. They do take their pants off."

"But not their underwear, right, Mom?" Cameron added with utter certainty that he was correct.

"Actually, they do have to take their underwear off... it's just how it has to work."

Both kids stared at me with mouths hanging open, disgust creeping into their eyes.

"But, Mom... *you* had a baby," Taylor said in shock.

Oh no. Oh no!

She literally whispered the next question, I kid you not. "Mom, did you take your underwear off with Daddy?"

I could see now that our relationship was forever going to be changed. No matter which way I played this, she was right. I *did* have a baby. Her beloved daddy and I had done sex... pantless... in the very home where she rests her head at night. And every single time our bedroom door will close from this point forward, she will assume we are doing sex all over again.

I started to feel very warm. And uncomfortable. Warm and uncomfortable.

"Um, that's how it works. If you want to have a baby, you have to take your underwear off. I don't make the rules. It's just how it has to happen."

"Do you have to take your shirts off too?" I felt Cameron staring at me like I was no longer the mother he'd grown to know and love.

"Well... sometimes. You don't have to, but sometimes people do take their shirts off."

Taylor literally laughed out loud. She offered no explanation, just cracked up for a good thirty seconds.

"What's so funny?" Cameron asked.

Choking back hysterics, Taylor responded, "I was just thinking how funny Mom would look with a shirt on but no pants!"

Cameron joined the laughter instantly.

Hey, now! Am I seriously getting body-shamed by my seven- and nine-year-olds?

"Guys, come on. Be serious here, would ya?"

They took a moment to compose themselves while I continued to push Wyatt in his swing. I watched him with envy as he enjoyed the spring breeze without a care in the world—no one demanding answers from him or picturing him half-naked. He's a lucky little guy, that one.

"Is sex the same thing as humping?" Cameron asked.

Oh my gosh, it's hot out here! What are we doing, breaking the heat record for the month of May already?

"Uh, yeah... same basic concept. But please never say that word again. Ever. It's inappropriate and... just... don't."

"Do you get a baby every time you do sex?" Taylor questioned.

"No. Then we would be China."

"Then why do people do sex since they won't always get a baby?"

I can't even... I just can't.

"Um..." I stalled for a good answer to magically appear on my tongue. And there it was. "Practice! They practice making babies."

"Does it feel good?"

Deep breath, Mama, deep breath.

"Sometimes..."

"Does it feel like when you have to sneeze, and it finally comes out? Because that feels good, but when I can't sneeze, it doesn't feel, good and I hate that."

"YES!" I said, a little too eagerly. "That's exactly right!

Good way to think about it!"

Yes. I did allow my child to compare sex to sneezing... I'd had enough truth-telling for one day!

A silence settled over us. My panic started to subside, the May weather seemed to take on a more refreshing temperature, and I no longer felt the need to pop a Xanax.

"So, will I do sex someday, Mommy?"

Oh, my gosh! Heart attack! Someone please call for a medic... I thought we were done with this conversation!

"Uh... you see... one day you will get married and you and your husband will want to have babies. Then and *only then* will you... do sex. Okay?"

Taylor looked at me with big eyes. I think she realized she'd hit a nerve. So she nodded her agreement and then went back to swinging.

Cameron, who had remained silent (probably fearful of giving more wrong answers), ended the conversation with this beautiful gem.

"Mom, I don't want to have kids when I grow up. So that means I don't have to do sex, right?"

"Cameron, that's exactly right." He beamed happily at the praise.

"Good... because I look really stupid without my pants on."

Bless these children... bless them.

Living with children with RAD, it has been an uphill battle trying to get them to attach to others in a healthy way. Are they bullying or are they being bullied? Are they using physical touch in an appropriate manner? Are they being too clingy when they meet strangers? Are they showing signs of grasping concepts such as respecting others, personal space, empathy, and love? Are they managing their anger or feelings of jealousy correctly or are they breaking things and hurting themselves instead? What does "playing house" look like to them? Are they being kind enough to our animals and nature, even when we're not looking? Will my children ever stop lying or is this going to be a forever battle? Are they showing any signs of grief when they lose a favored toy or a person in their life or do they still show no emotion at all?

These things and more are the questions that flood a RAD parent's head with each play date, sleep over, and school day. When we are at home, however, everyone usually lets it all hang out, as is the case with most families. And with everything my kids have been through together, you'd think they would be close to one another. But the reality is there's an awful lot of anger and jealousy between the two of them, even still.

My son, the oldest, tends to treat his sister with violence, manipulation, threats, and disdain. Not all the time, but enough of the time. And frankly, *any amount of this behavior is enough to cause retaliation on my daughter's end.* And let me assure you, she's very good at what she does.

It wasn't uncommon to hear screams and tears from both kids multiple times each day. Now, as a psychotherapist, I knew that I should try for the millionth time to work through the problems, using each situation as a learning tool. Yet, as a parent, I really just wanted them to shut up and stop screaming at each other! I knew I should encourage a peaceful reconciliation, but I'd find myself only having energy to yell for everyone to go to their rooms. "If you can't play together nicely, then you can't play at all!" (I'm sure I'm the only mom to have ever used that line. Ever.)

One summer afternoon, when the screaming had started for the thousandth time that day, my blood began to boil. I bellowed my all-too-familiar line and sent everyone to their rooms. *Ah... peace.* Except was it really peace? No. It was only a temporary solution—a mere Band-Aid on a gaping wound. I remembered back to my own childhood when my brother and I were at each other's throats (yes, I am very much aware that this is normal child behavior and not just RAD behavior!) and my mom couldn't take it anymore. I recalled her grounding us together. We couldn't do anything alone. We were stuck to one another like glue. *And it was awful!*

However, if the main goal was to help my kiddos build appropriate and healthy relationships, what better place to start than with each other? So, that's exactly what I did. I immediately called them from their rooms and explained to them that there was going to be a change that summer.

My husband and I were *not* going to spend three months listening to them fight. Nor were we going to tolerate bullying of any kind. And we certainly were not going to let them grow up to hate one another. If that was the only thing they did all summer long, that was fine, but they would practice love. *Period.*

I then told them the new game plan. Stage 1: They were to sit at the living room table together. They would eat their meals there, they would do their summer homework assignments there, they would read their library books, do puzzles, play games, read, write, draw, or craft. Together. There would be no talking to anyone else and no visiting with anyone else. For every intervention needed from an adult, another hour of together time would be added. And if they could manage this for two days, then they would move on to Stage 2.

I have to tell you, I had never seen my son cry harder than he did in that moment. I basically told him that he would have a constant play pal and be able to do a plethora of fun activities, but because it was with his sister, he acted like it was a death sentence! I kid you not when I say that he choked on sobs for a full hour while they played the first few games. It was actually quite pathetic, and I told him so. *When you have learned to love your sibling, then you may practice loving other people.*

And with that, I'd left them to work it out. As the hours went by, I'd noticed that the crying had stopped. What I also noticed was that there were unfamiliar sounds coming from the room next to me. What *was* that?

It was the sound of two children *giggling*. After all the games had been played, they'd made up their own game at the table, and they were laughing like children who actually liked each other! Could it be possible? Could they really be getting along?

The next day, two children awoke and anxiously asked to come out of their rooms so they could go sit at the table together. It was like entering an episode of *The Twilight Zone*. There they sat, all day, playing games, reading to one another, and helping each other with math problems. I praised them so much that they actually asked me to stop so that they could get back to their game. It was a wow-mom moment to be sure!

By day three, I'd announced that they were ready for Stage 2. That consisted of getting to play in each other's rooms with toys, something that would usually cause a war of epic proportions. The ground rules were that they would both clean up anything that was taken out and that they would both be given the opportunity to choose an activity.

After all, compromises are part of all relationships. I also reminded them that bickering would get them more time and possibly send them back to Stage 1. They assured me they could handle it.

Four hours later, they had built a Barbie kingdom out of Legos and blocks, blankets and chairs. Cameron was the contractor, Taylor was the decorator. The room was a disaster, and the kids had never been happier.

I'd decided that they were ready to move on to the final stage later that afternoon. It had *finally* stopped raining here in Western Pennsylvania (after many, *many* days), and the kids needed to get some exercise and Vitamin D. So, I explained the rules of Stage 3. They were informed that they could go anywhere outside but they had to stay *together*. There would be no wandering off to do separate activities. There were a few concerned looks as Cameron whined that Taylor would only want to swing, and Taylor bellowed that Cameron would only want to play in the mud. "Figure it out," I said.

With play clothes on, water bottles filled, and sunscreen applied, they were sent out into the yard to test their new skills. I was skeptical.

I'd seen too many times where good interactions quickly became bad ones when the great outdoors was interjected. They were further away from adult supervision and prying ears. They were out of sight at times, which usually ended with me playing referee for a rousing rendition of "he said, she said." But they had been doing so well, and I wanted to believe that things could be getting better.

I opened all the windows in the house so that I could keep better ears on them while Wyatt took his nap. It was a mere twenty minutes before the screaming began.

Crap.

I ran to window and stopped dead in my tracks. It had not been screams of anger or pain that I'd heard. Instead, what I saw was this: my son—in play clothes, muck boots, and his bike helmet— had attached a garden cart to the back of his bicycle with a bungee cord. And sitting on the garden cart was my forty-pound daughter, wearing her bike helmet and her brother's hiking boots. He was racing full speed down the driveway with his sister death gripping the cart behind him. I watched as the cart began to veer off the driveway and into the muddy yard. Two bumps later, my daughter lay sprawled in the grass, a muddy mess. And, guys, you're never going to guess what happened next.

My son jumped off his bike with lightning speed and raced to her side. He helped her up and asked if she was okay. (*Wait, was that empathy? Was that love?*) She began to giggle (not wail, not tattle), and they ran back to the cart and began figuring out a better way to attach it to the bike. They did this for hours. They climbed trees, played hide-and-seek, made a fort in the clubhouse, and hung upside down from the swing set. Cameron even let Taylor teach him some gymnastics!

The following day, my kids anxiously asked what Stage 4 entailed. I explained that there was no Stage 4 and that their lesson was over. In that moment, I witnessed two faces drop in disappointment. "Well, can we at least still play together?" My son, the one who had cried like a baby over having to spend time with his sister, was close to tears at the thought of not spending the day with her.

And that was when the angels started to sing the "Hallelujah Chorus."

I assured them that they were *more* than welcome to continue playing together, but that they were now also allowed to interact with others and have alone time as well. That's when they *chose* to play with each other for the entire day.

It was a good two to three weeks with only the most minor of spats. I was quite aware that this technique wouldn't have worked with them even a year before. However, parenting children with mental illness requires retrying interventions again and again, tweaking them until you find what works. And it may not work ever again, leaving you scratching your head in frustration and sending you back to the drawing board for more tweaking.

Whereas I know that my children are still going to struggle with their disorder and that their days of relational conflicts are far from over, I do continue to feel hopeful that change is possible.

Because sometimes Hope means shooting in the dark and knowing that eventually, you'll hit something.

The day came when Taylor had to have dental surgery. Let me start off by saying that anxiety-ridden seven-year-old girls who already have a high propensity for drama, mixed with the expectancy of teeth extractions, equals one hot mess! The poor thing was born into bad teeth. I know this because her biological mother had no teeth. Nada. Zero. Zip. Her biological brother, Cameron, also has terrible teeth.

She'd already had multiple fillings—caps and orthodontic work were a given—and extractions were a must.

Despite brushing twice daily and consuming very little sugary products, we still found ourselves in a stressful predicament. The days/weeks of nerve-wracking anticipation for the grand teeth pulling, the months of headaches, the gum pain, the tears... *oh, the tears*! Let's just say our dramatic princess had been even more emotional than usual!

My alarm went off at 5:00 a.m., and I'd staggered clumsily down the stairs to Taylor's room. I turned on her light and gently touched her arm to wake her. Before her little eyes even opened, the tears started slipping from beneath her long lashes. But there was no time for another cry session as we had to be out the door in fifteen minutes, so I hustled her along, and we were in the van without a moment to spare. She asked to watch a movie in the car. She chose *The Tooth Fairy.*

It seemed appropriate and kept her occupied on our one-hour trip to the surgery center. Miraculously, she held herself together through the intake process, even when we had to go through yet another explanation of her adoption, talking about her past family's medical health issues, and completing *another* change in guarantors on her medical forms.

Once we got back to the prep room, the nerves finally reemerged. Luckily for me (and now, for all of you), Taylor was given silly juice. And let me tell you, it lived up to every bit of its name! In less than ten minutes, my shy/nervous/clingy little girl had turned into the picture of a tipsy patron who had just emerged from a local establishment. She was, in fact, a walking margarita.

It started with the giggles. There she was, in her gown and cap and fuzzy socks, cracking herself up like it was amateur night at a comedy club. After listening to her cackle at six-bloody-thirty in the morning, I casually mentioned that I could really use another cup of coffee.

This was her response to me, "Mommy! Don't *ever* stop drinking coffee... it'll just ruin my life!"

Okay, I was starting to feel amused.

"Why's that, Tay?"

"Because of all the spaces!" "Because of what spaces, honey?"

"What spaces?" She echoed back to me.

"I don't know, that's what I'm asking you."

"What spaces?" She repeated with a hiccup.

I was trying not to giggle.

"I don't know honey, never mind."

Terror suddenly spread across her face.

"Holy crap, where *are* we?"

Okay, definitely starting to giggle.

"Honey, we're at the dentist, remember?"

"Oh... did Wyatt run away? Where did he go?" (She starts frantically looking around for the baby.)

"Taylor, Wyatt is at home with Daddy. We didn't bring him, remember?"

"Bring him where? Where are we?"

Okay, giggling is turning into all-out laughter. "We're at the dentist, honey. Here, you wanna play a game on my phone while you wait?"

I set her up with a kid's app that allowed her to practice typing, text message style. She typed her name. Five minutes later, the silly juice had kicked in even more as she typed me this little gem, slurring an explanation that this was a love letter to me.

Text #1 read like this: "Taylor"

Text #2 (one minute later): "i luv yuo"

Text # 3 (five minutes later): "i ijhbhhhjddeyyuu"

I thanked her for the lovely message... whatever it said. That's when Daddy called on the phone to say hi to her. She grabbed for the phone and started talking into it upside-down. I helped her flip the phone around as she proceeded to giggle and slur all sorts of silly things, spit slipping from the corners of her mouth in tiny bubbles. As she talked, her eyes began rolling in circles, and she told me that I have more than one head. (It was obviously time to take the phone.)

"Mommy... I wanna see the streen. The streen. The streen. The... I don't know. Do you have any lipstip? Lickstip? Litstick? Litstit? For my lits?"

And this is when I started taking videos. I don't care, you can call it exploitation of a child if you want to. But I call it *heaven*. When I die, I expect these recordings to be played on a continuous loop while I'm in that mansion in the sky, because this was my favorite thing ever.

Suddenly, my daughter raised her finger as if saying "Check please!" trying to get the attention of a passing doctor. "Exxxuse me? Where's my mudder? My mudder? My mother?" The doctor chuckled and made a comment about the fantastic powers of silly juice as I gently touched her arm and assured her that I was directly next to her— exactly where I had been for the past forty-five minutes.

She looked at me like I was an alien. Then, with sudden recognition, she goes, "*Heeeyyyy*. I see you there! Ha. Ha ha. Hahaha, hehe. Hum."

I remember thinking, *Is it wrong that I love her more like this? I mean, that is wrong, isn't it? It is. I know it is. Okay. Sorry. (Actually, no I'm not. This is fan-tas-tic!)*

And then, just when I thought it couldn't get even better, it did. As I was just finishing a text to my husband, I looked back up and noticed that my daughter was sliding out of her chair like a slippery fish. She looked like pure liquid as she seamlessly glided over each bump and curve of the big recliner. She landed in a puddle on the floor and laughed so loudly that nurses came rushing to see what the commotion was! I picked up my Jello-like daughter and tried to situate her back in the chair, but it was no use. She was a complete blob.

So I slumped her as best as I could and secured her pillow and blankets around her to keep her upright. And then... stage two of silly juice set in. That was where she started tripping.

"*Ah, ooh*... I don't want my teeth pulled!" (Sobs. Tears. Yells.)

"Where am I? Oh, my gosh, where am I?" (Fear. Terror. Hysterics.)

"*Mommy*! I'm having bad dreams!" (Hallucinations. Horror. Panic.)

"Hey, you look funny... I look funny. Ha, am I upside-down?"

"Don't let them kill me, Mommy... pleeeaaase!"

Okay, it had gone from hysterical to pitiful very quickly. The nurses said that I could pick her up and hold her until the gurney arrived. Taylor asked if I would "cubble" her. I was pretty sure she'd meant cuddle. So, I did. And when her bed showed up outside our curtained room, she wailed in fear.

Taylor screamed my name for all to hear as they wheeled her down the hall and out of sight. It was definitely not my favorite part. But I remembered back to a time several years ago when she used to scream for her biological mom like that. I used to feel so helpless. And now, even though her screams broke my heart, I felt a sense of warmth pour through me. I *am that mommy now*.

I returned to my place in the waiting room, sipping my sixth cup of teeny, tiny coffee as I patiently froze to death in the subzero temperatures of the office. My coffee tasted like dirt. I was contemplating a seventh cup when the doctor came into the waiting room and motioned to me.

"First off, your daughter did great. So no worries. Two teeth pulled, two capped, two filled. Uh, secondly, does your daughter tend to be a little dramatic? I checked her over good, and she's in great health, everything went well, she didn't even need stitches. But she's very difficult to calm down. Is that normal?"

"She got a paper cut once and wanted to go to the ER. And then there was the time she got a splinter, and I thought she was being murdered when my husband tried taking it out... he hadn't even touched her yet when she started screaming. So... yeah. Normal."

"Okay! Just checking. You guys are good to go, then!"

On the way home, she was every bit the gem I'd envisioned she'd be. I thought about taking her back to the hospital and asking them to keep her until the new teeth grew in, but that hardly seemed fair to their staff. Not that she wasn't in pain... I know it must've felt terrible! But once she started sobbing uncontrollably over the vanity of having caps and now looking "stupid like Cameron," I decided it was probably time for a mandatory nap!

She slept for over three hours. The final stage of the silly juice is apparently a coma. And for that, I was grateful.

We all have that *one child*, don't we? You know what I'm talking about, even if you don't want to admit it! It's the child that gets under your skin more than the others by either acting just like you or by acting such your opposite that you can't even fathom understanding what's going on in his or her teeny head.

It's the child that you wish would sleep just a little bit longer in the morning (by at least two hours) instead of greeting you the moment your eyes pop open. You wonder just how long they'd been awake, waiting for you to stir, as thousands of thoughts and ideas and outfit choices and questions come spewing from his or her mouth—the child that just can't seem to grasp that we need *coffee* before we can answer *all of the questions*. It's the child that follows you from room to room, so closely, in fact, that you have marks on the backs of your heels from the thirtieth time they've been gouged by little toenails that week. The child that requires all of your patience *all* of the time. No. Matter. What.

We all have that one child. And mine is my daughter. She's just a pint-sized shadow, a nugget of a human. She was seven (and a half... always add the half or they'll have your head), forty pounds soaking wet, and cute as a button. Cute as a button that's on a pair of pants that are three sizes too small. She's the child that I love, but whom I would probably love more if she would ever go away and give me a chance to miss her!

However, Taylor has always had many amazing qualities as well. She's adorable, athletic, resilient, and she loves to help clean, just to name a few things. But there were always those "quirks" that made me want to ram sharp objects into my eyes and ears, just so I wouldn't have to deal with them any longer. The make-up obsession (which led to stealing, lying, etc.), the passion for trendy clothes but the inability to stop wearing dirty ones from the hamper (again with the lies even when I could clearly see she'd layered like five dirty shirts under her jacket!), but most importantly, her need to mother—more specifically, her need to hold/carry other children. Infants, toddlers, other children her age, it didn't seem to matter. Strangers, people we knew, kids at the park, kids at school, babies picked up from strollers—if it was a child and could be lifted somewhat successfully, then she'd be all over it.

I know the deep-rooted issues behind each of these behaviors, really I do. My husband and I had tried a million and one therapeutic techniques (along with an equal number of not-so therapeutic techniques), and naturally three-and-a-half years later, she was still being grounded to her room for picking up the babies.

There are plenty of reasons I didn't want her doing this, not all of which I'll go into detail about, but most importantly, she's just too small and too immature to pick kids up safely. Children literally get hurt about 50 percent of the time that she touches them. Whether she's hovering so closely that she trips them, she sets them up on furniture and then walks away, or she downright drops them. I was constantly having to explain Isaac's and Wyatt's bumps and bruises to others just so they didn't call the authorities on us!

So, one blissful afternoon, Taylor had nearly given little Wyatt a concussion and then lied her pants off about it. Being the therapist that I am, I lost my mind on her. I banished her to her bedroom for the entire weekend. Meals and potty breaks—that was all she was allowed out for. It seemed the only way to keep the young ones safe since she'd pick them up the second I'd turn to do dishes or stir the soup on the stove.

Folks, she was heartbroken! *But I was not.* For a full weekend, I walked without heels being stepped on, drank an entire cup of coffee without having to answer (or ignore) two hundred questions, and I didn't have to apply first aid to anyone in the house! Thus, you can imagine my surprise when Saturday late afternoon arrived, and I started to *miss her.* (I know... it shocked me, too!) It was just so much calmer with her in a different room that I almost mistook my melancholy feelings for her as the flu.

After finding no fever, I deduced that it was definitely me missing Taylor. However, I am one for consistency. And I'd told her that she was grounded for the weekend, so how could I go back on my word without losing whatever ground I thought I might have with her? This is where parenting gets tough, constantly questioning every choice and weighing every option—wondering if I chose the right thing or not.

Strangely enough, it was in that moment of self-debate, standing at the top of the stairs, that I heard something coming from her room. *Was she talking to herself or to someone else?*

It didn't take long before I realized what was happening. Friends... my daughter was *praying.* She was praying loudly and boldly, just like I'd taught her to do. She was not prompted, nor was she encouraged to do it as a condition for "early release." As I stood there, tears streaming down my face, I heard these words:

"God, *please* make me good! When you say to do it, I wanna do it. I'll read my Bible and I won't wear dirty clothes and I won't pick up babies no more. I need to stop trying and start doing!" (A quote from me... she had been listening!)

"I need to move on and be who I gotta be. I don't want to go down the wrong path!" (I put daily Bible verses in the kids' lunch boxes, and Taylor had one earlier in the week about God lighting her path and showing her which way to go. So not only did she read it, she memorized it and *applied* it.)

This is where she randomly burst into song in the middle of her prayer with the correct amount of Taylor-sized drama. "Je-*sus*, I gotta do the right thing, Je-*sus*... I gotta take the right path, Je-*sus*..." Okay, so I stopped crying to crack up for a few minutes as she mooed like a cow going through the spin cycle, uttering those sweet words before returning to her prayer. Only this time, I could hear the tears in her own voice.

"God, I have such a long way to go, and my mom, she's not being mean to me by keeping me in my room. She's just trying to help me. If she dies, I'll probably end up in jail, so you *have* to help me, God! I need to do *my part* so everybody can be happy. Please! Please help me be good, God. Please!" Between heaving sobs, I managed to pull myself together and assess the situation with fresh eyes. The child who seemed to never learn her lesson, the child who seemed to only care about what she wanted, despite the harm it may cause others, the child who was *that child* to me... well, she was learning, wasn't she?

It's so hard to remember that her behavior is not always "defiant." Hearing her words to God reminded me that she's not trying to be bad. She doesn't want to struggle like this. Her desire to do the right thing is tantamount to her desire to over-mother the little ones, and it had caused a spiritual war inside of her, frustrating her, leaving her feeling like a failure. And where was I? Sipping my coffee and enjoying my healing heels. I felt so small in that moment, so broken for her little heart. I walked down the stairs, took a deep breath and opened her door. There she was, sitting on her bed, baby doll in her lap, tear-stained cheeks beneath watery eyes looking back at me. She suddenly burst into sobs all over again. I gently moved to her, grabbing her up into my arms, letting her just weep her frustrated, cleansing tears.

I think I felt closer to her in that moment than I ever had. I, too, do what is wrong, despite knowing what is right. I, too, sin repeatedly and don't seem to learn my lesson. I don't have RAD. What was *my* excuse?

We were able to have a long heart-to-heart over the next hour, my daughter and me. We talked about safety. We talked about consistency in consequences. We talked about love. And we talked about forgiveness. I explained how God's grace covers us fully and completely, no matter what we've done. I also explained how God uses just wisdom in order to teach us things in the middle of our sin. And I explained that I loved her, that I was so proud of her for letting God work on her heart.

Taylor remained grounded until the next day, and she understood why that decision was upheld. But I think she and I both gained a huge sense of peace in our relationship from that hour we spent talking on her bed. Although my heels went back to being marred and my state of mind back to that of frazzled, I am filled with hope at the realization that she is, in fact, learning and growing and trying.

Because sometimes Hope comes by recognizing that trying is, in fact, good enough.

Denial. Taylor, my seven-year-old, simply looked at me upon hearing the news and said, "Whelp, I guess he's not my brother anymore." We had waited to tell the kids until we had to, but the day came when we would normally pick up Isaac for our biweekly visits, and we had been told by Isaac's birth father that there would be no more interactions with our family. It had been sudden and without warning.

I remembered trying to keep myself composed, for the kids' sakes. I didn't know how they'd handle the loss, and I knew that my natural reaction to weep like a baby would only cause them to go into survival mode and not truly face their feelings. Yet Taylor, despite all the progress she'd made in emotional expression over the past several years, she still responded in the same way she always had. Emotional deadness. Denial.

She then hugged baby Wyatt and said, "At least I still have this baby brother." And that was it. No questions. No emotions. Nothing! Throughout the week, she would randomly ask me what time we were picking Isaac up that coming weekend, what we were going to do for his upcoming birthday party, and if I had bought him his presents yet. Needless to say, these constant reminders of his absence struck a chord in me. It was even more concerning that there was no reaction to him leaving, and that, furthermore, she seemed to hourly re-forget that he was even gone. It took several months of not seeing Isaac before Taylor was able to respond to her internal pain.

We had gone to my parents' house in Michigan—just her, Wyatt, and I. My folks had a meeting at their church, so the kids and I were visiting with my brother, when out of nowhere, Taylor stated that she missed Isaac.

We hadn't been talking about him, nor were we conversing about anything related to her brother. But there she stood, like a statue, head hung down and hair over her face. I knew she was crying because tears were landing on her bare feet, but no sound was being made.

It was just how she had always handled her emotions. Staring off at nothing and refusing to move had been her go-to response for a long time—it was her way of pretending that a hurt or loss wasn't there. But over the previous year, we had seen that particular habit slowly retire itself. Perhaps she had been feeling more secure, with less pain than she was used to. Perhaps nothing had hurt her badly enough for her to resort to the old method of coping. Either way, it didn't really matter. She was hurting, and it was my job to make it stop.

I went to her and put my arm around her shoulders as my brother and I looked at one another through tears. She was as stiff as a corpse.

I picked up her wooden body and set her on my lap. Carefully rubbing her back and trying to help her body loosen, I began to pray over her.

She instantly tightened again, and as I tried to brush the hair from her face, she swiftly moved a stiff arm and smacked my hand away. It was so very obvious that the pain she'd been pushing down for two months was no longer able to be hidden, but equally obvious was the fact that she had no idea how to handle such intense pain or *how to accept love while she was desperately hurting.*

Continuing to whisper prayers over her, I stroked her hair without moving it away from her face, leaving her veil of privacy intact. I made slow, circular motions on her arms and legs with my other hand as I put words to her feelings, letting her know that those feelings were allowed, they were okay, and they were necessary to heal. Her rigid body eventually began to loosen, but she still made no sound. When I ended the prayer, Taylor stood and walked to the bedroom she has at my parents' home.

We listened to her weep for over two hours.

I checked on her twice, and both times she turned away so I wouldn't see her pain. So I simply told her that I hurt, too. That I cry every day. That I know it feels like the worst thing in the world, but we have each other. Neither of us has to grieve alone.

She finally fell asleep, and when she woke the next morning, she was more cuddly than ever. My girl, who *adores* her grandparents, called for *me* to do her tuck-ins each night of our stay. She wanted to sit next to me on the couch and at the dinner table. All because she needed someone to help her feel... and for so long, I'd always worried it would be a friend or a boyfriend she would choose, or God forbid an addictive substance. My worst fear was that she would never learn to address her emotions and constantly chase after anything and anyone who could distract her from that pain.

But she chose me. And I was honored to be that someone for her.

It's funny how love can sneak up on you all of a sudden. It can happen so slowly and gradually that you're not even aware that it was there the whole time. I remember when I first started dating my husband. We were just hanging out, really. I don't even know if you could call it dating. But one day, I woke up, and I just knew... I loved

him. It wasn't butterflies or a crush, but a love that took it's time—
something that grew out of a friendship, something that came on
without me even noticing because of how subtly my heart had been
changing.

I've never had microwave love. The only loves I've ever known,
the only really good ones anyway, have all been developed Crock-Pot
style. They've simmered slowly for long periods, warming me from
the inside out, not the other way around.

Yet when the foster care system handed me kids and two seconds
later asked me to keep them forever and love them unconditionally,
I found myself looking at these crazy little strangers and wishing for
a pot roast instead of a Hot Pocket family. I was never blessed with
the privilege to get to know my older kids as they grew inside my
belly for nine months; I never got to anxiously await each prenatal
appointment and their upcoming arrivals.

I needed more *time*. I needed time to court them and get to know
them without the pressure of having to make it all work overnight,
with people who were already set in their ways... ways that I didn't
particularly care for. I needed time to *fall in love* with my children. And
after all we'd been through in those first several years, I felt as though
I should re-propose to them.

Would they take me to be their mother? Because I was finally
ready to commit, not just legally, but emotionally... completely... with
my whole heart.

The changes crept up slowly over the period of several months.
We'd done a lot of grieving and a lot figuring out life. And one
morning after the kids had gone to school, I caught myself smiling
as I remembered something funny Cameron had said. Another day I
laughed out loud at an utterly ridiculous joke that Taylor had told, and
it didn't feel forced or awkward in the slightest. Someone had once
said to me, "Can you even imagine the lives those kids would've had
if they hadn't come to you?" And for the first time, I couldn't picture
my life without them.

As a mother, you hate to say you're surprised when these things
happen, but those of you who have a similar story of your own,
you know the struggle—how we've all fought to connect and love

and be to okay with our thrown-together, emotional roller coaster of an existence. You know my resentments and bitterness, all the uncomfortable and unmotherly things that I've thought and said. And now, I sit here wondering how worse off my life would be if I didn't have these little people calling me mama.

One thing is for sure. Taylor taught me to love persistently.

God looked at the pair of us and said, "Ah, this is good." He gave us to one another so that as iron sharpens iron, we would both be changed for the better, and our abilities to love will have grown stronger and deeper than we could have ever dreamed.

Sometimes Hope means allowing God to make a beautiful meal our collectively broken pieces. And I'm so thankful that God gave me my pot roast.

ISAAC

It's at this point in a meal when your pallet needs to be refreshed. You've experienced lots of flavors, all jumbling around and creating new sensations for you to experience. But this next course is filled with sweetness and love beautifully mixed with sorrow. This, in and of itself, is your comfort food.

We knew the day was coming for almost a month; although, it was still not nearly enough time to prepare. CYS had come to us one afternoon and informed my husband and me that Taylor and Cameron's birth mother was pregnant and that she was due mid-October of that year, 2012. Baffled, we wondered how she'd been doing visits with the kids each week *without* anyone noticing that she was eight months pregnant! Either way, the baby was coming, and they were planning to place him/her into foster care immediately after birth.

They gave us time to think it through before we needed to give them an answer. Deep down we already knew our reply. We made our pro-con list, just to appear responsible. However, the look in my husband's eyes at the mention of a baby mirrored the aching in my own heart, and I knew we were done for.

We did discuss it, though. Bringing an infant into an already crazy home, finding daycare to accommodate our work schedules that already seemed to be impossible to navigate, and how we would deal with losing a baby—one that we had from birth, one that came to us perfectly innocent and fresh, right from the start. More so, how would the children handle yet another loss in their lives if their sibling couldn't stay?

These were the things that we asked our caseworker. What she told us was this: bio mom had already lost her four other children. Due to her legal, financial, and mental health issues, there was no way she would be granted the ability to care for a baby. We were also informed that she had been with a large number of men during that time as she needed housing and money for her addiction and that she had no idea who the father was. CYS expressed that they would test men that she could remember, but that most of them would more than likely not be an approved home for the baby in the end.

They told us not to count our chickens but to prepare for adoption.

As excited as we were, we tried to remain calm. Well, we tried to *appear* calm, all the while we were pacing around the house each day, waiting for this woman's water to break! Was it a boy? Was it a girl? Was he or she healthy?

What name would be chosen? There were just so many unanswered questions! Thus I began to use my nesting excitement to prepare for all things gender neutral and baby-related.

Finally, on October 23, at the exact same time that Taylor was being adopted, baby Isaac was being brought into this world. It's almost poetic how things work out, isn't it? The beginning of two new lives simultaneously occurring, all within the span of a few moments. The adoption went beautifully. Taylor was beyond excited to have everyone in one place specifically for her, and she was even more excited that her present was a new baby brother!

However, even though we weren't able to see Baby Isaac that day, it was amazing to feel 100 percent connected to a child whom we'd only just come to know about, whom we'd never met, and who may or may not be with us for more than a few months. Yet there we were— the perfect picture of connectedness.

When we found out that Isaac was born addicted to opiates, I know that I can speak for my husband as well, but our hearts were twisted into so many knots that even a boy scout wouldn't have been able to undo them. The doctors were keeping him for observation, and we were told to expect him home on Wednesday.

So, I took Wednesday off of work. And then Wednesday came and went, and we were told Thursday was the day. Thursday morning, I called off again as I wore holes in the floorboards by my constant movement from room to room, straightening the same towels on the racks for the millionth time and checking his bassinet with equal frequency.

Finally, we received a phone call stating that he wouldn't be home for one to three more days! The anxiety of waiting was more than I could handle, so I promptly went back to work to distract my racing thoughts. CYS and the doctors wouldn't give us information on if Isaac was okay, and the hospital was treating us as if we were the bad guys (because obviously his current health condition was our fault).

At last, on his third evening we were able to see him at the hospital for the first time, and he was beautiful! The nurses reported that Isaac's symptoms were much better and that he was one of the best babies they've had. I'm afraid that I monopolized most of our time with him on that first visit, never having had the opportunity to be a proper mother from the beginning of a child's life.

Over the next several days, Pat and I took turns holding little Isaac and staring at each perfect little part of him. We fed him, sang to him, and practiced changing newborn diapers. We asked the nurses a million questions, and they answered each one with encouragement, assuring us that we would be fine!

Sunday morning came and we went about our daily schedule as planned. As the worship leader of our small church, I was ready with songs for that morning and had just finished the microphone check as my cell phone rang. My heart leapt when I recognized the number on the screen. It was the hospital—and it was time to go get our baby!

I tried to feel badly about leaving our church members in a lurch without any music for the morning, but we all knew that I didn't want to be anywhere else than at the hospital as soon as humanly possible.

Our church family prayed over us and then sent us out the door with big smiles and congratulatory hugs. We dropped the bigger kids off with Pat's parents and headed to the hospital to officially welcome Baby Isaac into our family.

When we arrived, the police and a caseworker were waiting for us. I hadn't expected law enforcement, so my heart lurched quickly at the thought that something was terribly wrong. Little did I know that he was there to do a car seat check and nothing more (new mother problems)! Subsequently, we signed all the papers and made sure we had our little man secured perfectly in his seat before heading for the door.

"Hold on," a nurse said, coming up to me with a wheelchair. I looked at her with wide, confused eyes.

"It's protocol. We have to wheel you out of the hospital."

"Um, really? I didn't actually *have* a baby...I can just walk. It's fine."

"It's protocol," she replied.

I reluctantly sat in the wheelchair, and the nurse placed Isaac's carrier in my lap. I didn't expect the tears that came to my eyes. Slightly embarrassed, I began brushing them away in haste. My precious husband looked at me with a smile and whispered, "You may never get to do this again—just enjoy it."

Through the long hallways and past each lobby, my heart filled more and more with emotion. People smiled and congratulated me as they passed, and I had no idea what to say other than, "Thank you." When we finally reached the front door, my husband and I stood together, car seat between us, facing the world on our own.

Suddenly, I missed the wheelchair! An overwhelming feeling of "I don't know what the heck I'm doing" came over me, and I wanted to bring a nurse home with me to make sure that I didn't mess this baby up! I mean, didn't they know I had never had a baby before? How did they even know I'd be able to do this?

But the staff just smiled with confidence and sent us on our way. Oh, to have had half of that assurance...

Pat drove as I sat in the back with little Isaac, death-gripping the car seat at each turn and bump in the road. I'm pretty sure that I didn't exhale until the car was parked safely in our driveway.

Knowing my children didn't get the correct bonding experience with their birth families, my husband and I wanted to make sure we did everything we could to make Isaac feel safe. Sadly, because foster parents don't get maternity leave, I had to use my last week of vacation to stay home with Isaac. But I used that time to do nothing but hold him and love on him. Also during that week, I called the hospital about five times, just to make sure we were doing things right!

Shouldn't he wake up at some point? Why is he sleeping so long? Doesn't he need to eat? Should I change his diaper, even if he's not awake yet? How do I know if he's too hot... oh, my gosh, what if he's too cold? He's supposed to sleep on his back, right? Or is the latest health advice stomach-sleeping...? His blanket isn't too close to his face, is it? And how the heck do I do this swaddling thing!

It was a sleepless, worrisome week to be sure, but it was one of the most rewarding weeks of my life. Although I realized very quickly that I had more questions than answers. Questions like, "Why do babies wear clothes?" Because after several nights, I was seriously considering taking all of Isaac's new clothes back in exchange for pairs of long socks and a baby Snuggie. This kid pooped like it's what all the cool babies were doing, and he was desperate to fit in... that as *soon* as I'd change his diaper and get all the snaps done back up on the forty-five layers he's required to wear, I'd hear the familiar gruntings of the second bowel movement begin. At that point, working in the dead of night by the small glow from the baby monitor, I found myself cursing the maker of snaps.

Another thing I realized is that the nurses had lied. They should be punished. It's just not right to tell a brand-new mother of an infant, "Oh, your baby sleeps through the night like a champ!" Two words, medical professionals of a hospital that shall remain nameless: You're *wrong*. What they should've said? "Your child sleeps through the *day* like a champ. In fact, you'll probably think that he's in a coma, but at night, I'm sorry to tell you, he's going to be wide awake and ready to party."

I'd brought two bottles upstairs with me one night in that first week, figuring that we'd probably have two feedings in the night and then a couple of diaper changes. Well, I was sorely unprepared when Isaac wanted to eat *four* times and then pooped continuously throughout the night. And it was also rather unfair that the little nugget refused to look alive at all during the daytime but then wanted to coo and explore and be all cutesy and fun at bedtime.

Those same nurses told me to make nighttime feedings very businesslike (suit and tie?), no monkeying around, no cooing, no baby talk. Well, you know what? That's just not fair, *nor* was it possible. I couldn't refuse his cuteness at night any more than I could wake the sack of logs up during the day!

Although I'll never forget the morning that we had our first real "poop experience." I knew it was only a matter of time, but for some reason, I thought that I was immune. After all, I knew how to change a diaper, and I was certainly finding my way around those silly baby snaps by the end of that first week. But the inevitable finally happened.

My husband and I were co-changing Isaac's diaper (one person holding the binky in and keeping the hands from flapping, the other one changing the yuckiness... if this is the only reason you get married, it's worth it) when I realized that we had quite the load on our hands. We were experiencing smells and sights that had not yet been breached with this little guy. And lo and behold, there we were, on the living room floor, trying to keep his squirming to a minimum, when *plop!* In went his foot. His tootsies were covered in poo and he was rapidly cycling his leg, making it nearly impossible to clean him off (and to prevent flinging of gunk from his waving limb)! I finally latched hold of his foot, which transferred a big smear of gooey poo onto my hand.

Then, for whatever reason, Little Man's "smear" would not wipe off that day. It was as if he'd been eating glue or something. The consistency was different from his norm, and it was as if the brown sludge was immune to the powers of the baby wipe. The poor fella wailed heartily as his little body was exposed to the cold air and even colder baby wipes. And the thing about baby screams is that they chill you to the bone. I knew in my rational head that no one was dying in that moment. I *knew* that Isaac would survive that diaper change and that he would warm up, calm down, and eventually be the happy boy we'd come to love.

But that scream... that *scream*! It could turn on a level of panic inside that says, "You know what? Someone *may* actually be dying right now! *Hurry, hurry, hurry!* Get that diaper changed *now!*" And before I'd know it, I would be sweating and making silly mistakes, and my husband and I would be screaming at each other as dogs ran for cover. It was poo pandemonium, I tell you!

Yet despite his utter disgustingness, I had fallen in love with little Isaac. And it broke my heart to go back to work only a week after his arrival. I felt completely and utterly shorted. Those first several months would never be allotted to me again, and had I known my time with him was going to be cut short, I would've quit work in that very instant and just breathed him in until he was no longer mine to hold.

Hindsight will do that to you though. It will show you all the things you could never have foretold early on, and it will shame you into thinking you've made all sorts of mistakes. When really, we are all just people doing our best with the information we've been given. And so, I moped my way through long days at work and watched videos of a happy baby that my husband would send me during my lunch break. When I would finally arrive home, make dinner, help little ones with homework and clean up the day's mess, then it would be just Isaac and me—no one else. He would be my focus, and each night, he would steal my heart again and again.

Although generally beat like a rug by evening, I adored the fact that Isaac was wide awake and anxious to stare at my face, play with my nose, and give me a big, toothless smile. Because Isaac was only five weeks old, he didn't do a whole lot of talking yet. There were the occasional babbles, but mostly just an odd coo every now and again. That's why I'd spend a lot of our time together talking to him and using silly sounds to get his attention.

However, one night I decided to take his hands and put them on his cheeks while saying, "Isaac," and then I would take those same hands and rub them on my cheeks and say, "Mama." I did this about ten times with him, just staring into his little face, him staring back at me in full amusement. I completed this new game one last time, saying, "Isaac," by touching his own chubby hands to his equally chubby cheeks... and just as I put his hands on my face, baby boy tightened up his entire body and belted out a very distinctive, "Ma!"

Instant tears sprang to my eyes as I laughed and danced around the room with Isaac in my arms. It still amazed me that after having to work for motherhood status for oh so long, in just five short weeks, this tiny human was all ready to take me on as his "Ma."

Now, at the time, I knew in my head that babies that age don't really have an understanding of what they're saying... that it was mimicking at its finest. But in hindsight, once again, I now know that Isaac is *incredibly* smart, and he has language skills far beyond his years. So, I can claim his proclamation of my motherhood with full confidence that he meant it and had chosen me in that moment! And that thought was enough to get me through the long work days and each sleepless night.

There's something utterly fantastic about long weekends. And there's only one thing that makes a long weekend even more miraculous than it already is, and that is spending most of that time holding a three-month-old chunky baby. Isaac was easily the world's fattest creature. Although that may have been our fault. I mean, I tend to overwater plants until they drown; whoever thought I would know the correct amount to feed a baby was seriously mistaken. If he cried, we'd check for the usual culprits (wet diaper, bored, wanting to be held in a new position, etc.), but if nothing worked, we just fed him. A *lot*. This baby ate like he couldn't be sated for the first full year of his life.

And it's not like we knew he had a formula allergy that was causing his fussiness and crazy-demonic diapers. The doctors assured us that he was healthy each and every time we asked, yet they had us try an assortment of expensive formulas, all of which seemed to make Isaac worse. Finally, we decided to take matters into our own hands, switching to soy formula around three months old. Lo and behold, our chubster stopped fussing and crapping sixteen times a day. It looked like Mama really *did* know best after all, which boosted my maternal confidence greatly.

One of my favorite moments with Isaac one particular holiday weekend was discovering his love for the cooking channel. This was not going to bode well for his weight problem later in life, obviously, but it sure was cute to watch his entranced gaze as he hungrily sucked on his entire fist, probably wishing it was one of the gourmet burgers being made on *Diners, Drive-Ins, and Dives*. Interestingly enough, he also seemed to enjoy *The Biggest Loser*, leading me to think that he may be an athlete—you know, high caloric intake but willing to work it off in the gym. (I'm sure it has nothing to do with the fast pace of the show, bright colors, and loud sounds of the gym... not at all.)

However, over those next several months, I learned the art of mothering in reverse. Starting with older children and then moving to an infant was confusing at first, but it progressively got easier and easier once I realized that Isaac was a very effortless child to raise. Never had I witnessed a baby with such a capacity for learning. It was as if he soaked in every word, every picture, every place we traveled; he mimicked noises, practiced words, and responded consistently to conversations we had with him.

When teething hit, it really didn't seem much different than Cameron and his teeth coming in. And none of the kids actually slept through the night so that really wasn't anything new either. Plus, Isaac was fearless, so he would climb, jump, toddle, and run full speed at anything and everything. The child was a walking *bruise*, but he was just so curious, and to his credit, those bruises didn't slow him down in the slightest. Once he got the hang of his own body, we realized that he was not only brilliant, but he was also very coordinated.

In fact, it wasn't long before Isaac weighed more than Taylor and could throw a ball farther than Cameron, and he wasn't even one year old! Everywhere we went, people would either comment on the size of his gigantic thighs, his beautiful biracial skin, or remark about his incredible vocabulary. Isaac required constant attention (mainly so he didn't get hurt being a daredevil), but he also captivated our attention with his humor and magnetic personality. I was constantly guilty of watching him play for well over an hour, simply marveling at how his mind worked and at the complexities of his imagination.

Sundays had become a particular favorite for me and Pat. Early in the morning, before the rest of the house awoke, Isaac would waken and we would bring him into our bed. The room would still be dark, our sheets were still warm from the night's sleep. And in the darkness, we would place Isaac between us for our Sunday morning cuddles. He would take turns rolling toward one of us and giving hugs and kisses, chattering about anything and everything. Then, when we could hold them off no longer, the big kids would come in and lavish Isaac with love and attention.

Our Sunday blessings continued as we headed to church each week. Being the worship leader of a church as cozy as ours, I loved that I could hear individual voices singing along with me from the congregation. But what would make me melt was hearing my baby's voice, singing along to his favorite songs, raising his hands in the air from atop my husband's shoulders. Because what Isaac demonstrated from very early on was his love for worship. Anytime I sang, he sang. If I played the piano, he danced and made his own noises to accompany me. And at church, he joined in with the big kids or the adults each and every time, anxious to sing and dance for Jesus.

Parenting Isaac was, in a nutshell, *incredible*.

My husband tells the story perfectly when he says this: "The first moment I held him, I knew that whatever happened, whether he stayed or whether he had to go, I made a promise to Isaac. I promised him that I would love him with all of my heart and hold nothing back, even if it meant losing everything in return—because I loved him from that very first minute."

These words have been spoken and re-spoken over the past three years as we question if we did the right thing by bringing Isaac into our home. When we think about the pain our family has gone through and the suffering of our other children, we always go back to that promise we made to Isaac as a baby. And we know that while we endured tremendous heartache, we also endured tremendous love... and that we could hold our heads high, knowing that we loved fully and completely, if only for a short time.

There are stints in life when you're suddenly faced with the possibility of a horrible life event—the imminent death of a loved one, losing your job, or a grave financial disaster, just to name a few. But in each of these instances, whether the outcome is dire or whether it works out in your favor, the excruciatingly painful wait is the same.

In late April of 2013, my heart was breaking in half with the anticipation of a horrible life event. Isaac's time with us hung in limbo, pending the results of a simple mouth swab paternity test.

It was and still is so hard to think that a small piece of cotton mixed with a small bit of DNA could change my life and the lives of my family members forever. What was I to say to my other two children? How should my husband and I process the thousands of feelings raging inside? Who could we turn to that would have any clue what we were going through? The very answer to all that fear and anxiety was sitting on the end of a Q-tip in a lab somewhere.

Isaac has always held the key to so many spoken and unspoken prayers that have been offered up from my lips to God's ears. He was my favorite part of the day, my smile when I arrived home, and my precious cuddle at night. I'm the one who knew the position he liked to be held in just as he'd drift off to sleep. I'm the one who could tell if he had even the slightest fever with just the touch of my cheek. I'm the one who could read his smiles, interpret his cries, and find his secret tickle spots. I'm the one who gave him baby massages and trimmed his tiny fingernails, the one who cleaned out his ears and nose, lotioned his skin, and sang him to sleep. I'm the one he smiled at and the face that he knew. *I am his mother....*

And yet, how could I hate someone for possibly being his father? How could I be angry that he may take his child from me? No. I couldn't hate this man. What I did hate was that I had no idea where to place all of those awful emotions. Who would get to be the bearer of the mountains of blame that I wanted to pour out in a fit of tears and rage? Who would be the recipient of my gut-wrenching sobs and rants? No one. There was *no one* to blame. How could I possibly be mad at anyone for wanting this amazing child? Anyone who had met him loved him in an instant.

Perhaps foolishly, I'd acted like he was all mine. I selfishly fantasized about him as a Costa, his first day of kindergarten, what he will look like when he's in grade school, what type of man he will become. I unguardedly loved someone that was never truly mine in the first place. I assumed that this was God's gift to me because I had been unable to have babies of my own... but what if I was just a stepping stone to the rest of his life? What if I was there to love him unconditionally for a few short months as a holding place until he could be united with a man that didn't even know he existed?

If that was the case, if my *son* was to be nothing more to me than a temporary glimpse of the dreams I had always wanted to come true, then I would be left with a memory of what it is to have mothered the most wonderful baby boy in the entire world. And he would never remember that he had me as his mother at all.

I had no idea how to make my heart, mind, or soul understand such a tragedy. I didn't know how to grieve someone I wasn't supposed to fall in love with, someone that is still alive, and someone that would soon forget my very existence. His biological father had no idea what he was missing... but I would be painfully and desperately aware of Isaac's absence from my arms.

I will always want what is best for all of my children— for my son. But perhaps that's not me.

For every great feeling, there is an equally intense opposite. In order to know the fullness of one, you must, at some point, experience its opposite. Throughout that week of waiting, my husband and I lived through a plethora of heartbreaking emotions. When faced with the possibility of having Isaac taken from us at a moment's notice, it's unreal how our entire world started to swim. The complete fear, devastation, and grief that washed over us felt like an all-consuming tidal wave. The other things in life became foggy, the events of the day seemed tortured with waiting for that one life-changing phone call.

Finally, that phone call came. My husband was the one to answer. I was on my cell phone with my parents, driving to work, as my husband's name flashed on the call-waiting. When I answered, he shared the news that my heart had been anxiously waiting for. *The man in question was not our baby's father.*

In that moment, I felt the full weight of each emotion as it drained from my body and was replaced by the opposite feelings. Love. Abundance. Joy. Peace. *Hope.* And in true woman form, I sobbed uncontrollably before calling my parents back to sob some more. Thankfully, they're weepers, too.

Even though I was very much aware that this tumultuous process was not done with until we'd take that final picture with the judge celebrating Isaac's adoption, I was able to rest well that night, knowing that my baby boy was right there with me, just where he was supposed to be. And once again, I counted my blessings. One amazing husband, three amazing children, three insane dogs, a loving and supportive extended family, and a vast number of friends (and strangers) that would go out of their way to pray for a situation that was not their own.

Because sometimes Hope means momentary blessings, even if those blessings eventually must leave.

For as long as I can remember, I've believed in happy endings. I love the stories where the good guy wins or the girl finds her prince. But sometimes, in real life, happy endings are harder to believe in. *Sometimes* the good guy loses or the girl's heart gets broken. Life is *sometimes* a tragedy instead of a comedy, leaving our beloved hopes and dreams to fall short.

But along with my belief in happy endings, I had dealt with bouts of insomnia since I was a little girl. So to pass the time and try to induce sleep, I created a little game. I would lie in bed and think about the best dream I could possibly have, close my eyes tightly, and let my imagination take over. This fun game didn't always help me sleep, but it gave me plenty of time to plan my dream wedding, name my imaginary children, and design the mansion we were sure to live in. In fact, I kept my list of beloved baby names in my nightstand for years, scratching off choices that became "too trendy" as time went on.

At every baby shower, I played each game with enthusiasm, and (taking a moment to gloat) there was not one family living within a ten-mile radius from my parents' home that didn't have me on speed-dial as their number one babysitter. Yet the one dream that I believed in more than anything was that one day, I was going to be a mommy. You can imagine, then, my devastation when I saw my ob-gyn and was told that I have the leading causes of infertility. I was barely sixteen years old. With the pain I'd been having, I was actually hoping for something like colon problems or ulcers, not *infertility*.

At age 21, I finally had to have surgery to help relieve the excruciating pain that was starting to take over my life. It was at that time that the doctor strongly recommended I think about a hysterectomy. When I asked him if there was anything else that would help relieve my symptoms instead, he responded, "Yes... getting pregnant."

Well, ain't that a kick in the head! The one thing that could cure me was the one thing that seemed impossible to achieve. But despite the agony that kept exploding in my body every four weeks, I held onto my belief in happy endings.

As time passed, I lost track of my coveted list of baby names. I started a job working with children who had been abused and suffered mentally, emotionally, and behaviorally—surrounding myself with children that needed my help seemed like the best way to handle the whole situation. I forced myself to feel happy for all my friends who started having babies all the while becoming livid with those who seemed to flippantly have children without even trying.

Working with broken and hurting children increased my resentment toward those "mothers" who continually chose drugs, men, or their own conveniences over their babies. But I still held out hope that my story would end happily.

When I married my husband and we were unsuccessful at getting pregnant, we had landed on fostering as our way to continue helping little ones. And once Cameron and Taylor had finally come to us, we realized that life as we knew it was forever changed. Whereas I was so grateful for the opportunity to be a mother, I still felt that I had missed out on those first years of my kids' lives. I had never rocked a baby to sleep or experienced that new baby smell that mother's tell of. It appeared that my dreams of motherhood were once again going to be less than I had imagined years ago.

As it turns out, God had already worked out all my beginnings and my endings—He had just done them in reverse order. Because within minutes of holding Isaac, I didn't worry about the fact that I'd never read the book *What to Expect When You're Expecting*, because he was already here. And if he ended up leaving the very next day, I would ultimately be a better person for having loved him so strongly for just that one day.

By the time Cameron's adoption came, their mother had still not identified the correct father for little Isaac. We were told that if a birth father was interested, Isaac would be taken from us in a matter of days. Our fears came and went with each passing man she mentioned. We waited for the court orders to demand testing, for the results to be determined, and for the dreaded phone call. And with each passing month, I feared losing him even more. Finally, in May, the judge announced that the last two men identified would be the last two that the court would agree to test.

And so we waited again...

We had the fortunate opportunity to meet both men at that court hearing. Man number one assured us that he would never rip a child away from a family that obviously loves him so much. He said that he could tell we were good people and that he was glad Isaac was with his siblings, so if it was his baby, he would sign his rights over. Man number two was a different story. He began actively pursuing Isaac, calling the caseworker weekly, and creating pins and needles for me and my husband.

Six weeks passed before we heard anything. Six long weeks. I'd felt like I was back to that place several years ago, staring at each pregnancy test as the clock ticked by. Each time we received a call from our agency during those dreadful weeks, my stomach turned queasy. I could feel my heart pound in my ears as I waited for the news. Yet *still*, no results.

One warm Friday in mid-July 2013, I found myself at my dear friend's house, performing my maid of honor duties in preparation for her wedding the following day. For once, my mind was occupied enough to find rest in someone else's stress instead of my own! I glanced at my phone in the midst of the busyness and realized that I had multiple missed calls, followed up with a text message from my husband that read: CALL ME ASAP.

Had Cameron or Taylor been hurt? Did one of the dogs get hit by a car? Are our parents okay? I frantically called him back, fearing the worst of the worst. "What's wrong?" I'd asked with panic in my tone.

My husband responded with an unusual huskiness in his voice that sounded as if he'd been crying, "The DNA results are in...."

Oh God... oh God, oh God, oh God, please! Please, no...

"The first man is the father, and he agreed to let us keep him... he's ours... Honey, Isaac is ours!" My husband could barely get the words out as his tears got the better of him.

There is nothing that can explain the feeling that came over me. No words to express the gratitude, relief, and joy that overwhelmed me so completely. The moments spent staring at him as he slept, not wanting to fall asleep and miss one second of memorizing his face, just in case he left me... that was *over*! No more waiting, no more worrying, and no more wondering if I was going to get my happy ending.

I was given a child for each cause of infertility. *Take that, Uterus!* God knew what I'd needed way back when I was planning my seven-year-old dreams, and He took those dreams, ground them into dust, and then recreated them into something more beautiful than I could have ever imagined. To top it off, I could *finally* make my OBGYN's dream come true and get that hysterectomy!

But things... they change so quickly. In a moment's time, you can be given everything you've ever wanted... yet in the very next moment, you can't catch your breath because your world is being shattered. And in a word, that's how I felt in August 2013. Shattered.

Within thirty-six hours of Isaac's father confirming that he would sign his rights over to us, he sent our lives into a tailspin. Isaac's dad informed us that he "might as well just take the baby." This man went from being pleasant and jovial to irritable and hostile. We had no idea what had happened; all we knew was that he had now decided to keep Isaac.

Our caseworkers were unwilling to confirm nor deny what was going on; additionally, on several occasions, they outright lied to us about the situation, leaving us to simply wait for a phone call once again.

And as the days grew closer to Isaac's adoption into our family, my husband and I realized that we would never make it to that final moment with the judge—the happy one where he'd shake our hands, congratulate us, and we'd take a family photo. No. Our last day with the judge would be one of two grief-stricken parents, saying good-bye to the baby they had planned to know and love the rest of their lives.

Finally, the wait was over and the call came. The worst news in the world was confirmed to me as I sat at a rest stop in the middle of Ohio, on my way to visit my parents in Michigan. I was alone with my three, soon to be two, children. I pleaded with the voice on the other end of the phone, begging for a different answer, but they simply hung up and seemingly went on to forget that I even existed.

I rolled up the windows of our Saab and screamed until I couldn't make any more sound. Isaac somehow slept through my wailing, and the older two stared at me with large eyes until I could formulate the words—the words to tell them that their baby brother was being taken away. Cameron cried instantly—a cry that came from deep down and wasn't intended to be muffled. It was a cry that broke my heart even more.

I drove the rest of the way to my parents' house, using every last ounce of my energy to focus on pressing pedals, using turn signals, and breathing. Honestly, I'm not sure that I did any of them well. I spent the next few days trying to remind myself that this man could change his mind again. He could realize he's too old and not in great health as it is. I spent time begging God, rationalizing, and analyzing every word of every conversation—trying to give myself hope so that I could make it to the end of each day.

When I'd finally returned home with Isaac, after leaving the older kids with my parents for the rest of the week, I met my husband, and we hugged with a tiredness that couldn't be put into words. I watched my big, strong man sink to the floor, unable to speak past the sobs. We both knew it was over. There was no more begging to be done. There was no more praying for a change in this man and our situation. There were only prayers that we would survive it. That somehow, each day, we could get out of bed and feel proud of the love and life that we gave to Isaac, even though he would never remember our names nor recognize our faces if he saw us in the street. He was too young to remember that he loved us. And we were too old to forget.

My emotions took turns appearing in unexpected waves. Anger. Despair. Rage. Disbelief. Gut-wrenching pain and weeping. Frantically seeking out countries without extradition. Those moments cycled rapidly and frequently. If I saw a child in a stroller, I dissolved into breathless tears. If people asked me about my baby, I tried to not throw up, sometimes more successfully than others. If I saw a dad holding the hand of a toddler as they walked down the street, I felt bitterness at the thought that I would never get to see Isaac's first steps and my husband would never get to walk with him hand in hand like the picture before me. Those moments had been stolen from me by a man that shares nothing more with my baby than his DNA.

I held Isaac when he was sick. I rocked him to sleep. I suffered his colic and fell in love with his smile. I had every inch of that perfect child memorized... yet I had to graciously hand him over to a man who couldn't even find it within himself to thank us for taking care of his son.

As you can see, I was a whirlwind of ups and downs during those months. My mind raced like that constantly, and then my emotions would cycle all over again. I found myself having those moments while working, at the store, in the shower, sleeping. To this day, I still haven't found a way to escape them. But I would have strong moments, too. In those moments, I was able to recognize that Isaac would be raised by his biological father, who seemed to have a lot of family that were interested in helping with Isaac, and two other sons that lived with him. Isaac would get to share his laughter and his incredibly loving personality with a town that is in desperate need of God's love. He would get the opportunity to be a light to his new family and to his community—and whereas he may experience a rougher life than he would have had with us, maybe that is what God needs him to endure in order to be who he's meant to be.

In my strong moments, I felt like I could go to work and still be a good therapist, maybe even a better one, because I had experienced something that many of my clients had also endured—loss. I felt like I could continue to lead worship at my church and bless those around me. I felt like I could parent my remaining two children with just enough grace to get me through to the next day.

But my strong moments kept fading in and out. They'd get gray. Cloudy. I sometimes couldn't see them through tear-blurred eyes. I couldn't find the strength to grab at them as I was clutching my heart at the same time. I knew God's strength was still there somewhere, even when it was hiding. And I knew that the love of our family, friends, and all who had shared with us in this journey were still there, as well.

Our last day with Isaac was set for August 12. He had three one-day visits and an overnight visit before he was to leave us for good, and we still had to attend the fateful court hearing on the August 16, just to make it final. Each of those days was the new hardest day of my life. And then each day after that was a process to figure out how to grieve a child who didn't die, but died to me.

August 12 came and went. When I woke up the morning Isaac left, my eyes swollen from crying and my body weary from restless sleep, our family was informed that Isaac was going to be picked up at 8:30 a.m. I had an hour and a half left to hold my baby, smell his skin, and kiss his chubby lips. But there was no amount of preparation that could be done to get ready for a moment like that.

My parents, my in-laws, our grandmother, my husband, my kids, and myself all stared at Isaac with solemn faces as the clock ticked loudly on the wall. Our Baby Bear played happily, excited to have so much attention, not understanding that he was going to be leaving the only family he'd known in a matter of minutes.

Will he be scared? Will he think we don't love him or that we abandoned him? Will Isaac's dad and brothers keep him safe? Did they read the 4½-page letter I'd sent with all the necessary information about our baby, or did they toss it in the trash? Will he remember us? Will he remember me?

My mind swam with questions as I played with the dimples on Isaac's feet for the last time. It was so hard not to worry—so hard to muster up the amount of trust needed to send our most precious possession into an unsafe world, with people he didn't know, and to a man that was engaging in illegal and abusive activities. How was I to stand strong for my family when I was already collapsing inside?

Even still, I tried to keep my tears in for the sake of my other babies. Pat asked my father to pray over Isaac in our remaining five minutes. It was then, as we held him tightly, that my little girl's heart finally broke and she began to wail with unharnessed tears—tears that she had not been able to shed until that moment.

With that, all bets were off. There was no more being strong. Hearing her cries and watching my other son's chin quiver while I felt my husband's shoulders quake was more than I could bear. Our circle of nine surrounded Isaac with freely flowing tears as the car arrived to take him from us. I tried desperately to stop choking long enough to get another smile from him, but as Pat placed him in the car, Isaac began to scream and cry.

I wanted so badly to grab him from that car and just start running, as fast as I could, knowing that I wouldn't get far, but feeling like it was the only option I hadn't yet tried. I wanted to take away his tears and hold him forever. But I couldn't. In that moment, I had to give up my role as Isaac's mother.

The next twenty-four hours were a roller coaster. As a family, we tried to keep the kids occupied (or maybe we did that for ourselves). Taylor learned how to ride her bike without training wheels, and she regaled us with children's songs, pleased to have an audience. Cameron helped cut fire wood and showed us how he could ride his bike standing up. But every time I walked past the empty high chair or glanced at Isaac's picture on the wall, I realized that my home now felt hollow. We were missing a vital part of our family, and each of us was painfully aware.

Despite my desire not to move anything from its place, or even to wash the last of his dirty clothes for fear I'd lose the memory of his smell, I knew that my family needed me to pack up some of his things. The constant reminders in each room were too much for any of us, and we needed to get his belongings ready to send to his new home.

And so, the day after he was gone, I started the process. Numb and hazy, I finished filling out his baby book and added to his life book that was made by the caseworker with the intention of him being adopted into our family. It was then that I realized something... Pat and I had never written our letters to Isaac that would be displayed in his life book.

To leave it empty seemed disloyal to Isaac in some way, but how could I write one *now* knowing that he was gone? How could I write him a letter when I was hurting so badly? And if I sent it, would his biological father throw it out or keep it from him? So, I came to this substitute conclusion. I would write the letter to my baby and post it here... and maybe one day he would find it—or maybe one day I would have the chance to give it to him face to face. Or maybe I just needed to write it for me.

August 14, 2013

Dear Sweet Baby Boy,

My first glimpse of you was through a glass window. You were swaddled tightly in a blanket, sleeping soundly. Your daddy and I were outside the hospital nursery, waiting anxiously to be let inside so that we could start a relationship with you that would forever change us. As we touched your little fingers and kissed your tiny toes, we knew that no matter what, you had our hearts. We promised to love you unconditionally, and that promise we have kept. You found a way to make me a better mommy before you could even speak, and you left your stamp on my life and on this family in a way that cannot be put into words.

When I would hold you in my arms, I would pray over your life. I prayed for safety from sickness, danger, and bad decisions. I prayed for wisdom to always do what was right, no matter what the cost. I prayed for love to find you at every turn... and it's safe to say that every person that's ever met you has loved you.

I also prayed for happiness and laughter to be in your heart, not because the world is always happy or funny, but because Jesus has put a joy inside of you that can never be tainted, broken, or destroyed. Baby, your name, Isaac, means, "he laughs." Your birth mother didn't always do everything right, but what she did do was pick a name that fits you more perfectly than any other could. Your very name is a testimony to the effect that you have on others. The joy that pours out of you, even as a little one, has overwhelmed everyone that you meet, giving them that contagious smile that won't quit.

We gave you the nickname Bear when you outgrew Bug, which was rather quickly! Your size and outgoing personality, along with your many grunts, seemed to make the name stick. You were my Baby Bear, my cuddle bug, and my sunshine. Every smile pulled me in deeper, and each laugh turned me to mush. It kills me that I won't be able to tell you these things myself, but these are some things I want you to remember:

1.   You are so smart, and I hope you always believe that. I won't be there to help you with your homework or to teach you how to ride your bike, but you have such an amazing ability to catch on to things so quickly; you can do whatever you put your mind to, so never give up. Try your hardest and let others help you when you need it.

2.   There's an incredible spirit inside of you. From the time you could make noise, you figured out your singing voice. Each time I sat at the piano, you calmed instantly. When I sang, you sang. When there was a beat to be heard, you found a way to make your own beat to join in. And when it came time to worship, you were at full attention. Praise Baby DVDs would put you into a trance and church would get you shouting. Always worship that boldly, Isaac – unashamed, unharnessed, unleashed. Let it out, and always be passionate about whom you serve.

3.   There will be lots of things that sound like good ideas. Many of them won't be. People in your life may offer you things to "help you loosen up" or to let you "have more fun." Remember that every action has a consequence and every seed planted eventually gets sowed. You're awesome just as you are. Don't let anyone make you feel pressured to act a certain way in order to fit in. You be the leader of the group. You be the example that others want to follow and fit in with. And in moments when you feel tempted or you slip up because you have a weak minute, don't throw in the towel. Every wrong can be righted, and you'll figure it out. I have faith in you. And remember, I'm always standing next to you in prayer about any problem you have... you're never alone, baby boy.

4.   Women are tricky. So just take one, okay? No one has ever made their life better by sleeping around, having a string of loves, or a full little black book. Know what you want before you start dating, and be the type of person that you want to attract. Start praying for your wife as soon as you hit puberty. Chances are she'll need someone covering her in prayer during those crazy years, as well. Respect her, love her, romance her, and put her before yourself. You'll know you chose right if she is doing those things for you in return. Never settle. A moment of fun is never worth missing out on true love.

5.   The final thing I want to teach you, baby, is that you will never go wrong if you love the things that God loves. He loves humility, so be humble. He loves a peacemaker, so make peace. He loves the brokenhearted, so help pick up someone's pieces with them. He loves forgiveness, so don't hold grudges. Be kind to everyone, especially the underdog. Always show gratitude to others, stay away from pride (but be confident, Bear, you've gotta be confident!), and love endlessly. If you follow God's heart, you'll never ever lose. Love always wins.

When I first found out that you were being taken from our family, I was devastated. Our lives were never going to be the same because we were going to be missing our Laughter. When trying to make sense of the grief I was experiencing, I opened my devotional and read the Bible lesson for the day. It was about Sarah and Isaac. (It's funny how God always knows what we need to hear, when we need to hear it...

don't forget to look for those moments He gives you, because those moments will get you through the toughest times in life.)

Most of the time when we hear the story of Isaac, it's about how God asked Isaac's father, Abraham, to sacrifice Isaac in order to show his dedication and obedience to the Lord. At the last second, God sent an angel to stop Abraham and to thank him for his faithfulness. I feel like I can finally relate to how Abraham must have felt when he was instructed to sacrifice his son! The helplessness, the questions, the sorrow... but the Bible lesson I wanted to share with you was about Sarah, not Abraham.

Sarah was very old, and she was unable to have children (that's me, without the old part... yet). She prayed for decades to be able to have a child, but it never happened. Finally, when she was one hundred years old, she gave birth to her only child. She named him Isaac because his birth brought Laughter to her soul. The lesson went on to share how Isaac's name was referred to as Isaac's laughter at times, and in other passages, it referred to the laughter of his parents.

The devotion then showed something interesting. In the middle of Abraham's preparation to lose his beloved son, it referred to Isaac's name as giving laughter to his parents. In the middle of the worst experience of their lives, God reminded their hearts that Laughter was already there. In the middle of utter loss was the ultimate joy.

Sweet Boy, you are my Laughter. Even in losing you, I have gained so much. I wouldn't change a second of my time with you, nor will I regret this experience ever. My secret hope is that you will one day come back to me. But I know that even if that can't ever happen, I will never ever stop loving you with my entire heart. I will continue to pray over your life, just as I did when I held you each night. And I will find a way to trust God more than I trust myself, knowing that He can keep you better than I ever could.

Remember that you are special. You are chosen by God and loved by so many; it's no wonder everyone wanted you for their own. I may have lost out on getting to watch you grow, but because of you, I have grown myself. Thank you for your amazing spirit, pure joy, and endless laughter.

Always in my heart, Your Mama

If I could change the child welfare system, I would do it in a heartbeat. There is no end to the distress any given family experiences at the hand of caseworkers, judges, and lawyers.

Everyone passes the buck, and no one takes responsibility for their actions; they simply blame it on "the system." Biological parents can have children as long as they are *"functioning addicts" and they aren't breaking bones when they "discipline" them*, a caseworker had told me.

One minute the system is on your side, the next minute, you're chopped liver. One hearing you're looking at adoption, the next you're looking at termination. There are so many ups and downs in this program, it's a wonder they haven't started handing out medication and psychiatric business cards with the foster parent sign-up packets! Even with all the irrational craziness my own family had gone through in the previous two years, nothing prepared me for that final court hearing my husband and I attended for Isaac.

Originally, it seemed unfair, almost cruel, to make us attend a hearing for the child we had to give up just days prior. Still grieving our loss, we showed up and were greeted by the sweetest sight these eyes could've seen. Members from our church were sitting in the lobby, ready to surround us with loving arms of support, prayers, and blessed distraction. Even though they couldn't come into the courtroom, there was so much love radiating from our friends in the hallway that it was like they were right there in the seats next to us.

When the hearing had finally started, we sat and listened to testimony after testimony as lawyers discussed Isaac's father, determining if he was fit to parent an infant. After being told we were not allowed to have a lawyer of our own to represent us, we were asked in that court hearing where our lawyer was. With questioning glances, CYS told us that we absolutely could've had our lawyer attend, despite the fact that we had the letter from them stating that we couldn't. So being the only ones unrepresented, I'd felt a little unarmed and defeated before we even began! (Particularly after each party, including Isaac's father, was allowed to read the letter that we had submitted to the judge, stating our concerns about this man caring for a child... nothing like awkward.) Isaac's mother perjured herself on numerous occasions that morning, Isaac's father made us seem like quibbling nitwits for writing our letter to the judge (despite that the information was based on first-hand knowledge I had on the man from my work in the community), and the CYS caseworker reported inaccurate fact after inaccurate fact.

All in all, it was like being tied to railway tracks as we watched the train approaching at full speed.

The hearing began to wrap up after an hour and a half, which made my upset stomach grateful. Each lawyer presented closing arguments and each lawyer also recommended that Isaac be placed in his biological father's care. My heart sank and my belly soured.

And then it was time for the judge's declaration:

"After hearing the closing arguments, it seems that everyone is in agreement. Everyone except for me."

Wait, what? I found myself staring at the man dressed in black with my mouth hanging open. I looked around the room, and it appeared that I was not alone. "I am here for the best interest of *Isaac*. And I feel that it is unfair to the Costa family, to Isaac's biological siblings, and to Isaac himself to sever ties so abruptly."

The judge then addressed Isaac's birth father. "Furthermore, you have two older children that will be starting school again very soon, and you said they were very busy with extracurricular activities. Your schedule is going to be changing quite drastically, and you need to make sure this is something you can handle. Therefore, I have decided that Isaac will remain in the foster care system for at least the next month. During this time, he will reside with his biological father from Monday through Friday and he will spend Saturday and Sunday with his foster family. This is scheduled to begin this Saturday—tomorrow. We will meet back here in a month to assess the situation again."

I'm pretty sure we could've heard a pin drop in that courtroom. I was prepared for everything but joint custody... is that even something they do? I mean, children who have been with foster families for much longer than ten months get ripped away and placed with their criminal parents all the time. But I'd never even heard of this and neither had CYS nor the lawyers nor the other judges. Apparently, this was an unprecedented ruling, one that left everyone baffled.

I want to say that I was elated. My baby was coming home the very next morning! However, there was a part of me that felt angry at the judge. I had already gone through saying good-bye once... and now I had to do it over and over again each weekend? The grieving process was something I'd already started. It's like saying that the child you buried may not have been as dead as you thought when you buried him. I mean, he still may be dead and all, but you have to wait at least a month to know for sure what the end result would be. *How would my family deal with that*?

In the end, I chose to look at this ruling through a more eternal perspective. God knew the results of this hearing from the beginning of time, so obviously, He had a plan. I had absolutely no idea what that was, mind you, but I knew that there was one. Therefore, I chose to take these extra weekends with my baby as a blessing, knowing that in the end, I may be forced to say another final good-bye and go through this pain all over again.

Perhaps this was the judge's way of giving Isaac's dad time to adjust. Or perhaps it was his way of giving him time to prove he was not able to do this after all. Or maybe he saw my eyes and knew that *I* needed more time to hold my little boy. I don't think I'll ever know the reasoning behind his decision, but I'm grateful for time to smother Isaac with more kisses than he could stand.

Saturday morning arrived quickly, and my husband, the bolder of the two of us, met with Isaac's birth father for the Great Baby Transfer. I stared at the clock, waiting for them to return home, anxious to see my chubby cherub and his toothy smile. And when the car pulled into the driveway, it was like he had never left. We played the same, we cuddled the same, and we loved the same.

Cameron and Taylor were elated that they would get to have visits with their baby brother. In fact, I was worried that this change in plans would put them into an emotional tailspin. But I have to say, I'd never felt more proud of two kids than I did as they went through such a tumultuous ordeal. They taught *me* a thing or two about coping and grieving. They also showed me to be grateful for each moment. My kids weren't worried about what saying good-bye to Isaac later would mean for them. They were just so excited to have him for the next two days. I was inspired by their ability to live in the moment and to enjoy this special gift with abandon, holding nothing back.

As expected, it was hard to let Isaac leave again at the end of that first weekend and every weekend after. Yet each time, I was able to console myself with thoughts of the following Saturday. I was able to focus 100 percent on my job, my husband, and my other two children during the week, leaving us to lavish all of our love, time, and attention on Baby Bear throughout the weekends. I had no idea what the end of this situation would hold, but I knew what I held.

Hope.

One more weekend. That's all we had left before it was all going to be over. We picked Isaac up Saturday morning and spent the entire day trying not to cry. My life was beginning to feel like a broken record, and my emotions started afresh each weekend as if I were living through the movie *Groundhog Day*. We took Isaac to church with us one last time and tried to take a mental snapshot of each moment so that it could forever be ingrained in our minds—*our last weekend with Isaac*. Saying good-bye week after week had been so emotionally trying, almost as emotional as the fact that it took our baby boy longer and longer to warm up to us with each passing visit. He was forgetting us already. I was hoping I would never have to see that process, but apparently saying good-bye once was for the weak; we must be awfully strong if our family was given the task of doing it over and over *and over again*. (At least that's what I kept telling myself.)

It's the small things that no one thinks of when they picture good-byes. I mean, all your senses are fully engaged in those hard moments.

When we would return Isaac each weekend, people understood that we were hurting, but no one was there to see how difficult it truly was.

It took such mighty strength to be friendly to a man that had yelled at me, lied to me, and then broken my heart—yet I smiled. I did what I had to do as I handed Isaac over to his birth father. Baby Bear kept reaching back for Pat and me, crying for us the entire time. Even as we finally broke his grip from us and we got into our car to leave, he swiveled his head back and forth, trying to get his last look of us.

Before closing my car door, I could hear his father curtly scold him. "Enough already. Quit your crying!"

He was not even one year old, and he was no longer allowed to show his feelings. It was heartrending. And yet at the same time, I couldn't help but wonder about the man that was now going to raise the child we loved. *Who had hurt him? Who caused him to think that people shouldn't feel?*

We didn't even make it out of their driveway before the flooding began. Needless to say, we only made it two blocks before we had to pull over as neither of us was fit to drive.

A few months prior to all this, my grandmother and my hero had passed away after a lengthy illness. And between the dogs running away and Isaac coming and going every weekend, it was a real struggle for each of us to find our way and to clasp on to happy moments once again.

My precious husband may have been taking things the worst. He was the one who was home with Isaac all day while I'd worked, and by the time I got home and Pat left to do his shifts, Isaac was flooded with attention from his siblings and our evening routine. But it was Pat who spent the most one-on-one time with him each day.

Some women complain about their husbands not wanting to help out when they have babies. That was never something I had to encounter! I married a man who will change the dirtiest diaper, give baths, wear a baby carrier on his chest, and get up in the middle of the night when a little one wakes up. At church, people struggled to pry Isaac from Pat's arms—not because Isaac was wary of strangers, but because his protective daddy struggled to know what to do with himself when he wasn't holding onto those chunky baby rolls!

I think that is why my husband often cried in his sleep—a habit that still occurs when the memories become too painful, even years later. Never one comfortable with showing his tears, he made it a daily ritual to go up onto the hill of our forty-acre farm to cut fire wood. Even though we could hear his wails echoing off the hill, we'd shut the windows to block out the sound. It felt like the only way to give him the privacy and freedom to grieve the way that he needed to. I'd tell the kids not to mention it to Daddy, but just to pray for his heart instead.

Unfortunately, my husband had one more devastating blow. His beloved pet toad of four years, to whom he fed bugs and played with while he worked out in the garage, was tragically stepped on late one Sunday night. It was a gruesome fatality that refused to wash away, and my husband was obviously crushed (although not as crushed as the toad...) I was worried that the nature of the event, so sudden and grotesque, may be the straw that would break my husband. I watched as his eyes filled with tears before he steeled himself against them and his face regained control.

That night, Pat exercised in the basement and didn't speak another word of his friend.

Luckily, my family decided to fill their hearts' void by taking in stray animals. *All of them.* After one of our dogs cornered a kitten on the front porch, my weak-for-animals spouse felt the need to nurse her back to health from her bone- thin, flea-infested frame. And for whatever reason, he and children started walking about with gaiety in their steps and smiles on their lips, talking about the kitty this and the kitty that.

Pat maturely offered to "make a call to the Humane Society," which consisted of him not making the call and playing with the cat instead, so I looked like the bad guy when I suggested we find a nice home for the kitten.

Three hollow and shell-shocked faces abruptly popped up and stared at me with mouths gaping. I felt like Hitler, standing there commanding them into the gas chambers if they didn't hand over the feline! Oh, for heaven's sake... *fine*. "We'll keep the darn cat!" I'd yelled. No one but me seemed to care that we already had *three* large dogs and that we could barely keep the house clean as it was. But I was clearly outnumbered.

Since we had to keep the little critter, we figured we might as well come up with a name for her. We held a family meeting and decided to take suggestions:

"Puddles," that was all Taylor, and it seemed too foretelling of something I did not want to clean up.

"Cuddles," Taylor again; they were learning rhyming in kindergarten that week.

"Patrick," Cameron thought it would be flattering to name the cat after his dad.

"Esmeralda," – Pat's lovely suggestion.

"Persephone," Pat offered again. Apparently, he wanted his cat to be a Disney character or a Greek goddess.

All were interesting options. However, the name that beat out all the rest was a nomination made by Cameron in honor of his and Taylor's favorite movie, *Matilda*. (But the kitty was not named Matilda.) The new name for our furry little feline was Miss Honey. She was a goldeny-orange color, and she was very, very sweet (and sticky from the poo that had clung to her matted fur), so the name fit like a glove. It was an added benefit that I didn't have to yell "Persephone!" every time I tracked cat litter up the stairs.

In addition to Miss Honey, Cameron happened upon a salamander in the basement (yes, we have gross things in our house) and decided that he couldn't live without his new friend. It was becoming clear that it was going to take many animals to fill the Isaac void, and who was I to stop the healing process? I informed him that he could keep the salamander as long as his friend lived outside and at least one hundred yards from my house. Cameron reluctantly told his spotted, red pal that his mom's a *big meany* and that he'd come visit him in the yard. And then he promptly asked my husband to try not to step on Sal the Salamander.

Later that week as I sat in the living room, plunking away on the piano, Pat burst through the door looking like a kid on Christmas morning. Holding his hands together in front of him, he thrust them out at me and said, "Look, Bubba! I found a new toad!"

Just as the words were leaving his lips, the giant amphibian leapt from Pat's fingers and toward my face. Toad dampness flung and hit me in the mouth as the gross little creature landed at my feet and hopped across the floor. "He's a big fella, ain't he?" My husband was so happy, and despite my disgust, I couldn't help but feel a bit happy for him, too. Even though Miss Honey, Sal the Salamander, and Toad-the-Sequel couldn't replace what was lost to our hearts, I was grateful that the ones I love were able to find joy in the moment.

Because sometimes Hope means living in a zoo to make your loved ones happy again.

September 18, 2013, my husband and I walked the steps of Judge Dohanich's courtroom for the last hearing. No matter how many times we entered the courthouse, still I would get a knot in the pit of my stomach. At the last ruling, our gracious judge had granted us an unprecedented gift of five precious weekends with Baby Isaac. We couldn't figure out why he'd made such an unheard of call, but as time went by, we began to realize that it was more than likely his way of giving us time to come to some sort of peaceful terms with Isaac's biological father.

Thanks to my husband's smooth people skills, he was able to befriend the man in a way that I simply could not. They talked football and kids, fishing, and general "man stuff." And it was just enough to have made the weekend transitions productive and not as depressing. Pat shared tidbits about what could calm Isaac down if he was upset, what songs he responded to, what books he liked to have read to him. He taught him basic care-taking needs that Isaac had and the importance of not smoking in the house around him due to Isaac's asthma. It helped me to know that the man was at least appearing receptive to the information needed to keep Isaac happy and healthy.

With raw emotions and grief over the finality that the day's court hearing was to bring, we sat and listened to the testimonies of everyone involved as they made their recommendations for Isaac to be removed from foster care, yet again. There was nothing left to be said, nothing left to be done. The judge then proclaimed the final verdict: Isaac was now to be permanently in the care of his birth father, and Child Welfare Services were no longer necessary. He thanked Isaac's father for stepping up to take him when most fathers wouldn't. And then he thanked my husband and me for wanting Isaac when no one else was there to want him. He stated that he hoped an amicable relationship could continue for us all.

As we all walked from the courtroom, choking back sobs, we acknowledged Isaac's dad with congratulations and best wishes. He shook Pat's hand and then pulled me in for an awkward, side hug. In that surreal moment, something lovely and unexpected happened. The man that my husband had built a relationship with over the past five weeks offered us the best gift that we could hope for in a situation that seemed overwhelmingly unbearable.

He asked if we would still be willing to do weekend visits with Isaac. He realized that Isaac loves us, that we love him, and that he has a brother and sister who adore him. He also appreciated that he'd get free babysitting on the weekends! And we *all* noted that Isaac deserved as much love from as many people as humanly possible.

And so, our second "final good-bye" turned around once more! It's not what we had hoped and prayed for, but what kind of God does what my puny little heart wills when He can see the biggest picture of all and knows what needs to be? Isaac would now be a part of two families—he would be loved and cherished doubly. He would get to keep going to church and singing his little baby heart out in worship each week, and he'd get to take that awesome, Godly spirit into a home that may not have ever had the opportunity to see it any other way.

Since the big picture in life is not who lives where or by what name I am called by a child, but in seeing each soul come to Jesus, then it seemed that God had found a way to bless us all. How could I be angry when He'd so beautifully and creatively formed a path where there seemed to be a dead end? Could this man go back on his word? Absolutely. At any moment he could decide to never let us see Isaac again. But I believe that God used my husband to bond with Isaac's dad. I believe that God knew what we all needed, not just what I wanted. So, when it comes time for me to worry and stress about this current situation, I choose to remind myself of this one faithful thought: *Hope has no end when it involves a very Big God... and in a very Big God, I trust.*

You don't realize how much you need a purely lovely day until you wake up and it's right there, staring you in the face, inviting you to join the festivities. And Isaac's first birthday was that day. Despite having our family party for him the previous weekend, Isaac's birth father suggested that we take him for his actual birthday, which happened to fall in the middle of the week.

Incredibly grateful for any extra second we got to spend with him, I promptly took the day off work so that I could enjoy some needed one-on-one time with my little guy, doing the things that he loved to do. To top things off, October 23 was not only Isaac's first birthday, but it was also the one-year anniversary of Taylor's adoption. So after sleeping in (just a little), I leisurely made my way downstairs and began prepping dinner and dessert for that evening. Taylor's favorite food is spaghetti, so I made a delicious spaghetti bake with glazed lemon pound cake to enjoy afterward.

I felt very maternal and (gasp) organized as I did my prep work in the kitchen before the sun was yet awake. I even multitasked by choosing that week's worship songs as the meat browned and the smell of lemony goodness wafted toward me from the oven. I felt like writing, I felt like reading, and I didn't even feel like I needed a nap first! Having the house to myself, taking time away from work, and feeling productive doing things that I actually wanted to do, I realized an important thing: I was starting to feel like myself again. Actually, I was starting to feel like a better version of myself.

Pat and I had found out that I was pregnant the evening of what we thought was our final visit with Isaac. And since that time, my body (and my emotions) had been taking turns doing somersaults of excitement and nausea in between waves of grief and healing. But even in the midst of the gazillion changes that were taking place both in and out of my body, I was indeed feeling like a new woman.

The day went from wonderful to fantastic when my sweet boy's face beamed at me as he came through the door in Pat's arms. Not having to wait an entire week to see him again was like magic and chocolate and rainbows all wrapped up in one chubby little package. His full grin and slobbery kisses were all I needed to know that the day was going to keep getting better. As he crawled around, laughing at everything and playing with the balloons left over from his birthday party, we got our bags packed and headed to the YMCA.

No, we were not nearly motivated enough to work out, but the YMCA near us has Isaac's favorite thing in the world—a pool. If all babies liked water, then this baby was a maniac for it! He'd splash in anything he could from the shower, to the dog's water, to the toilet. Give this kid some water and you'd watch him go bonkers!

And that's exactly what he did. We enjoyed three hours of splishing and splashing as Little Man made his way from pool to pool, saying "Hi" to everyone he met and laughing so much that he was easily the main attraction at the YMCA that day.

Chubbiness aside, I think he may actually turn into an excellent swimmer. He has always had, literally, no fear of the water, and he was constantly willing to shove his head straight under without bothering to take a breath first; he would then pop his little head back up, and there would be nothing but smiles all over his wet face. He even began to paddle his arms instinctively while Pat was holding him on his belly, moving him across the pool. Isaac was in his glory, and so was I.

After a short nap, the kids arrived home from school, and it was time to get the rest of the dinner finished. We had grandparents arriving to help us celebrate, so we tidied up while the kids entertained the baby with his new birthday toys. Together, we enjoyed a lovely meal as Taylor gobbled down her spaghetti bake and Cameron gagged down some salad. Even Baby Isaac discovered that spaghetti may very well be his new favorite food, just like Sissy! In the midst of leisurely enjoying our dessert, we remembered something— our beautiful day was ending. It was time for Isaac to go back home.

Taylor began to cry, and I became irritable once more. As I shoved pots and pans back in their places and busied myself with the task of cleaning up from dinner, snapping at Cameron and Taylor for arguing yet again, I realized that the gratefulness I had felt earlier that morning had been replaced by bitterness.

If Isaac was ours, we wouldn't have to say good-bye week after week. We would know that we would get each birthday with him and not just hope for a weekend at a time. If I didn't have to go back to work tomorrow, I wouldn't have to do all these stupid dishes right now... I could sit down and do something to help me cope with Isaac leaving. If this... if that... if only life were perfect... if only I were perfect...

Maybe it was the pregnancy hormones. Or maybe it was just the stressors of life. But whatever it was... it had to go. I was helpless to change the circumstances I felt so burdened by, which I knew was part of the problem. The circumstances would never be perfect, my life would never be perfect, and I (most certainly) would never be perfect.

So once again, I found myself reaching for that hope that sometimes got lost under piles of laundry and in tearful good-byes. I reminded myself that today was a purely lovely day and that each day must come to an end. Tomorrow may be more lovely or less lovely than the previous day, but it would still be another day where hope would find me.

As the months went on, my belly continued to grow, and we continued to get our weekend visits with Isaac. When Christmas rolled around, we were so blessed to be able to bring Isaac with us to Michigan for a visit. We attended our family Christmas parties and watched him open all the presents from us and our family before having to return him to his other home on Christmas Eve.

Isaac continued to call us Mama and Daddy, while calling his father by his first name. It didn't seem to be an issue to the man, so we continued treating Isaac like he was our child, just one with whom we had partial custody. Pat worked relentlessly on building his relationship with Isaac's dad, and we all did our best to find peace in our new arrangement.

Once Christmas and Taylor's birthday party were safely behind us, we began to work on the nursery for our new little nugget. Taylor moved downstairs to the bigger bedroom because it had pink carpet and a floral border. We had asked both Cameron and Taylor who wanted to move to the main floor from upstairs, and Taylor jumped at the opportunity to expand her world of pinkness. So, we used her old room to put Isaac's crib and make preparations for the new baby to join him.

And Isaac, because of his sweet nature, would rub my big belly and say hi to the baby each night as we cuddled in the rocking chair of his new room. It always amazed me how quickly his young mind grasped difficult concepts—he knew to be gentle with Mama's belly, he knew that we prayed over the baby, and he understood that Mama got very tired very quickly and that she needed more cuddle time than rough playtime those days.

However, Isaac never seemed to mind cuddle time. In fact, after he left our home, he seemed to have great difficulty separating from us at all. There was quite literally not one Sunday that went by where he didn't sob upon being put back into the clothes he came to us in and returned to his father's home. And as he grew, Isaac began adamantly verbalizing that he wanted to stay in our home. Hating to see him so distraught week after week and also fearing that his father would become tired of the tears, we tried our best to remind our little guy that his father loved him and that we would see him again in just a few days. However, our words provided little console to a toddler who wanted nothing more than to be held, comforted, and loved on.

That's why we couldn't walk from the room, go get the mail, or even use the restroom without panic rising up in him. And trying to get him to sleep in his own bed? Not a chance. When he was living with us, Isaac slept in his crib. But upon returning to us for weekend visits, there was no way to get him to nap or sleep alone. In fact, I would often awaken in the night feeling as if I were being strangled by limbs because he *had* to be touching one of us at all times, even in his sleep. Which was fine, until I became incredibly large with pregnancy! It would be on those nights that I would find my way to the nursery to sleep on the extra bed, only to hear Isaac start crying and calling my name moments later. Sleep is a small price to pay when you love your child and want him to feel safe and loved in return.

The week that Wyatt was born, I was released from the hospital on a Friday. The following morning, my husband went and picked up Isaac at the usual Saturday morning time. We never once wanted to miss a weekend with him, so whether we were sick, we had plans, or we were just coming home from the hospital, we made sure that one of us was always available to get Isaac for our visits.

When he walked in, his eyes went instantly to his new baby brother. Cautiously, he approached me as I sat propped up in the overstuffed chair of our living room, cradling Wyatt. Isaac peered at him and back up at me with a look of wonderment on his face. He gently poked Wyatt's forehead with a chubby finger and practiced the baby's name. "Wy-it," he'd say and smile.

It was a name he grew very good at saying over the next several months. When Wyatt would take a toy from Isaac's hands, when his flailing arms would smack Isaac in the head, when Wyatt would spit up... each time Isaac would say his name with such articulation. "Wy-it! Stop it!"

Even when our new little guy would make a particularly gross diaper, Isaac would crinkle his nose and look the baby in the face while saying, "Aw, Wy-it... you're yucky!" And Wyatt would think this was the greatest reaction in the world, because he would giggle and laugh every time Isaac said his name in disgust. Everywhere his big brother went, Wyatt's eyes would follow, watching him closely and trying his hardest to make his body get closer to Isaac.

Because everyone, even the baby, was drawn to Isaac's magnetic personality. We couldn't go out in public without people stopping to talk to Isaac, ask us his age, and comment on how advanced he was. Even as a young toddler, Isaac would shake hands, hug, or kiss anything that moved. And he never met a stranger that he wouldn't greet with a smile.

So when Isaac would come to our house with incredibly dilated pupils, suddenly showing violent behavior, using foul language, and mimicking sexual acts, we became highly concerned. *What was he being exposed to while he was not with us?* When we would lovingly redirect that behavior and remind him that that's not the way we act in our home, he would look ashamed and start weeping.

It was very obvious that Isaac didn't realize that these things were wrong, and his feelings were greatly hurt thinking that he'd done something to disappoint the people he loved. I would regularly sob with grief over the fact that he wasn't even two years old and facing adult situations that he had no business being exposed to. He also bore physical marks that had no business being on his body. Not that it made any difference to "the system." In their eyes, this had been a successful reunification—a gold star for their books. But in my eyes, there had already been an innocence that was lost, something that could never be regained. Because of that, I did all I could to cover Isaac in prayer and demonstrate as much love to him as possible.

And to that, Isaac's little soul always responded.

There's something about little boys that makes my heart go pitter-patter. Boys and their rambunctiousness, growling, ability to make car sounds, and contentedness to just run full speed into nothingness is what makes them so special. Cameron, unlike his sister, can amuse himself with a tennis ball, a few toothpicks, and a paper towel roll... for *hours*. I'm not kidding. The boy goes into his room and comes back with some sort of creation made from garbage, Lego pieces, and disassembled toy cars. *Every time!* I *love* this about him. Just yesterday he showed me a couch that he designed from a paper plate. A paper plate. And no, it wasn't a clean *paper plate* (naturally), and yes, he did spill cookie crumbs across two rooms as he brought his creation to my spot in the living room. But he was just so proud of this couch that I couldn't say anything to discourage his imagination. I mean, isn't that why we have three big dogs anyway? They'll eventually stumble upon that trail of cookie crumbs and happily take care of the mess.

Yes, creativity in sons is amazing. As is their ability to see my pre-coffee need for quietness in the morning and behave accordingly. In fact, I used to cringe when my bladder would wake me in wee hours of the morning—that time when you know that, if you hurry, you can be back in bed and still get another half hour of sleep. Not having an on-suite master bath, however, meant leaving the safety of my own room to venture out and meet the Little People before I was ready to start conversing. You mamas know what I mean—no coffee, still groggy, not ready to talk. I'm basically good for grunts only during those first few minutes.

But daughters are different. My daughter especially. She would listen for my sheets to crinkle as I prepared to get up from my bed and run across the hall to the bathroom, undetected. And there she was, every time, always quicker than I. No sooner would I have turned the door handle and Taylor would be right there, begging for someone to talk to (probably because she sleeps a total of four minutes per night and she'd been awake for hours just waiting for attention).

"Hi, Mom, how'd you sleep? Did you have any dreams? I dreamed of strawberries and ponies, and I made up a song to tell you about the dream, but then I forgot it and had to make up a new one, but then I forgot that one too, so I sang 'Jesus Loves Me' until I remembered that I love to color... can I have my markers now? Oh, wait! Let me sing 'Jesus Loves Me' to you first, and then I'll color you a picture of strawberries and ponies, and hey! I remembered my dream, wanna hear it?" Oh. My. Gosh.

I just wanted to pee... but instead I realized that I'd be forced to purchase adult diapers so I no longer would have to leave my room before I was good and ready. That was before Taylor's bedroom was moved downstairs. Thankfully, God granted me a baby, and the Taylor issue was solved. After that, it was just me and the boys upstairs. So, when I felt the urge to pee, I could open my door freely, because Cameron is just as groggy by morning as he is creative by day. He'd see me, nonchalantly wave a hello, and say, "Hey, Mom," to which I'd respond, "Hey, Cam," and we'd go our separate ways. It's practically magical. This is why I love little boys!

When Isaac came on the weekends, we'd get to see an entirely different side of boys—the I'm-loud-crazy-and-wild-but-can't-be-bothered-to-care side of boys. On the weekends, we would always try to have a fun event planned. It would give Isaac exposure to things he may not get to otherwise do, and it would allow the kids to have fun bonding experiences with one another. So one weekend, we had set our sights on going to the Science Center in Pittsburgh. However, due to a Pirate's baseball game, we were unable to find parking and decided to go to the Ballocity Zone at Fun Fore All.

The Ballocity Zone is a massive indoor climbing structure where kids can go through small passages that scale higher and higher, slam into netting, scream loudly while going down tube slides, and bash themselves off of hanging mats. Oh, and there are lots of balls. Everywhere. These foam balls come flying at you from air guns as well as from a huge volcanic structure in the center of the Ballocity Zone. The volcano fills with balls and erupts when a button is pushed, sending balls raining down with a loud whoosh! Needless to say, this was the perfect place for a rabid little man like Isaac.

Once he got past his initial intimidation of larger kids shoving their way past him as whoosh-ing occurred every few minutes, he began to fully submerge himself into his surroundings. I took him into the Zone, and he walked straight up to the ball volcano, clenched his fists, and he growled/shouted/yelled with all his might for about ten seconds straight. This was before he ran head first, as fast as his chubby legs allowed, into a netted wall. That was followed by about ten more seconds of growling/shouting/yelling (naturally). At one point, he bit a chunk out of a ball with a crazed look in his eye that sent a small girl running in the other direction.

This. Is. My. Son. And he sometimes resembled Animal from *The Muppets*, which was ironic, because he used to have a T-shirt with that very character on it. Do you see why I *love* little boys? Their rugged, dirty, primal beings are just like little cavemen, and it's awesome.

However, that same little caveman proceeded to pee all over me and his bedroom floor later that evening. And when I say pee, I mean pee. It was as if he'd saved all the water from his body for just the moment that I tried to wrangle him after his bath, before I'd had the chance to diaper and PJ him. Sure, I shouldn't have left him for those two minutes, diaperless... but he looked so stinking cute blowing his toy trumpet, huge grin on his face, naked as a jaybird. He walked over to me, and just as I lifted him up to set him on the bed, he let go of all that was within him. Promptly setting him down, I ordered him to stand still while I grabbed the towel... but what you have to know about twenty-two-month-olds is that they can't follow you with their eyes. Oh, no. They follow you with their entire bodies. Thus, Isaac proceeded to pee in an arch as he watched me move swiftly across the room. I sighed in exasperation because, honestly, what could I do but stand there and let him finish? Once there was enough urine on the floor to legally call his room a parking garage, he threw his hands in the air and said, "Uh-oh!" (Ya think, kid?) I sufficiently sopped up the mess with his bath towel before running to the bathroom to plunk it in the tub.

And that's when Isaac shut the door and locked me out of the nursery. I mean, seriously, you can't get this kind of action with a little girl! I'd spent the next few minutes pleading with my almost-toddler to "open the door for Mama," in which he alternated telling me "Okay!" and "No!" as he'd laugh. (Boy moms everywhere, hear me when I say this: keep a tool kit on every floor—if you have boys in the house, you're going to need a screwdriver to pop open locked doors.) When the door finally opened, there he was, still standing in all his naked glory, smiling widely. "Mama!" he exclaimed as he gave me a big ole birthday suit hug. This is why I love little boys.

When Wyatt came along, Taylor was completely outnumbered, but I expected her to go into full-on baby mode. Which she did. Every second of every day. She wanted diapers to put on her dolls, make-shift baby carriers, and she would even put on a "shawl" so she could feed her baby with privacy.

What I *didn't* expect was Isaac to be just as infatuated with babies. Not only was he constantly bringing me clean diapers, "gently" putting Wyatt's binky back in his mouth, and singing to him while rubbing his head, but he also decided to take up nursing. And since he didn't have a baby doll in his room, he chose to nurse his stuffed dog instead. Knowing that my husband would have a heart attack if he saw his all-boy son nursing his toy dog, I tried to tell him that boys feed babies with a bottle and only mamas can feed a baby with their bodies. But Isaac was not to be deterred. He insisted that he was the dog's mama and that his dog was hungry, so he'd lay down, prop himself up on a pillow, lift his shirt, and put the dog under his armpit.

You guys, it was hysterical. I would try to talk, but he'd "Shush!" me and rub the dog's head, occasionally asking the pup if he was done. When his dog had apparently finished ingesting Isaac's armpit, my little boy then burped his puppy dog and laid him on the pillow, covering him with a blanket to go to sleep. It was so precious. And it was over so quickly...

Seconds later, Isaac body-slammed the dog like a professional wrestler, screaming, "Wake up!"

And *this* is why I love little boys.

In January 2015, for some reason that we will probably never know, Isaac's birth dad became angry with Pat and I. He accused us of things that didn't make sense, and he was acting erratic, even towards my husband, whom he'd always favored. He threatened to take visits away and said that we had something to do with him losing his unemployment, which he was apparently receiving while he was employed. But he blamed us for things that we couldn't have possibly known about—things that we couldn't possibly have done.

And therefore, as our punishment for loving and caring for his son, he moved our weekly visits to biweekly ones.

I was convinced that my heart would never quite heal because of how many times the scabs had been pulled away. It's impossible to know for sure, because I was finding it hard to feel anything at all. There was probably worry lodged in there somewhere. And fear. Definitely sadness. Presumably anger. But we'd been down that road before. We'd seen those road signs, passed those landmarks.

For no reason other than to remind us of who was in charge, Isaac's biological dad decided that we were all too happy in our previous arrangement. We'd tried to talk to him, tried to gather some understanding as to what had gone wrong. However, logic, reason, and understanding weren't to change this outcome.

How was my heart to *stand* this? How would I face Saturday mornings without seeing my beaming two-year-old scramble through the front door and into my arms? I just didn't know how any of us would *do* life without getting those coveted thirty-six hours each week. We all still cried when he'd go back each Sunday as it was! I still ached when I'd look back at pictures from our last full week with him in our custody. I craved that little boy day in and day out... but once again, my happiness was being stolen by someone else. And we had done absolutely nothing to deserve it.

My husband, whose heart breaks even more for Isaac than mine does (a thought that is difficult to comprehend), did not deserve this. My children, who turn down plans with friends on the weekends in order to be with their little brother, did not deserve this. And most importantly, the little boy that we leave frantic, screaming, and clinging to us each Sunday night... he most certainly didn't deserve this.

Whatever was going on behind the scenes, and whoever was involved in aiding this negative situation, we may never know. But we were the ones left in the wake of the storm, waiting for the next wave to hit... the final wave that would wash us out to sea, ending our visits completely.

Yet, in my numbness, I still have to say this: *It was my happiness that was shaken, not my hope. At every turn of this crazy road, there has been a plan in place, one that I cannot see and cannot predict. Each time a wave hits, we choke and we flounder and we cry (oh, do we ever cry), but we do not drown. We will not drown. I will scream it if I have to, but we will not drown! I have no aces up my sleeve nor magic ball to turn to. However, I do have hope in a God that has brought me through so very much. And He has never left me to die. He has allowed pain and more grief than I thought I could handle, but He always saves the day. That's why He's the Savior and I'm not.*

Later that night, I did my best to try and feel. I made myself begin to go through those stages of grief for the hundredth time, praying that it would be the last but knowing that the answer to that prayer wouldn't change the fact that I'd have to do it anyway. Then I decided to lift up all of my children before the Lord, even when remembering Isaac caused me more pain than I could express. Still, I vowed to do my best to love on my other three as we prepared them for the news. Finally, I reminded myself that Isaac's dad was not the enemy.

Sometimes Hope means praying for those who do you harm, even as they continue to break you. Because when all is said and done, only God can fix a broken heart.

Eventually, whatever conflict we were facing with Isaac's father passed. Although his more stable mood did not restore our previous visitation schedule. If we'd make a parenting suggestion or if Isaac cried too much upon his return home, the man held those visits over our heads, seemingly trying to put us in our rightful place. The bigger kids, who had been filled with tears and rage at losing half of their monthly time with their brother, were rewarded with playdates we'd set up or fun outings to occupy their minds each weekend that we were without Isaac.

Taylor would cry each Saturday, asking if Isaac knew why we weren't there to pick him up. She'd wonder if he was standing at the door, waiting for us like he would always be. And I couldn't put her heart to rest because I, too, was wondering those very same things.

After a while, we again grew used to our new routine. We would work birthday parties and family events around Isaac's visits, and he was still able to come to Michigan on occasion, if we asked very humbly and without making eye contact. To say we walked on eggshells is an understatement, but what other choice did we have? As long as we still had contact with Isaac, then he would still be taught about love, safety, family, and Jesus.

We noticed yet another drastic change in Isaac's behaviors once the visits lessened. There was a definite increase in physical aggression, inappropriate language and mimicking, and he became harder to calm down after a tantrum. It was at this time that Isaac began craving me—craving a mom. Someone who would cuddle him, kiss his boo-boos, and sing him to sleep.

I know that my husband's feelings were hurt when I became the preferred parent for those months. But we both knew that Isaac's fragile heart needed a motherly touch. He began coming to us with more and more injuries, was sick often, and his breathing nebulizer to soothe his attacks would blow pure cigarette smoke into his wheezing lungs. Isaac also began to regress by slipping back in his potty training, stumbling over words that he'd never had trouble saying, and by refusing to sleep unless I was holding him tightly and singing his favorite song to him.

Despite the tension, Isaac's father let him come to our house for a midweek visit to celebrate Pat's birthday in March that year, and he was given to us once again for Wyatt's first birthday in May, joining our family pictures we'd scheduled for that day. (We had pictures taken regularly and always made sure to get some of just Isaac— pictures that we would develop and give to Isaac's father as a gift.) That same year, when Father's Day rolled around, we realized that it fell on our weekend. Yet when we asked Isaac's dad if he would rather have him that day, he told us to keep him... that we'd probably celebrate it and he "don't do that kind of thing."

We wanted to make sure we did something *spectacular* to celebrate being together as an entire family, and on a holiday at that! As usual, we had no idea what to give my husband or how to commemorate the day. The kids and I had racked our brains the entire week trying to figure out a good gift—something that would be thoughtful, useful, handy, funny, *wanted*.

New dress shoes? Practical, yes, but not very desirable for the man who would rather wear a ratty T-shirt and boots, cutting up firewood in his spare time. A new ax? Desirable, yes, but he probably has at least twelve other axes lying around in the garage... and I don't know the first thing about ax purchases. Is there an ax store? Do they have more than one kind or can you just walk in and ask where they keep the ax? I didn't know (I didn't care).

We decided that it would be best (even if it lacked a little creativity on our end) to let Dad pick out his own gift. So, he thoughtfully bought himself a new hard drive for his computer. (Why didn't I think of that? Um... because no wife would... ever.) He selected his own gift, and we got to pick the activity we thought would best celebrate his special day.

We chose the circus.

When I broke the news to my husband, I think he thought that I was kidding. He giggled and then asked, "Wait, are you serious?" I'm betting that he had visions of the two of us trying to keep the toddler from being eaten by a lion, the baby from chucking his cuppy at the row in front of us, and the older two from literally trying to join the circus. I'm sure these thoughts ran through his mind at least once before he agreed to the adventure. But for good measure, we invited his mom as reinforcement.

We arrived at the circus and saw a sad-looking tent surrounded by a few llamas, some skinny ponies, and an annoyed-looking camel. There was one snack stand, two port-a-johns, and an even smaller tent where three tiny horses were hooked up to a metal spokes system, giving children rides.

Swell. The kids had never been to the circus before, and I had talked it up as if we were going to see the Ringling Brothers. It was apparent that I had spoken too soon. There would be no tigers, no rings of fire, no tightrope walkers. There would be an emaciated petting zoo and stinky toilets. For this, we paid $45 and two babies missed their naps.

But since we were already there, we tried to make the best of it. After all, it was only 300 degrees (in the shade) and all the attendees looked to be carnies, themselves. We made our way through the sea of bearded women and toothless men, over to the "petting zoo." I use this term loosely because the skinny animals did not seem to enjoy the whole "petting" part of the experience. Apparently the hungry little suckers thought that my kids' fingers and limbs were carrots. Isaac was the first to cry, stating that the horsey had bit him. Like any good mom, I assumed he was exaggerating. Surely the horse had licked him or given him a little nibble—a horsey kiss, perhaps.

But then, I watched (and photographed) as Wyatt stood there, minding his own business while a particularly famished-looking pony attempted to eat him, starting with his fingers. My baby began to scream. I started to panic. I gave a gentle tug to see if I could get his finger loose, but no such luck. I didn't know what else to do. So, I slapped the pony. I was just getting ready to give him a firm upper cut when he finally released Wyatt's fingers.

For the record, I will literally beat up any animal that tries to eat my children. Just in case anyone asks.

I grabbed my children, and we began to flee the petting zoo. And that's when the camel turned and spit all over us. Apparently he was ticked off that I'd slapped his friend. Never in my life did I want to dropkick an entire lot of animals like I did in that moment. I dared the camel to take one step closer as I mentally threatened to turn him into a camel-burger. (Please don't call PETA on me... I'm the nice one here. These animals were jerks.)

Next, we had decided to make our way to the pony rides. Why? Simply because there was nothing else to do while we waited for the show to start... other than visit the port-a-johns. These guys looked less hungry and much more in control of themselves; so, we watched as our children awkwardly rode atop the slowest-moving ponies that I'd ever seen. Maybe it was the heat. Maybe they'd lost their will to go on. Either way, my kids smiled, and we took pictures.

No sooner had the small people begun to pester me for money to jump in the bouncy house when it suddenly deflated. Parents ran to rescue their children from the collapsed vinyl as toddlers sobbed in fear. Yeah... *no.*

Finally, it was show time. We made our way into the Little Top tent and found seats near the front (which wasn't hard to do, as *all* the seats were near the front... it was a really, really Little Top). There we sat, huddled together on mud-covered bleachers with about a hundred other sweaty people and their equally sweaty children, not a breeze to be had beneath the shelter of the tent. We fanned the young ones with Father's Day cards and poured water over all their heads as we awaited what would be the worst circus in circus history.

And then, all of our dreams came true.

The music began to thump. The ringleader began to announce. Jugglers juggled. Contortionists contorted. Acrobats acrobatted. Magicians did magic! There were stunts, clowns, incredible tricks, and death-defying acts (I'm not kidding!). Even the camel and llamas made an appearance. But I didn't clap for them. I was still bitter.

For nearly two hours, four children and three adults sat enthralled with the show. At intermission, we attacked the snow cone guy, shoveling the shaved ice into our mouths as fast as we could manage. But neither the heat nor the vexatious animals could spoil our fun.

The circus was haphazard. It was unexpected. Unconventional. But it was *amazing*. It was just like our family. Now that I think about it, there could've been no better way to spend Father's Day.

As luck would have it, we were blown away when the Fourth of July rolled around and we were granted an extra-long weekend with Isaac. We were all so thrilled, but then I remembered something...

Holidays in our house are bonkers with a capital B. If you have a child, you're nodding your head in agreement. If you have more than one child, you are still shaking from the amounts of coffee you drank to keep yourself standing until bedtime. And if you have children with any sort of mental health diagnosis, you are most likely sitting in a corner coloring on the wall with markers and putting Cheerios up your nose.

After such chaos that holidays bring, I, too, regress back to childhood for the next day and quite literally lose the will to go on as an adult. That weekend, in a nutshell, was one of the craziest weekends of my life. There was no prep work needed like for

Christmas or birthdays, there was no traveling out of state, no packing and unpacking of luggage.

So, *why* was Independence Day weekend so Bonkers (remember, capital *B*)?

Because holidays, no matter what they entail, cause the people in my house to feel *big* feelings and act on those big feelings with all their might.

There's heightened anticipation, unrealistic expectations, always wanting more, struggles to cope with schedule changes, and oh, let's not forget about the sugar—oh, the copious amounts of sugar and caffeinated beverages that are poured onto our children and their fragile little nervous systems from morning till night, keeping them up for hours past bedtime. Not that they would be able to sleep anyways, since fireworks are a nightly ritual for the *entire* Fourth of July weekend apparently.

My kids, for as far as they'd come, they still had such a hard time just relaxing and having fun. The Hubs and I answered no fewer than fifty thousand questions that weekend. Questions about times, activities, who would be there, how we'd get there, what we would eat, would it be time for bed when we got home, would they be allowed juice for the day, would the other kids like them, how long would the fireworks last, would the fireworks be loud, would bugs crawl on the blanket while we were watching the fireworks, would there be time to play the tablets when we got home, would we hold their coats/sweatshirts/sunglasses/flags/water bottles/shoes/bubbles/ headbands/ corn dogs/napkins, etc., etc., etc.!

Here's an idea, kids. Pull your bottom lips up over the top of your heads and then swallow.

For the love of all that is good and holy, couldn't we just relax and have fun like all the other families? The adults would be the adults, and we'd take care of all the things that needed attending to. All these kids had to do was play!

Anyone else's children end up in tears when they're given money to spend at the festival? If your kids are extra crunchy like mine, the answer is yes. Because they want to spend every last cent, but they can't find anything worthy of using the money on—despite the fact that they want all the things they see. Even when the lovely booth owners bartered with my children, lowering the prices to a more affordable seven-and nine-year-old range, my kids *still* walked away shaking their heads in disappointment—the stress of spending money simply too great for them.

And then there was the toddler. Dear, sweet Jesus. It was as if the Tantrum Monster had bitten Isaac while he was sleeping, turning my precious little boy into the Incredible Hulk, wreaking havoc and destruction on the world around him. He ran into people, jumped on expensive furniture, threw toys, dumped food all over, chucked rocks, hit, kicked, screamed, threw himself down, and all-out defied every little rule set before him. He was a human wrecking ball.

So many fits, so few naps.

I may have lost my mind and yelled a little that weekend. (Like what I did there? I made it sound like that was something out of the norm, and that yelling "a little" was all I did. Smooth, huh?) What I meant to say is, I *did* lose my mind, and I screamed, barked, and stomped my feet in all-out rage that weekend. At all of them.

And *then*, I scared them. I stood there and just started to cry. All these eyes just looked at me. They had expected groundings and executions, not befuddled tears and heaving sobs.

I cried because I just couldn't do holidays anymore. I couldn't *do* tantrums, I couldn't do repeating myself a trillion times, I couldn't do reminders to flush toilets or change underwear daily or pick up their toys. I couldn't do good mommy things, but I also couldn't do mean mommy things. I just couldn't do *any* thing else but cry.

It's the worst feeling because I hate yelling at them. I hate scolding and feeling like I'm constantly showing them all the things they do wrong when I just want to be a normal family! I just wanted to enjoy a festive occasion, with laughing and smiling and hugging and not doing all the crying.

But, I cried because I know they can't help it, really. I know Isaac was acting out because he sees all sorts of things he shouldn't during the time he's away from us and he feels all sorts of things he shouldn't have to feel—rejection and abandonment that we have to leave him after each visit, separation anxiety, fear that every time we get in the car he has to go back, stress over sleeping and missing out on the limited time he has with us before he'd have to return to his home.

How could I scold him and feel good about myself? Especially when each tantrum was followed up by a sloppy kiss and an, "Aw, I just love you, Mama!" seconds after he'd thrown his snow cone at me?

Guys, this is why I'm crazy. I told you, markers and Cheerios, in the corner. The roller coaster of emotions from all those small people and all those missed naps. The poor baby, he just road along in a stroller, tried to grab at the fireworks in the sky, and chewed (then promptly spit out) all the new foods I'd put in front of him that weekend.

Wyatt's tiny little face was just the poster of the napless child. He looked confused and exhausted, ready to collapse the entire weekend. He just wanted his normal mama time, complete with cuddles and rocking and playing with toys, doing his puzzles, and reading his books. In fact, he gave me *I Love You, Stinky Face* to read four times in a row. That means nothing to you, I know, but to me, it meant that he needed a break from chaos. It was his markers and Cheerios.

So, after a late night of fireworks anticipation, fear of fireworks, and disappointment that fireworks were not all they had hoped for and more, I'd decided to let everyone sleep in. Obviously, that meant that the Littles were up at 6:00 a.m.

The morning was filled with kisses and hugs and sweet, gentle words... until it was time to get Isaac ready to go back home. And then came the hitting. Naturally, the screaming and throwing followed. I literally had to chase him through the yard while death-gripping the baby and slipping in the dewy grass, just to get him into the minivan. (Don't worry, my neighbors know about the Bonkers thing already.)

The kids and I drove him home. He kept asking me to turn around and go back to my house. He asked if we could run away. He said please. He meant it.

And as we pulled into his driveway, the tears began to flow freely from all of the kids. Isaac clung to me as his dad told him to stop being a baby, yet again. I set him down, and he clawed my legs trying to keep his grasp, screaming until he could no longer breathe. I kissed him, told him I loved him, reminding him that we'd see him soon. I tried not to look back as I walked away, but he was throwing his whole little body onto the screen door of his house while screaming my name.

It was more than I could handle. I turned and blew him a kiss as I choked on all the emotions that I'd been trying to keep from pouring out of my eyes. I wanted him to see me be brave. I wanted my other kids to see me be brave. I wanted to believe that I *could* be brave.

I got into the car, and a song came on the radio that brought the tears that I'd fought so hard to keep inside. Driving away from the house, I turned up the music to stop the screams from following me. And once my eyes were mostly dry, I let my gaze slip to the rearview mirror. My eldest's eyes met mine.

He gave me a knowing smile and nodded. My kids... they aren't great for holidays. But they know. They feel the big feelings, too. They're there to nod their heads and smile when they see bravery crumbling. They may not know how to meet new kids on the playground, but they help the little ones climb the stairs to the slide and chase a stray one that makes a run for the road. They get clingy and ask a billion questions and have unrealistic expectations, but they love.

Having two toddlers in the house, even if it was just every other weekend, was always interesting. By Sunday night, it generally looked as if a bomb had gone off in each and every room of our home. Thankful that I had a flexible work schedule at my church and was free to use Monday mornings as a power clean-up session, I usually just left the mess, shielding my eyes from all the grossness until the next day. After all, two toddlers equals one buggy-eyed mama!

Now, as a parent, I feel that I've always had a pretty strong stomach—unusually so. In fact, I was always given the grossest tasks when I worked in residential treatment because my coworkers were weak and squeamish. They simply couldn't handle the bodily fluids/lumps/or chunks, leaving me to do the clean up when the kiddos got sick.

But even the strongest people have their limits. And one day in late summer, I'd reached mine at least twelve times. To set the stage, it's important to note that most of our household was currently getting over that lovely end- of-summer cold, complete with all things that Mucinex is supposed to fix but doesn't. Additionally, the humidity was approximately 2,794 percent, and my clothes were sticking to me like they'd been attached with a gallon of Elmer's glue. Along with my hair. And everything floating through the air.

We'd started the day off at church. The weather was still somewhat cool, and we were all freshly showered (a rare occurrence, really). By the time we'd left the service and made our way to the park for our annual church picnic, the sweat started attracting an array of flying insects—insects that get stuck in your hair and eyelashes and that find their way up skirts and make you swat at your unmentionable parts. My main goal was to avoid looking like a lunatic and disgracing the family name.

It wasn't long before toddlers started revealing to us that naps were needed *immediately*. They demonstrated this need by throwing hot dogs and by dumping my plate of macaroni and cheese onto my lap. *Because I just wasn't sticky enough.* The smallest of the group then made a run for it and fell face first onto the muddy road. Covered in scrapes and donning a hefty lump on his head, I ran to Wyatt and scooped him up, cuddling him into me as I tried to assess his marks. Thankfully my Sunday dress served as a magnificent towel. It soaked up his mud-covered front side rather well.

We finally arrived at home, and nap time could not come quickly enough! We sent the Bigs to their rooms and prepped the Littles for sleep as fast as possible. The husband and I laid down as the weak air-conditioner in the window finally started working its magic. Isaac rolled into me for a sleepy cuddle, and I happily wrapped my arms around him. And then, just as heavy eyelids were starting to close, he sneezed a handful-sized ball of snot all over my chest. I couldn't get the words out fast enough.

"Don't touch...!" But it was too late. Chubby little hands wiped the remaining snot all across his gooey face. And then he sneezed about eight more times with equal amounts of boogers connecting and stringing to me like a spider web.

Wyatt started screaming from his crib, awakened by Isaac's power-sneezes, and Isaac obviously needed to be power-washed, so I gave up on the hopes of a nap.

Isaac was sent to the bathroom as I grabbed the baby and brought him into the restroom with his brother so at least Pat could rest. After all, he had done the dishes, cooked breakfast, *and* did all of bedtime routine the night before. The man deserved a medal, but he settled for a nap instead. When I returned to the door, Isaac had stripped down and was peeing on his potty chair.

"Good boy!" I said to Isaac with enthusiasm, setting Wyatt down. Only there was a sticky suction sound that popped in the air as I detached from my baby. And there was an orange substance gracing my stomach, arm, and hand that had held him. Carrots? Yams? Nope. One sniff answered all my questions. *Crap.*

It's really something when poop works its way into the crevices of your wedding ring, isn't it? It's also fun when you're in the process of changing a baby's diaper and he shoves his fist *and* a toy into the mix. Meanwhile, trying to keep the poo splattering to a minimum, Isaac finished his toilet endeavors and insisted on emptying the contents into the big potty by himself, despite my repeated pleas to "Wait for Mommy!"

"I do it, Mama, I help you..." In the rush to change the baby, I notice that I had set my cell phone on top of the toilet lid. Isaac, however, failed to see this. He lifted the lid and dumped pee everwhere. Sure, some of it got in the toilet. And some of it got on my phone—the phone that fell off the lid and knocked over the toilet brush holder, spilling grimy toilet nastiness all across the floor and my phone. Wyatt happily splashed in his orange crap, laughing at his big brother while I hastily finished up the diaper change and hand-sanitizing. That's when I felt sprinkles landing on my neck, coming from somewhere behind me. I turned in time to see Isaac fondly petting the toilet brush, sending flecks of grossness everywhere while he giggled, "It tickles, Mama!"

As chemicaled poop water rained down on me, I contemplated the very real possibility that this was the worst day of my life. If not the worst, it was certainly the very grossest. I couldn't take another second of it.

"*Stop!*"

For a moment, both the little ones stared at me and stopped smearing, spraying, and splattering. They gazed at me with wide eyes and still hands. For a full two seconds, I felt powerful. It had *worked*! It *never* works, but today, God smiled down on me and had pity.

It was Isaac's sneeze that broke the silence. And of course, he wiped the rest of it across his face, along with all the toilet germs he'd accumulated in the previous five minutes. (Okay, so maybe it didn't *actually* work.) Disappointed and exasperated, I scrubbed the babies down and hustled them to the playroom. Isaac immediately began building his train and pulled me to the floor to help him. After ten minutes, we were rather proud of our track and ready to start up the engine.

The trains were making their first loop around our newly-built creation, and both boys were mesmerized. Isaac made train sounds and Wyatt clapped his hands while gasping at the sight of a train car getting closer and closer to where he was seated. It was more than he could handle. He had to grab it. And just as Wyatt bent down to snatch up the passing car, he projectile vomited everywhere.

"Aw, Wyatt!" Isaac bellowed. "You're gross!" (He obviously hadn't seen his snot-covered face.) I grabbed the tracks and rushed them to the sink, dripping white chunks of stomach acid down my arms as I ran. *We are* never *having sex again*, I thought to myself as I tried to undo the baby-proof latch with slimy hands—the very latch that was keeping me from my highly-needed bleach products. *Curse these latches! And curse trains! And motherhood! And vomit!* But as I finished up with my final curse, I noticed pink gooey crud all over the still-to-be-washed train tracks. "What the heck is *this*?" Isaac climbed up on his stool next to me at the sink, looked around my shoulder, and said to me as innocently as possible, "Well, it *might* be yogurt."

Of course it was. Why *wouldn't* it be? I scrubbed it clean and brought it back to the train room. Bending to wipe up the floor, two raisins fell out of my hair. They were warm.

You have got to be kidding me!

My hubby came downstairs just in time to save me from banishing all raisin/grape products from our house forever. He was there to help, but he just needed a drink first. Upon opening the fridge, he pulled out the milk, only to find that the lid had not been screwed on tightly and that milk had poured through the entire lower refrigerator and the crisping drawers. Yep. That helped my day *tremendously*.

And then, as he pulled out the first drawer, I noticed a brown sticky puddle spanning the entire width of the fridge. It took me a while to realize that it was teriyaki sauce, you know, because it was covered in milk and all. In my haste to clean it up, I grabbed the rag covered in baby puke. Because that's how I roll. (Please know that if you choose to eat at my house or use my bathrooms, I make no guarantees that you will not die of E. coli or C. diff. This is why I don't host parties. That and because all my appetizers are hiding in my hair somewhere.)

We cleaned up the mess as best we could, but it was time to get Isaac ready to go back to his dad's house, and I needed to get the puker outside where he could run free. And run he did. He ran well, but I did not. I ran straight into a pile of dog poop. I didn't know it right away, but Cameron informed me that I had it all over my foot and my leg. I grabbed my only tissue to wipe my calf but remembered too late that it was the one covered in Isaac's snot. It smeared the poop and seemed to help it adhere to me, creating some sort of *super-poop* never seen before.

I kind of wanted to cry. And I kind of wanted to vomit just a little bit. I very much wanted to shower, but I wasn't about to put that dirty baby in his crib before giving him a bath. However, I've learned the hard way that showering with him loose in the bathroom leads to all my things being put into the toilet. *All of them.* So, I washed my leg in a mud puddle and put the baby in his swing. With a few hearty pushes, he was giggling with glee. As I was contemplating the fact that he could very well throw up again, I started feeling itchy on my legs. I looked down, and my legs were swarming. I had stood on an ant hill and was apparently being overtaken by its colony!

That was it. I could handle no more. I screamed bloody murder and swatted at my legs so hard that I left marks—marks that I couldn't see until I had killed at least fifty ants. This was more than anyone should have to bear, honestly. It was practically the plagues of Egypt all rolled into a five-hour period—all directed at me. There I was, in dirty garments and a bug-filled land, trying to lead my sick children and dogs across our forty acres of Ellwood City wilderness. *I was basically Charlton Heston.*

The thought of a nice hot bath was quite literally the only thing that kept me from pulling my clothes off in the middle of my yard and scaring my neighbors half to death. The husband returned home after dropping Isaac off with his dad, and I immediately took my leave. Since the baby needed a bath as well, I decided to kill two birds with one stone and joined him in the tub. He played with his train and washcloth. I soaped myself and let the suds marinate my skin. Naturally, Wyatt peed in the bathwater. But I didn't care. It was the cleanest thing I'd touched all day. I allowed myself to think that the suds would protect me from all things. The magical suds that were washing away the grossest day of my life.

Snuggled into bed an hour later with my computer and a bottle of Nyquil, I made my list of tasks for the following day:
1. Scrub *all* floors.
2. Sanitize *all* counters.
3. Wash *all* laundry.
4. Disinfect both bathrooms.
5. Clean fridge.
6. Buy new toilet brush.
7. Spray for ants.
8. Clean dog poop from yard.
9. Burn house down.
10. Purchase forty thousand condoms.

Because sometimes Hope means believing that things couldn't possibly get worse than they already are.

However, it seems that things can always get worse. And worse they got. In fact, I would've relived that grossest day of my life every day until my last breath if it would've saved my family from enduring what we've had to face since that time.

Had I known that the very next Isaac visit was going to be our last, I often wonder if I would've done anything differently. But looking back, I can see that it had only been a matter of time before the end was to come. Isaac was too smart and too verbal. He was able to tell us too much.

Isaac's father had asked us to get him a day early because he had plans that weekend. So, on Friday, I arrived to their home, only to find that no one was there. While I was standing in the yard, the drunken next-door neighbor yelled over and slurred a question, asking what happened to the girl living in that house? I had no idea if he meant Isaac's dad's girlfriend or if he was referring to the girlfriend's three-year-old daughter who also lived there.

I didn't get to ask my question because just then, Isaac's father came barreling down the road, blowing through each and every stop sign as my almost three-year-old bounced around in the front seat—no car seat, no seatbelt—despite the dozens of times my husband (and the police) had addressed that very issue with him.

When Isaac got out of the car, his father told me that Isaac had wet himself while they were out and that he'd take him inside to get him cleaned up. I stood in the warm sun and listened as Isaac got yelled at for peeing in his pants. And when my little boy emerged, he simply climbed into my van without a hug or hello, barely making eye contact at all.

It was only one of the stranger things that happened during that last weekend.

Always trying to be polite and social, I asked Isaac's father how his job hunt was going. The man became agitated, saying that our society is pathetic for not giving hardworking people jobs just because they have drug charges and acts of violence on their records. Then, for reasons I will never truly understand, he told me this (which is not a direct quote, as it was far too vulgar to write):

"All those women try to press charges on me, but not a one of them sticks. 'Cause I always know how to get women to drop their charges..."

How the heck was I supposed to respond to that? I stood there staring at this man, wracking my brain for some sort of retort that wouldn't come out negatively. All I could come up with was, "Well, I'm sure you'll find a job doing something soon. So, has Isaac eaten lunch yet?"

And we went on from there. In hindsight, there's a part of me that wonders if he was threatening me to tell what he suspected that I knew. The way that he stared me in the eyes... the way that he brought up his history of violence toward women while he and I were alone, him only inches from my face... it was as if he was daring me to tell on him for the drug paraphernalia in his home, the violence his other children and girlfriend had reported to us, the many times Isaac had spilled the beans about his father's aggressive outbursts.

But I simply hooked Isaac into his car seat and pushed the uncomfortable conversation from my mind. However, we weren't halfway home when Isaac started sobbing. I asked him repeatedly what was wrong, but he just kept repeating that he didn't know. When we finally arrived home, I noticed that Isaac's father had simply changed his shorts, but that his shoes were filled to the brim with urine, and his shirt was still wet.

I took him upstairs to the bathroom, and Isaac instantly peed all over the floor. It's unusual for a boy who is just under three years old to be fully potty-trained, but Isaac was always so advanced for his age. So, when he had two accidents that afternoon, it was rather odd. After putting him in the bath, one of Isaac's favorite activities, he just stood there. He wasn't smiling, and he refused to play. I washed him down, and then he instantly peed again.

Deciding that pull-ups were a necessity that day, I dressed him and brought him downstairs. I quietly told my husband about the odd interaction I'd had with Isaac's dad, but we were interrupted as our little man peed again, this time overflowing his pull-up. In fact, he wet himself every ten minutes off and on for the next day and a half. There was no blood, and he said it didn't hurt, but we texted his father, encouraging him to make a doctor's appointment as soon as he could, sure that Isaac had a urinary tract infection.

And then suddenly, Isaac's irritable, nonresponsive, weepy mood changed in the blink of an eye. We heard yelling from Taylor's room and ran to see what was wrong. Isaac had her by the hair and was punching her in the head over and over, yelling an obscene phrase at her—one of the same horrible phrases that I'd heard his dad say on many occasions to his girlfriend. When I grabbed Isaac and tried to tell him that he couldn't do that to his sister, he immediately started hitting me.

I was taken aback. It was a surreal moment because my little boy's eyes were not looking at me with love. They were dark and distracted. I could barely react because I was so stunned. Pat helped me get Isaac to the living room, and we sat and held him firmly, stroking his hair and whispering that everything was okay—that he was going to be all right. It seemed like forever before he finally relaxed into us, accepting our comfort. Yet when he looked up at me, there was my little boy again. There was the love. I gave him a hug and kiss, and he told me that he was sorry, and then he apologized to Sissy.

Later that evening, my mother-in-law and I had planned to take the kids to her church's outdoor carnival. After putting Isaac in a full-fledged diaper because he just kept wetting through the pull-ups, we loaded into the van and headed the short distance to her church. When we got there, we saw baby animals, a swing set and jungle gym, and carnival games that were so easy even my uncoordinated kids could win prizes.

I let the big kids loose to play the games while I pushed Isaac and Wyatt on the swings. It was starting to feel like we were settling down and getting back to normal. But suddenly, Isaac's mood changed yet again. He moved from happy and lovable to hyper and impulsive... so much so that he was throwing baseballs at children, hitting them with the bats in the carnival games, stealing game pieces and running away with them so the games couldn't be played. He threw my phone, and hit me repeatedly when I'd try to retrieve anything he'd taken. Isaac then began throwing himself onto the ground and screaming horrifically while people stared in our direction. If I hadn't been so concerned about what was going on inside my child, I would've been mortified. Needless to say, we had to cut the night short because Isaac simply couldn't be managed. He wasn't safe to have outside as the sun was setting and cars were coming and going. He was just too unpredictable.

That night, after finally getting everyone else to sleep, Pat and I snuggled Isaac into our bed between the two of us. My husband was the first to fall asleep. Isaac, however, was wide awake until well after 11:00 p.m. My mind suddenly went back to the drunken neighbor.

"Isaac," I'd said. "Where's your dad's girlfriend?" "I don't know, Mama."

"Are you sure? Did something happen to her or her daughter?" (I'd called them by name as not to confuse him, but I won't be using their names here for privacy's sake.)

And again he repeated, "I don't know, Mama."

Finally, Isaac fell asleep. He felt like deadweight lying on me. Scared to move and wake him, I decided to just try to power through and sleep uncomfortably. However, Isaac didn't sleep in that position long. Because for the next six hours, Isaac screamed and cried in his sleep, he rolled, he kicked and hit, and he peed.

I began to realize that Isaac didn't have a UTI. The signs of trauma were so obvious that you could've checked off his symptoms from a psychology textbook. It struck me hard that I am a therapist, specifically one that works with trauma patients. And I am the only mother he's ever known. Had I become so used to turning my eyes against the trauma in order to not rock the visitation boat that I had neglected to see what my child needed this entire time? Sick to my stomach, I held his crying little frame against me as he fought in his sleep. I stayed up and prayed over him until sunrise. I fought the enemy on his behalf and would not stop until my son was calm.

And calm he finally did. He was able to sleep for a few hours of peace before waking up. Continuing to urinate frequently, we just put him in another diaper and gave up on toileting for the weekend. We stayed at home and watched Isaac's moods ebb and flow, changing with the wind. Whether he was cuddling, hitting, or sobbing, I just loved on him and prayed over his heart with every ounce of my soul.

Later that night, we had plans to go to a friend's annual pig roast, which we knew the kids always enjoyed. By evening, Isaac had finally stopped peeing, he had stopped hitting, and he was being his normal self once again. Relieved, we enjoyed the night together. The last one that we would have.

Isaac slept like a baby that entire night. He didn't move a muscle, he didn't cry out, he didn't scream. And in the morning, he woke up and smiled his big, beautiful smile at me and said, "Hi, Mama!" Following that lovely greeting, he spontaneously told me that his dad's girlfriend was in jail.

"Wait, what?" I was still waking up and wasn't even sure I knew what we were talking about. Isaac repeated that his father's girlfriend was in jail. When I asked why, he said that she and his dad had been "fighting real hard." I asked if they were fighting with their mouths or fighting with their hands. "Both," he said. And then he asked for breakfast.

After getting him something to eat, I was able to call the jail, and sure enough, Isaac was right. She had been brought in Friday morning after a domestic disturbance and being turned in for a warrant that was out on her. My mind was reeling as I sat speculating the events of the weekend. We had been called to come get Isaac early, and Isaac's dad randomly told me that he knows how to make women not press charges. *Did he beat her up again and then turn her in for her warrant when she'd threatened to press charges against him?* It wouldn't have been the first time. Isaac had obviously witnessed the event, which made sense as to why he was so distraught and violent the previous two days.

We went to church and did our normal Sunday things. Finally, it came time to put Isaac back into his dad's clothes and send him home. Isaac instantly started peeing on the floor again. In fact, he peed three times before we left the house to take him back. He cried hysterically and fought us getting his clothes on. He kept saying that he hated his dad, calling him by his first name. This was not the first time he'd said these words, not by a long shot. However, we'd always told him that his dad loves him and that he can't say that he hates people just because he's sad.

But that day, I couldn't correct him. I didn't have the emotional strength, nor did I think he was wrong for his feelings. Whatever had gone on in that house had scared the heck out of my innocent baby... and he was free to hate in that moment if he needed to. The first half of the car ride, Isaac sobbed and begged me, "Ask him if I can stay with you, Mama. Please, ask him if I can stay." My heart broke as I choked down my own tears.

"Okay, baby, I'll ask."

And then, halfway to his home, Isaac's eyes went dead as they had so many times before. He was helpless to turn the car around. He couldn't fight his return. So, he emotionally shut down and resigned to his powerlessness.

I feel the same exact way, Sweetie... the same exact way. Worn-out from all the big emotions he'd exerted that weekend, Isaac had fallen asleep a few minutes before we arrived at his home. That gave me the chance I needed to talk to his father one-on-one before Isaac's tears started up again. I'd mentioned that Isaac's behaviors had been very erratic that weekend and that he had a lot of nightmares. I also mentioned that he was showing significant signs of trauma. And then I point-blank asked the man my question: "Did anything happen this week that would've scared Isaac in any way?"

That man stared me straight in the face for several seconds before answering. "Nope, nothing that I can think of."

"I just know that even if it may seem small, our actions can really affect little kids, you know?"

"Nothing happened," he repeated with finality.

I woke Isaac up, and he cried as we kissed good-bye. It was the last kiss I would receive from his little lips. The last time he would call out my name and I would be there to hear it. The last time I would see his face peering back at mine.

I hadn't even pulled out of the driveway before Isaac's father texted my husband and said that we would never see him again. And to this day, he has kept his word.

Those phrases from before were repeated again by those within the child welfare system—"functioning addict" and "no broken bones." I dejectedly realized that the people who are entrusted with the most precious of God's creatures have failed the little boy that I used to hold in my arms each night. He is labeled a success in their books because he was reunified with a biological parent that hasn't broken his bones yet and can function in his addiction some of the time.

And if Isaac's physical body is not being looked out for by the broken system that makes the rules, how could I ever believe that his mental, emotional, and spiritual body would be cared for? What of his extreme intelligence and self-esteem? What about his courage and athleticism? Would they fall by the wayside too? Would he ever get to go to college? Or would he become another statistic, simply proving that our child welfare system is inadequate at best, negligent, and abusive?

I don't know that I will ever have the answers to these questions. I don't know if the system will ever find a way to change the decades of ruin and devastation they've caused to so many families and children with their ancient, decrepit laws. But one thing that I do know is that Isaac taught me how to love freely and fearlessly, with no holding back. He didn't grow in my belly, but he grew in me a selfless kind of love that will forever leave me changed as a mother—as a person in general. He opened my heart when it felt closed off and scared. And then he went on to show me that, even in his leaving, my heart will be forever opened to love.

Because sometimes Hope means loving without seeing; it is the otherworldly Faith established in our worldly hearts. And it requires all of my Hope to believe that my child is being held by a God that loves him more than I ever could.

WYATT

Wyatt is my dessert to an otherwise heavy meal. He came at just the right time, with just the perfect amount of sweetness to lessen the bitterness that had come before him. Discovering that I was pregnant on the same night that I thought I'd lost my other baby boy was one of the most poetic and miraculous moments of my life. If you're not one to believe in miracles, I'd strongly encourage you to reconsider your opinion on the matter. From having three causes of infertility, to not responding to fertility medication, to losing a child and then finding out an hour later that God was blessing us with another, one that couldn't be taken away...

Sure, nobody rose from the dead. But I can assure you that our hearts were as good as dead in those moments of loss that we were facing. We didn't know how to carry on or how to even take one more breath. And in our moment of complete ruin, God showed up and breathed new life into a broken womb and dying hearts.

If you're looking for more of a miracle than that, then perhaps your expectations of what God can do in your own life need to be altered. When God shows up to perform a miracle, it's usually very personal, very timely. He renews us in the times when darkness tries to steal our very souls.

Because sometimes Hope means finding an open window after a door has been closed.

I don't know why I didn't expect it, but my pregnancy was terrible. Just... terrible. There aren't even enough words to describe how much my body hated it. Now please, don't get me wrong. I was grateful *beyond belief* to be carrying my little miracle inside of me, but it was seriously the longest nine months ever. I cannot understand why people have multiple children, because women are quite literally being punished for Eve eating that apple all those thousands of years ago. (Which is why her name was not in the running when it came choosing time.)

Consider yourself forewarned, but if you're squeamish in the slightest, you may just want to skip to the end of the book. I mean, every day my body did something just a little bit grosser than it did the previous day. I knew this to be true because my doting husband reminded me of how disgusting I was after I'd informed him of each bodily change. However, facing my current health issues, and knowing that they increased the chance of miscarriage by 50 percent, I didn't feel comfortable keeping those changes to myself!

What if, God forbid, I was to spontaneously pass out? My husband would be forced to rush me to the local emergency room and would have to attest to my every symptom. How would he know that my poo was green *if I didn't tell him*? And how could he report to the ER doctor that I'd had a terrible rash on my bottom *if I didn't tell him*?

You see, I was doing this for mine and the baby's safety.

Sure, it may have killed the mood a bit at times, but no more than my puking or ultrasensitive body parts, so what difference did it make? Thankfully, my sweetheart of a gynie prescribed me Zofran. It was the delicious nectar required to sustain me each day, and it made it possible to move without barfing on my clients at work. Sadly, my lovely doctor was the only one helpful in getting me this miracle med I so desperately needed. The pharmacy and the insurance company proved to be not only unsympathetic to my nauseous plight, but they were downright *rude*!

Who in their right mind gets rude to a pregnant woman with morning/all-day-long sickness? There had to be some missing rule in the Ten Commandments forbidding people from ticking off a hormonal gal... "Thou Shalt Not Withhold Zofran" or "Thou Shalt Not Ruin a Lady's First Week of Knowing She's Pregnant"! But obviously, the people at my pharmacy were not Bible readers, and they certainly didn't care about womankind in the slightest.

Yet sick or not, our regular date night arrived. Despite my lack of interest in intimacy those first two months, my blessed mother-in-law offered to relieve Pat and I of our parenting duties one evening, which was the best present in the world. It was especially necessary since our two little rugrats, Cameron and Taylor, had decided to make my supposed-to-be happy week a treacherous one. Grateful for the date night, I made plans to do one thing—*sleep*. My husband, *bless him*, had made plans to do other things on the bed.

However, just in time to ward off romance, another symptom emerged. Good-bye, diarrhea. Hello, constipation! I went from chewing Imodium like it was candy, to sucking down stool softeners just to relieve the bloating and pain. As it turns out, my miracle Zofran was the culprit of this new and unfortunate symptom. And the only solution was an enema—on date night (not exactly the type of sounds Pat was hoping for that evening).

Two years ago, date night would've consisted of passionate kisses, decadent food, and a night on the town. But then we had all those kids and I got pregnant and all my parts started getting really gross... now all that was left was me bending over as my husband played doctor, but not in a good way. To say I was mortified is an understatement. Yet, despite the humiliation that shall forever haunt me, my gratitude for a husband who's willing to go the extra mile in a marriage cannot be measured. I fear we may never be able to look one another in the eye again, but still... there's the gratitude.

A few days later and feeling better than I had in weeks, I ate a box of pierogies. The *entire box.* That was not my intention when I set out to make dinner one night. In fact, it was the last thing on my mind when I came home from work. My husband took the kids to see my niece perform in a play downtown, which left me home alone for the first time in *forever.*

Knowing that I could take a nap, eat whatever/whenever I wanted, or enjoy a relaxing bath, I chose to nap. The couch just looked too comfortable to pass up after a very long day at work. Before I knew it, I was cuddled up with the pillows and my soft, green throw, waiting until sleep overtook my fattening body.

Just as I was about to drift off, I felt a very intense and familiar pull coming from deep inside of me. I recognized it immediately as the *pangs of hunger.* Pre-pregnancy, I would've ignored such a calling and moved on with the nap (actually, pre- pregnancy, I wouldn't have dreamed of taking a nap in the first place, so, scratch that – I would've eaten anyways).

However, since my belly now had a life of its own (literally), I'd learned to eat whatever I could get my hands on and as soon as possible when the pangs arrived. If I chose to ignore this hunger, vomiting was sure to follow! So, I jumped (heaved) up and ran to the kitchen in search of something non-nauseating.

Salad? *Ugh, gag...* Mac 'n cheese? Eh, *that was so yesterday's accident.* Tuna fish? *Oh, my gosh, never again!* Pierogies? Pierogies! Ah, yes! Butter, onion, Parmesan, garlic, potatoey-noodly-goodness? I needed it in my stomach as of ten minutes ago, so I whipped out my ingredients and fired up the skillet.

And that was where my problem occurred. I tore the top off the pierogi box and began dumping in an amount that looked satisfying to this mama that had been puking on and off all week, unable to eat nearly enough to even begin dealing with the third bout of constipation that had been threatening to creep in. Needless to say, I was hungry.

Perhaps a bit too hungry.

After I finished pouring, I went to re-close the box, only to find that a meager three pierogies remained. Three, lonely pierogies, destined for freezer-burn, stared back at me in a plea to be warmed in a butter bath. *Ah, crap. I can't just leave three—that's not even enough for an appetizer!* So I did the only thing that could be done, and I plopped the remaining potato noodles into the skillet. There was a satisfying sizzle as they thanked me.

Fifteen minutes later, I sat with my platter of food as I caught up on that week's episode of *Parenthood*. I dug in and was doing pretty well, until the wall hit me. And guess what? There were three pierogies left on my plate. Those little buggers had tricked me! They knew there was no way I was going to finish them, but they just *had* to be cooked, didn't they!

I pushed my plate away in disgust as nausea stopped by to say hello. As I sat there cursing my dinner and pleading with my stomach to take a chill pill, I vowed never to eat another pierogi again. I took the plate into the kitchen before curling back up on the sofa for another twenty minutes, willing my insides to settle. Thankful for the eventual relief, I returned to the kitchen for a glass of water.

"*Ooh*, pierogies!" I said to myself excitedly, and then I housed the three noodles down like I'd been in a prison camp for the last decade. I'd like to say that I was ashamed of myself, but I know that if I had to do it over again, the results would've been the same. So, I accepted my fat- kid status and moved on with my life. I mean, come on, my stomach is an idiot if it believed my vow to never eat another pierogi again anyways, so it had what was coming to it.

Never being one to keep such an exciting secret to myself, it may come as a shock that we were able to fool our families into thinking that Baby Bean (as we had lovingly named our unborn) had his/her legs crossed during the 5-month ultrasound, making it *impossible* to get a clear gender reading. Little did we know, Baby Bean almost pranked us with this as well! After an hour and a half of unnerving picture-taking suspense, the little fella *finally* uncrossed his legs just long enough to get a rump shot... and there was really no doubt about it. This baby was 100 percent boy!

Was I disappointed? No. Was I shocked? *Completely*! I'd spent the prior five months convinced that I was carrying a little princess bean, only to find out that I was going to have to drop the double S at the end. So no, I wasn't disappointed, but it was a concept that took some getting used to.

To help me adjust to the idea, I made myself find the silver lining to the news:

1. I will never pass on my cracked-out uterus problems to a boy. He will never feel a cyst on his ovary rupture, know the awfulness of menstruation, nor have to have any surgeries to laser ickyness off of his innards.

2. Boys tend to be closer to their mamas, whereas girls tend to love on their daddies, and I wanted this baby to be a full-fledged mama's boy! Well, at least until it causes him to get beat up... and then I wanted him to just snuggle with me secretly and kiss me a block away from the school yard, like any other closeted mama's boy.

3. We already had so much baby boy stuff that this news would make my baby shower so much simpler! (And yes, I got to have a baby shower for the first time in four kids!)

Okay, back to the secret we kept from our families. For a full week, we knew the gender of our little nugget, but we painfully fibbed to our parents, telling them the leg-crossed story. After all, I wasn't able to tell my family in person that I was pregnant because of our geographical distance, so I wanted to make sure I could tell them this news in person and in a special way.

To do this, I wrapped up the ultrasound pictures in blue tissue paper and homemade blue and white confetti, complete with an announcement that we were having a baby boy. I then wrapped the gifts in regular Christmas paper and planned to have my family open their gifts simultaneously at our Christmas party. Pat's parents would do the same at our Costa family party the following week. I also wrapped two little boy gifts for both Taylor and Cameron to unwrap— gifts that they could keep and give to the baby once he was born.

Sounds sweet, doesn't it? Well, there seemed to be a bit of confusion at the *grand revealing*. I anxiously watched my parents' faces as they opened their gift. My brother and dad caught on right away, but my mother stared at the gift in wonderment, almost as if she were thinking, "Huh... what an odd gift of a random ultrasound picture that reads 'It's A Boy!' Hmm...."

I waited and waited for what seemed like minutes, but in reality it was probably no more than five seconds before my mom yelled out in realization as to what the gift meant for her as a grandmother! All were shocked, but happy... all except for one small family member named Taylor.

My almost six-year-old looked at me with a frown and told me that she no longer wanted a new little baby in the family if it was going to be a boy. Immediately following her disdain, Cameron let out a whoop of enthusiasm that he was going to have another boy "on his side." However, his excitement was promptly followed by a look of confusion as he asked, "Hey, is the new baby going to be black like Isaac?"

My husband chimed in with an abrupt, "He better not be!" as I decided against having a birds and bees talk with Cameron in the middle of our family Christmas party. We informed Cam that this baby would be white, and Taylor that this baby would be a boy, and that if anyone doesn't like it, they were free to file a complaint with God, but that all negativity was banned from spoiling the moment.

Our reveal to Pat's family was much simpler. His father was excited to have yet another Italian male in the family, his mother suggested we start a family basketball team, and his grandmother turned up her hearing aid so that she could hear what was happening. Needless to say, all were happy for us! Except for my grandmother, who had bought the new baby little pink socks before his gender was revealed. She got even with me by telling the room (rather loudly) how large I'd gotten so quickly in my pregnancy...

Sometimes Hope means knowing that the rest of the party guests would *eventually* stop looking at me like a gigantic freak of nature. Eventually.

The week of my first baby shower was quite eventful. From the exhilarating T-dap vaccine to my parents coming into town, life had been a whirlwind! It seemed that overnight my stomach had grown at the same rate as the speed of light. It felt as if Baby Boy was ready to bust on out of his current home with each punch and roll he made. By the end of each day, I felt thoroughly and utterly worn out. But I have to say, family time was just what I needed.

My husband and dad stepped up and watched all the ragamuffins that attended the shower so that the mommies were free to enjoy some grown-up time and delicious food. It was so wonderful to feel such a vast amount of love that day from family, friends, coworkers, and church members. My lovely friend who hosted the shower had everyone fill out a sheet that allowed each guest to write down their wishes for Baby Boy Costa. And as I read through them later that night, I was filled with such happiness knowing that my baby, who wasn't even here yet, was loved by so many.

Sunday came, and it was time to say good-bye to my family, which always leaves me feeling a bit empty for a few days. Luckily, right as I entered my third trimester, my company switched us to mandatory twelve-hour shifts instead of our usual eight, so I never really had time to think about such things as emptiness, sadness, hunger, or the constant need to urinate. I would just go-go-go until my body fell into bed minutes after walking through the door at the end of the night.

Thankfully, the new schedule also allowed for a day off in the middle of the week… which just meant that I'd spend the entire day doing work at home that I wasn't able to do over the weekends while we had Isaac or on the days I'd work long shifts. So naturally, I pushed myself too hard and ended up on the couch, elevating swollen ankles, resting my aching back, and warding off nausea.

Since the homework had been done, dinner was cleaned up, and the kids were actually playing together nicely upstairs for a change, I felt justified to take a few moments to catch up on episodes of *A Baby Story* that I had recorded earlier that week.

Now, let me just say this. I find this show equal parts horrifying and gratifying, and I'm not exactly positive that it was a healthy thing for me to watch, since it would cause my worrying mind to go into overdrive. Yeah, remember those panic attacks? *A Baby Story* did those no favors!

But something about the show was just like that car accident that you stop and stare at as you drive by super-slowly—you wanna look away but it seems impossible to do so. And that night was no different. I was halfway through the second episode when Taylor came downstairs and stopped, just in time to see the mother on TV begin her series of labor pushes. I watched my daughter's face, her little eyes as wide as saucers, mouth hanging open.

"Oh. My. Goodness," she whispered to herself. I couldn't help but giggle as she watched the mother scream in pain, nurses hustling and bustling every which way. Then, as she pushed the baby out and the doctor lifted the little boy onto his mama's chest, Taylor's face burst into a huge smile. "Oh, wow! It's really a baby!" she said, still glued to the television. She was literally transfixed until the commercial break... and that's when the questions began.

"What was all that stuff on the baby? Where is the hole that the baby came out of? I didn't see a hole on the mommy's tummy... will her belly stay that big forever? When is our baby coming?"

"Okay, okay, okay. First of all, that stuff on the baby was inside the mommy too, and it was keeping the baby nice and warm while he was in there. And there's no hole in the mommy's tummy because the baby came out of her privates. That's why girls have the parts they have – so that babies can come out."

"Oh... well, that's just a little bit gross, I think. So you will be naked when you have our baby?"

"I won't be able to have pants on, that's right."

"Oh, my goodness... so Dad's gonna see your vagina?" (The shock was priceless.)

"Uh, yeah. And the doctors."

"But it's okay for doctors to see us naked, but not boys, Mom!"

"It's okay for daddies to see mommies naked."

"Well, if the baby's gonna be naked, then everyone else can be naked too, I guess!"

"No, not everyone, just me and the baby."

She seemed to accept this reasoning and moved on.

"So, when's the baby gonna get here? How many more years?"

"Not years... although it feels like it. Just about two more months. Remember, it's winter now, and the baby will come in the spring. You'll still be in kindergarten."

"I'm gonna be in kindergarten for that many more years?" "No, Taylor, it's winter now. In the spring, I will have the baby. Then, in the summer, you will be done with kindergarten. It's only two more months, not years."

"Are you gonna be old when you have the baby?"

"No, I'll be thirty-two in two weeks, and that's how old I will be when the baby is born."

"Yep, you're still gonna be old..."

Thankfully, the commercial break ended, and the show had fast-forwarded one month, showing the baby in his new home. I noticed right away that the parents of this particular episode named their little boy the same name that my husband and I had been contemplating. We hadn't told the kids this name yet because of their struggle with fixating on things, so we'd held out until we were certain. However, Taylor looked me square in the eye and said, "Wyatt... I like that name. I think we should name our baby that, too!"

We decided to watch one more episode just as Cameron came into the room. He took one look at the woman on the screen and said, "Hey, Mom, she's not even as fat as you, and her baby is already coming out?"

Awesome. Thanks, Cam! He quickly became just as transfixed as Taylor had, eyes glued to the screen, but with a much more confused look on his face than Taylor had shown... and then the questions started all over again.

"She's making weird noises... why is she making those sounds? It gross!"

"Cam, she's just in pain. Labor hurts, bud." "So, she gets to eat ice cubes and drink juice?"

"Yep, this mama gets to. She needs it to help her get through the delivery."

(Enter the tub for the water birth.)

"You get to go swimming when you have a baby?" Taylor asked excitedly.

"No, it's not a swimming pool. It's a tub, and some women have their babies in the water."

"No fair! She gets to eat ice, drink juice, and take a bath!"

Cameron, *my son*, was actually pouting over the "fairness" of labor.

"Cam, it's not like she's having a party, man. She's in *pain*, remember?"

"Cameron, I'm not even going to tell you why she doesn't have a hole in her tummy!" exclaimed Taylor.

And just then, with the final few pushes, the baby emerged into the water.

"Hey, where did the baby come from?" Cameron asked in confusion.

"Mom!" Taylor whispered loudly. "Don't tell him the baby came out of the V-A... Mom, how do you spell vagina?"

"Taylor, you're so gross! Babies don't come out of there!" Cameron looked at his sister like she was utterly ridiculous.

"Actually, Cam, they do. That's why mommies have the parts they have. God made us that way."

He stared at me for a few seconds as if processing the information he'd just learned.

"Well, at least you get to have some juice."

That was his final statement before leaving the room, probably to go hunt down some juice. However, at tuck-in that night, he did ask me if he would be allowed to tie that cord into a bow and make the belly button. He was rather sad when I informed him that doctors went to school for eight years to learn how to tie that special kind of bow and that he wouldn't be allowed to do that part. He sulked his way under the covers as I shut off his light, all the while praying that he would marry a very patient woman someday.

Perhaps it was all the running around I'd do throughout my day or the normal child neediness of my six- and eight-year-olds when I'd get home or the fact that I'd had a whirlwind trip to Michigan for my second baby shower and maternity photo shoot – or possibly it was the fact that I had the flu for five days and ended up sitting in the Triage unit getting pumped full of fluids and meds... or maybe it was just a combination of all those things that had me worn and ragged during those final days of pregnancy.

So, in honor of having a day in which I *did not feel* like death, I decided to try to knock a few things off my to-do list—that ever-growing list that seemed to multiply by 10 each time I crossed one thing off—the list that haunted my dreams and made me sleepy before I'd even begun. If I wasn't puking, then I needed take the opportunity to be productive. Unfortunately, everything that I touched that day broke (quite literally).

Pay the bills? Sure! Except that our Internet connection refused to be cooperative for the first half of the day. Then, when it did start working again, wouldn't you know that my bank's Web page froze on me twice and pop-up ads almost led to the demise of my computer? *Forget bills*, I'd said to myself, *I'll vacuum!*

I shook out all the rugs onto the floor and, after spending twenty minutes untangling the cord (ooh, someone was so going to pay for that injustice when they got home!), I plugged in my brand-new vacuum and started in one corner of the first room.

I was just branching out of my corner when I noticed a sea of dead ladybugs in the window sill. I hooked on my new handy-dandy wand attachment and sucked those little ladies right up! Feeling pleased, I put the attachment hose back into its place and realized that I was unable to release the base of the wand from the main vacuum. I checked for special buttons, read the manual, and prayed for miracles... but still, nothing.

That attachment was stuck like cement on the end of my handle, making it impossible for me to use the vacuum for anything else.

Looking at my one clean corner in my one lonely room and noticing that I had just shook out the rugs of all the other rooms in preparation for The Great Sweep of 2014, a wave of anger washed over me. My calm, rational "There must be a way to figure this out" self flew right out the window, and a crazed, hormonal woman that I barely recognized appeared.

That day I found great comfort in beating the vacuum wand off the arms of the couch. I may have also found it rather therapeutic to scream at the top of my lungs, sending all three dogs, tails between their legs, running up the stairs with panic in their eyes. And then finally, the vacuum cleaner won.

In a fit of exhaustion, I flopped myself down on the loveseat, and I sobbed. I'm talking, those were uncontrollable, face-swelling wretches that increased every time I looked back at the sweeper. I didn't even try to stop them. For some reason, I'd needed the release, and I let myself have it. Several minutes later, I was feeling slightly better, braver even, and I was ready to try again with fresh eyes. I looked back at the vacuum cleaner and spent about ten seconds pondering the situation before I chucked the wand across the room and screamed in rage, *"I'm pregnant, don't mess with me, dang it!"* And then I screamed some more and dissolved into a second fit of tears.

It had become obvious to me that I was unwell. So, I decided to call my mother-in-law, the woman who'd bought me the evil vacuum cleaner, to see if she had any ideas. Before she arrived to give the sweeper a try, I gave the machine one last stab, sending myself into such a tizzy that my nose began to bleed. By the time my husband's mother arrived, I was drenched in sweat, my eyes were almost swollen shut, and I was nursing my nose. Slightly embarrassed, I pointed her in the direction of the broken piece of crap that was once called my vacuum cleaner.

Twenty minutes later, my mother-in-law was in the same state as me... except she used cool things like pliers and hammers, butter knives and liquid soap while she did her ranting—none of which worked, all of which caused her to yell and hit the wand off the same couch that had taken the beating earlier. In the end, we did what we should've done in the beginning. We called customer service. This was their reply: "Why don't you wait for your husband to come home and have him fix it?"

Excuse me? For one, this isn't the 1950s. And two, unless my husband is the Incredible Hulk, he isn't going to be able to get this stupid wand off either! So, I yelled about that for a while, too. And after two hours, my mother-in- law gave up, as did I, and I continued with my to-do list. I started to unpack baby gifts from my shower and put them away. Because that would be fun *and* productive, right?

Which it was, until I bent to pick up the first bag and my back went out. You know the drill... I cried for a while, although carefully, as not to aggravate my nose again. I hobbled down the stairs to let my frantic dogs outside while I rested on the beaten couch. When it was time to bring them back in, I knelt slowly, keeping my back as straight as possible, my belly sinking low between my thighs. And just as my left knee touched the ground, I heard a pop and felt pain shoot up my leg.

Unable to bend said leg, stand upright, vacuum, or accomplish *anything* on my to-do list, I retired back to the couch and cried for the millionth time that day. I'm still not sure if it was the flu, the traveling, the long days at work, or the multitude of lovely pregnancy symptoms that had me down, but one thing was for sure... in the battle of hormones versus rationality, it was very apparent that the hormones had won.

By the way, my husband fixed the vacuum in less than two minutes. But we don't really need to tell the customer service lady that, now do we?

The long-awaited maternity leave had finally begun. No, there was no baby yet, but my health had been deteriorating quite rapidly, and I needed a break to help prepare my rotund body for the vigorous workout that is labor.

Frankly, I'm not sure who was more nervous about that whole process, me or my husband. He routinely informed me that he couldn't rest because he was anxious with not knowing the when, where, and how all of it was gonna go down—like we were waiting for a nuclear attack or something.

In fact, when I was having contractions one day, he demanded that I tell him if the baby was coming right then or not... as if I knew! And then later he informed me that I was no longer allowed to call him during the day because he would immediately assume that I was going into labor. In the meantime, he'd wake me up almost nightly to ask how I was doing. Now, I thought all men had an innate sense of self-preservation that warned them away from ever waking a pregnant woman, especially when she was in her ninth month. Apparently I was wrong.

To top things off, Pat would just stare at me while I was in the shower... and not in the way he used to stare at me, but in an entirely new way, as if he was watching (in astonishment) as the world's largest woman attempted to shave her legs without falling and taking the curtain down with her.

Even little Isaac was amazed at my big belly. He regularly tried to climb the mountain that had become his Mama, and he'd lift my shirt to try to poke my "button" back in. He'd then rub my stomach while saying, "Baby," like it was a magic lamp. Isaac was also quite taken with my equally enlarged "upper area" as he tried to push those "buttons" back in through my shirt, as well... I think he was pretty convinced that everything in my torso was a baby, the entire womb-concept proving to be a bit too much his eighteen- month mentality.

Cameron and Taylor were just excited that I was no longer working. There were actually cheers complete with fist pumps when I'd informed them of my last day of work. Even if I had to spend half the time lying down while they're home, you could see the happiness radiating off them. Taylor was *thrilled* that I got to watch her in gymnastics once again and Cameron's homework began to improve greatly.

Not to mention my own health was improving, just in that first week off ! My feet were far less swollen and my back pain was more manageable. Even my tonsillitis, which the doctor's told me would probably require surgery, had nearly cleared up with the final antibiotic.

And then, it was just a matter of time. The wait was agonizing, but the end result would be miraculous! Just knowing that my cervix was softening rapidly helped me come to grips with the few stray stretch marks that had made their way from my hips to the lower left side of my belly. It didn't help the fact, however, that I was nearly two hundred pounds and that my groin felt like I had pulled every muscle in the forbidden zone.

Still, it was almost over. Would I miss it? Not being pregnant, heck no! But feeling him move around inside of me? Possibly. All I knew was that I would have my little man in my arms, and I'd feel so grateful to have had this experience. I knew it was one that I'd never want to repeat, but I'd have gone through the greatest miracle of my life—one I didn't think I was capable of having.

Because sometimes Hope comes in small, baby-sized packages.

May, 2014. There I was, 216 months pregnant. Big and hormonal, sweaty and not giving any craps about anything.

Holding one baby on my hip and another in my gut, I looked like the redneck woman's pregnant best friend. Even my toddler couldn't believe I was still pregnant. Wyatt was supposed to have been here days before, months really, if you take into account the size of my watermelon-esque midsection. He wasn't supposed to wait that long, get that big! I mean, he had to be the size of an NFL linebacker by that point. And I didn't have much experience in the way of labor and all, but I was pretty sure that linebackers didn't come out all that gracefully.

To be honest, I was 100 percent terrified. I was one half terrified of him coming out, and the other half terrified that he'd stay in... scratch that. Maybe it was more like 40-60. Either way, there were some serious fears going on. I kept crying. And then I'd puke a little. And then I'd double over for forty-five to ninety seconds, and then I'd cry some more. I hadn't slept in days!

Literally. I mean, I had not slept for three nights straight.

And the fourth night wasn't looking too promising either, with all the cramping and puking and contracting and crying going on. But this was how my four-day labor started...

Past my due date and convinced that he was never going to come out, I decided that I was tired of waiting around for him. It was a Friday night, and we planned some family time, so we rented the beloved movie Frozen to watch for the evening. Halfway through the movie, I started to have contractions (not that I got too excited, because who knew if they were real or just another set of Braxton Hicks).

Either way, I decided to pull out my handy-dandy contraction tracker app on my phone, just to see if there was a pattern to those annoying pains. After several hours, I realized that there was no consistent pattern, but that I was averaging a contraction once every fifteen to twenty minutes. I'd already had one false labor scare, and my poor parents drove all the way from Michigan just to sit on my couch and watch me remain pregnant, so I certainly didn't want to make that mistake again by calling them too hastily. I'd decided to just go to bed and see how I felt in the morning.

Except trying to sleep through contractions is kinda like trying to sleep through an earthquake. Some things can't (and shouldn't) be ignored! By morning, the contractions were averaging ten minutes apart, but still there was no set pattern to them, which I was told was a sign that they were Braxton Hicks. So, on I labored (I just didn't know I was doing so). We picked up Isaac for our weekend visit and hung out around the house for the day, just in case my body did anything too crazy.

Besides that, I was exhausted from not having slept at all the previous night. Never having pulled an all- nighter before, my body was stuck in zombie mode. Finally, by around 5:00 p.m., my husband encouraged me to call my parents to come out. The contractions were getting stronger, but still all over the place. And as sure as I sat there, about an hour after making the call, the pains slowed down considerably.

Great, I'd thought. *Another false alarm as soon as my parents got on the road!* However, being several days past my due date, Mom and Dad decided to keep driving because it was only a matter of time before I would have to pop, right?

They arrived at 11:00 p.m. on Saturday night, and we all decided to "get some sleep" just in case things were to pick up again. Sure enough, moments after placing my head on the pillow, the contractions went from about fifteen minutes apart to six minutes apart (but still irregular!). I laid awake monitoring frequencies and strength of the pains as Pat sawed logs next to me. But once I had two episodes in a four-minute span, I promptly woke him and my parents up at 1:00 a.m., and we began the hour ride into Pittsburgh where my hospital was located.

Thankfully, there wasn't a whole lot of traffic in the middle of the night, and our trip was quicker than expected. Long story short, the doctor examined me and found I was only half a centimeter dilated. Seriously. He had me walk laps for an hour to keep the contractions coming strong. They were two to three minutes apart when he checked me again, but I had only increased to one centimeter. The option to induce labor was mentioned by the nurse, and I'd promptly told her that I didn't want to do anything that would increase my chances of having a C-section.

It needs to be said that I have a horrific fear of needles and knives. The thought of being cut open was so treacherous for me that I could barely catch my breath. So, after almost eleven hours at the hospital, the doctor gave me a shot of morphine to help me sleep (and apparently hallucinate), and he sent me home to finish laboring there.

I managed to get two hours of sleep, although somewhat interrupted. My hubby's nerves through the whole process had the poor man sleep-talking and asking me random questions; he didn't even remember shaking me constantly to ask if I was okay every few minutes. When I woke from my nap, the contractions had slowed to about one per hour. *Awesome.*

I spent the rest of Sunday evening power walking up and down my driveway, and my patient and sleepy husband even took me on a bumpy quad ride to try to get things going again. But all of it was in vain. There was nothing left for me to do other than wait until my OB appointment the following afternoon. Feeling defeated, I went to bed.

I managed almost four hours of sleep before contractions woke me up again, keeping me hopping until midmorning, at which point they decided to hibernate once more. I was starting to become very angry at my uterus. Maybe it was the lack of sleep or maybe it was the mostly consistent pains I'd been experiencing for almost three days, but I had just about had it with the whole pregnancy thing! Hanging on by a very loose thread, my hormones just couldn't take it anymore. By the time my family and I arrived at my doctor appointment on Monday afternoon, I was a frazzled, nervous mess. My doctor checked and informed me that, guess what, I was 1.5 cm dilated.

Oh, my gosh, for real? All those contractions for three days, and I was only 1.5 cm and 50 percent effaced? There had to be some mistake! My mind was reeling and my doctor could tell I was going to lose it, so she offered up some more bad news, just for good measure.

"I hate to tell you this, but I'm usually not wrong about these things. Your baby is very high and isn't dropping at all. I'm a little concerned about the cord, and you need to prepare yourself for a C-section." (Cue the waterworks.) Too tired to contain myself, I let the sobs take over. When I could finally catch my breath, I politely begged her to get my baby out of me... immediately.

Lucky for me, she was the on-call doctor for the following day, and she was able to schedule my induction for 7:00 a.m. the next morning. *Thank God!* Finally some good news!

However, as the day went on, I became increasingly petrified of my baby's cord possibly being wrapped around his neck, him not dropping, and having to go under the knife. Frantic, I began to try all the old wives' tales I could think of. I did squats, bounced on my yoga ball, ate spicy foods, and my husband and I even made some very unlovely love that afternoon—*anything to get my baby to drop!* But nothing worked.

The only thing I knew to do from that point on was to walk. Well, waddle. I was going to waddle a trench down my driveway if it was the last thing I did. And since I was already pretty convinced that I was dying, it felt very likely what it would be the last thing I did!

I waddled down the drive. I waddled up the drive. (Quick pee break while near the house.) I again waddled down the drive and then waddled back up the drive. (Another pee break. Rested ankles for a minute while I contracted.) Then I waddle down the drive and waddled up the drive. I didn't quite make it to the bathroom that time, but I was not to be deterred. So, I waddled down the drive once more. On the final go of it, I waddled halfway up the drive, collapsed midway, contracted for a minute, and then rolled around for a while because I'd fallen and couldn't get up. I cried. I also decided that I would deliver the baby at home, in the driveway. And then I decided I didn't want the neighbors to see my vagina. So, I rolled some more. A gust of wind and labor fairies help me up. I finished my waddle up the drive, and then I gave up waddling altogether.

My plan was to sleep well that night so that I'd be in better shape for delivering a kid into the world the next morning. But, true to form, as soon as I laid my head on the pillow, the contractions picked right back up. Ten minutes apart... seven minutes apart... five minutes apart... *Shoot, I gotta puke... oh no, both ends? Really? Oh, Lord in heaven, make it stop!* Four minutes apart... *Time to go, but I can't bring the toilet with me...*

May 13, 2014. By 5:00 a.m., we were in the car, barf bucket in one hand, contraction tracker in the other. We made it to the hospital in time for me to book it to the bathroom. It was later that morning that I learned my mother-in-law and oldest son had both come down with the flu, which I had probably caught on my delivery day, as luck would have it. But since my contractions were moving along steadily on their own, the hospital staff decided to wait on the induction and just let me labor for a bit. I was two centimeters dilated and having strong contractions two to three minutes apart.

Since I'd already been in labor for the previous three days, I was basically a pro. I did my breaths, showed my cervix to every Tom, Dick, and Harry wearing a doctor's coat, and I prayed for Wyatt to drop.

My husband held my hand for the next few hours through the breathing and trying of new positions to see what would help alleviate the pain. And then, he shocked me and asked when I was going to start yelling at him. I guess he thought I was going to be a monster during labor, screaming and yelling and writhing in pain. I told him I didn't think it would help and he didn't do anything worth yelling at, so what would be the point?

He sweetly stayed by my side and kept telling me how proud he was of me for doing such a good job. I don't know why, but that meant more to me than anything else. By early afternoon, I was only at four centimeters and ready to talk epidural, despite my desperate fear of a large needle being shoved into my back. But I was so tired, and the thought of going on for six more centimeters was too exhausting. I just needed to rest for a little bit...

The lovely nurse Shelley assured me that my progress would increase once my body was more relaxed. Even though it was against protocol, I made the doctor promise to refrain from explaining the procedure to me, and the nice man agreed to let Pat stay in the room for the process. Convulsing uncontrollably and quite *dizzy*, I was overwhelmingly proud of myself for not passing out!

And sure enough, an hour later, I was at six centimeters! However, six centimeters is where I stayed for the next five hours. And that's when Wyatt's heartbeat went away. And everything seemed to fade a bit. The pain grew small, and the doctors grew quieter as the heartbeat in my ears thudded louder and louder.

"I need you to flip, *now*," the nurse ordered me—a woman who hadn't been able to roll over independently for at least two months. My husband, the nurse, and my momentous girth got me flipped in a colossal team effort—an effort we exerted every fifteen minutes or so, each time we lost the heartbeat. We did this for hours. Then the doctor had to hook a little coil into my wee baby's scalp to better keep track of his heartbeats, also inserting a probe into me to monitor the strength of my contractions as they tried to find the right dose of Pitocin that would keep me progressing without risking Wyatt's health.

"Try to sleep," they told me as my baby's heart rate blipped inconsistently on the monitor next to me. "It may just be the cord wrapped around his neck, which is really quite common."

Sleep? Really? Tell me, exactly how does one sleep when their baby's life is in danger!? Pat was watching me stare at the monitor, eyes bloodshot and tense, refusing to rest. Thankfully, my incredible husband told me that he would watch the monitor for me and would wake me if anything was wrong, but that he wanted me to rest.

And so I tried... not very well, but I think I got a few minutes in here and there. Finally, my doctor came in and told me that we had given it as long as we could. Wyatt was still far too high for whatever reason, and I was not dilating any further. It was time for the C-section. Nurse Shelley held my trembling hand, stroking it with compassion as she said, "You've been so strong all day... honey, it's okay to cry."

And cry I did. I couldn't keep it in any longer. My greatest fear was happening, and there was nothing I could do about it. I couldn't get Wyatt out any other way and his heart rate was still posing a concern; it had to be done, but how was I ever going to force my mind get through it?

I looked over and saw my husband, still holding my other hand, crying right alongside me. He knew I had tried so hard all day and that I was scared beyond belief. In that moment, it was as if he felt my pain and helped share it with me. My parents joined the circle that had formed around my bed and began to pray over me and the baby one last time.

All of a sudden, the nausea came back with a vengeance, and I felt like I was on fire. Out of nowhere, I had spiked a fever, and the puking returned. But there was no time for this, because prep work had already begun, and I was being wheeled to the operating room. Pat wasn't allowed into the room until the very last minute, and I laid there, shaking like a leaf, arms in restraints, unable to move anything from my neck down.

I vomited through the entire prep; throw up ran down my cheek and rested in my ear, my hair, and down my neck. The all-too-peppy anesthesiologist didn't see this as a problem and just kept chattering on to me about how a nice alcohol wipe to the forehead was just what

I needed. *No, what I need is for you to unclog my puke-ear and get out of my face for a few minutes,* I thought bitterly. (This was one person I *could* get behind yelling at during labor.)

Eventually, Pat was allowed into the room, and they began the procedure. He held my hand, and I found myself getting dizzier and increasingly convulsive as the minutes ticked by, my entire upper body bucking uncontrollably at the restraints. My dream delivery was to have worship music playing, my mom and husband next to me, and for me to immediately hold my baby as he came out. I pictured myself crying joyful tears and planting loving kisses all over his face.

But my reality was far less lovely. There was no music, just the sounds of steel instruments clanging and doctors exchanging words I didn't understand. My mind felt heavy and my body felt sick and out of my control. And when I finally heard little Wyatt's first cries, I felt nothing. I didn't see him until everything was over, but even then, I couldn't keep my eyes from crossing, and my mind couldn't register that I had just had a baby.

The nurses wheeled me into recovery and shoved Wyatt's little face onto my breast, telling me long instructions of how to feed him as I stared blankly at them, unable to make words that even resembled English come from my mouth. Machines began to beep frantically behind me and doctors ran in and out of the room, injecting more and more medication into my IV.

What is going on? Why all the beeping? Why is this lady telling me to feed my baby when I can't move anything below my neck? Why am I so confused? Apparently, my blood pressure had decided to plummet, and they couldn't get it re-stabilized with the medications. Since I had thrown up so much during delivery, the doctor told me that they had given me literally every single nausea medicine they had in stock at the hospital, none of which made a difference. Not to mention the anti-anxiety med they injected to help me stay calm and the high dosage of Benadryl that probably aided my overall feelings of confusion.

They finally got my BP somewhat stabilized (although since when is 68 over 44 stable?) before sending me upstairs to my new room. It was *then* that I was able to actually meet my new little man without my eyes rolling back into my head. And as I looked at his little face,

I realized that he was perfect. Well, mostly perfect... he had a bit of a cone head from sitting in my pelvis too long earlier that day. As it turns out, Wyatt had been sunny-side up with his head cocked to the side. There was no way he was ever going to come out naturally, and he had the funny-shaped head to prove it!

After four sleepless days and nights, it was finally time to rest.

Or was it? Due to the low blood pressure, the nurse had to come in and check my vitals every thirty minutes, and due to some bleeding issues I was having, the doctor had to come use my uterus as a trampoline every hour, pushing on it as though giving it CPR while I gagged in pain. And at 4:00 a.m., apparently my bleeding was a bit more than they had planned for. I heard a code go out over the loudspeaker as no fewer than twenty nurses and doctors charged into my room to look between my sprawled legs, push on my uterus some more, and discuss with each other my state of "gushing."

I looked over at my personal nurse and told her I was starting to feel like a $2 whore. "Oh no, honey," she said with a smile, "you're worth way more than $2!" Instantly, I knew that we were friends. Once the bleeding stopped, it was time for vitals again and then to feed Wyatt and then to have my uterus jumped on and then vitals and so on and so forth.

It had now been five days with only six hours of sleep. My blood pressure still teetered on and off in the safety zone, and my fever wouldn't go away. Unfortunately my blood count was also rather low and the word "transfusion" was flippantly tossed out there. *Good heavens, this was getting ridiculous*, I'd thought. To top things off, the local anesthesia they gave me refused to wear off, and I couldn't properly use my legs for almost two full days, *and* I had an allergic reaction to all the tape they used on my skin.

Have I mentioned that I will never be doing this again? Despite his obvious exhaustion, Pat stayed by my side for three days straight, refusing to go home to sleep. All he kept telling me was this: "As long as you're here, I'm here. There's no other place I'd be." On that Friday, Pat, Wyatt, and I were finally released from the hospital, a full week after the entire labor began. My parents were in Pennsylvania to help out, and my husband had been a Godsend. In fact, before we left the hospital, Pat looked at me and told me that he loved me more than he ever thought possible and that after going through this experience, he had never felt this close to another human being in his entire life. Even months later, he'd tell me daily that I was doing a good job, that I'm a good mother, that he's proud of me.

I don't think I would've made it through quite as well without him being my faithful cheerleader and backbone. Still tired, still sore, and still kinda sick, I was at least in my own home with helpers all around me as I learned how to be a brand-new mom in a way that I hadn't had the privilege of experiencing before.

Were there tears? Um, yes. Were there a few breakdowns as I stared into the refrigerator at 1:30 a.m. not knowing what to eat, but recognizing the somewhat familiar pangs of hunger jabbing at me as my baby refused to sleep? Yep. But we got through it.

Cameron and Taylor loved their new sibling, and Isaac eventually worked through his feelings of "dethronement" with a little extra love. And then there was Wyatt... he was so big... so long! At birth he weighed eight pounds, ten ounces and was twenty-three inches long. He came out looking like he needed a big, juicy steak. But all I had was milk, so he settled for a liquid diet and continued to grow rather nicely.

For quite some time, I felt incredibly saddened by his delivery. I never got to experience that initial bonding—his skin on mine or take in his tiny little features while planting kisses on his long fingers. I've always felt sad, even cheated that I'd missed out on the best moment of my life.

But as he grew, I finally realized that I didn't miss out on the best moment of my life. Because each day with him is my new best moment. I constantly caress his soft skin as he's cuddled up against my chest. I admire those big, beautiful, brown eyes and memorize the heartwarming tone of his laughter day in and day out. And I have planted no less than a million kisses on those long fingers, tiny toes, and every other kissable inch of his perfect little frame. His conception was a miracle, his delivery was a miracle, and his smile reminds me that each day, is in fact, a miracle, as well.

I became suddenly aware that my life consisted of little more than putting people to sleep. Day in and day out, I assisted in nap schedules, bedtime routines, and midnight soothings. We'd eat our nighttime snacks, we'd say our prayers, and we reminded short people to brush their teeth. We'd then put on footie pajamas, sing all the songs, and read all the books.

Please, don't misunderstand... I'm not complaining!

There are worse things in the world than making sure your family gets their rest. After all, without adequate sleep, there would be no learning in school. And without the learning in school, there would be no graduating from high school. And without the graduation, there would be no college and no job and *no moving out of my house someday*. Trust me when I say that it is with the greatest of pleasures that I'd ensure bedtime happened and that it happened well in our home!

My one question, however, was always this: *When do I sleep*? A question that was especially difficult to answer on one particularly exhausting weekend. With all four kids in tow and a husband who was sick and cranky (in a way that only a husband can truly be), I waded through a sleepless fog, trying to break up sibling spats and clean up toddler messes and change umpteen diapers. But despite my best efforts, it was apparent that naps were in order—*for all of them*.

But you can't call them "naps" and get the result you want. Oh no, not with the big ones! This was not my first rodeo, friends. This was the time to pull out the psychology degree and convince the children to take a nap without them knowing they'd been fooled into sleeping. Phrases like, "You don't have to take a nap or anything, gosh, no! Just take the tablet to your room and play real quietly, maybe on your bed, so that I can get the babies to sleep."

Meanwhile, I'd spray the house with lavender-scented Febreeze and let "Rock-a-Bye Baby" play loudly over the baby monitor. Ten minutes later, the big kids and husband were down for the count, and it was just me and the little ones left.

Getting all the other kids to sleep is a walk in the park, however, compared to the toddler. You see, Isaac had developed an internal clock that told him it was nap time, yet that same internal clock continually fought with his internal need to *not sleep... ever.* But that weekend, I chose to use a little more creativity than normal.

Just as the terror of Sleepy Isaac was in full force, I laid down on his big boy bed and cuddled up with one of his stuffed animals. When Isaac poked my face, I pretended to snore. This made him laugh hysterically and, unfortunately, caused him to poke my face repeatedly and with increasing firmness. I learned quickly to tone back the snoring so that he would get bored, which he did.

I then deliberately rolled away from him and curled up once again. The sound of small feet climbing onto his truck to get onto the bed with me was heard, and moments later, I felt his warm breath as he whispered into my ear, "Mama?" I whispered back that Mama was so sleepy and she needed a tuck-in. I asked him to get me the blanket, which he did. I asked him to cover me up, which he did. I asked him to kiss me good night, which he did. He kissed my lips, my cheeks, my hair, my leg, and my elbow. I then asked him to read me a story. He pulled his book over and said his 1-2-3s, which are part of a different book entirely, but I didn't argue. And when I felt we had reached a level of calmness needed for the final stage, I swooped in with the big guns.

"Isaac, come cuddle Mama to put her to sleep, okay?" And that little guy didn't even know what hit him. He cuddled up to me and patted my back over and over, saying, "A'night, Mama. A'night, Mama." I had my eyes closed, but I could hear the yawn, that sweet baby yawn that makes getting tired sound so amazing. His head began to lower onto my shoulder, and I knew it was only a matter of seconds before I had won.

With one final motion, Isaac crawled onto my chest, laid down, and looked at me with heavy, sleepy eyes... and then he farted. Long and loud. Smiling sleepily, he whispered, "I poopin'." Then, he put his head on my shoulder and instantly fell asleep. I laid there for a while, trapped, holding my breath as long as I could before the need for air overtook me. And then I realized what had happened. I had been dutch-ovened, toddler style. It was he who had won the battle, not I.

Luckily, Wyatt was still too young to win battles with this mama. Once I was able to weasel my way out from underneath Isaac, I took advantage of Wyatt's need to nurse, knowing that he would be out cold after ten minutes. And naturally, I was right. That doesn't mean that he didn't get his win later that night when he and Isaac tag-teamed me by waking up seven times in seven hours. Seven in seven.

There was one point when I'd put a baby down and look at the clock only to realize that I had slept for a mere four minutes before the next baby woke up wailing. And thanks to the Benadryled Hubs, I was on duty all night. Well, all except for the fifth time. The fifth time involved me punching him in the back twice and whisper- yelling, "No! I won't do it again! *You! Your turn!*" And he did, waking up the other baby as he went.

It was a magical night.

But this I can say, no sarcasm involved, is that one of the brightest and most beautifulest gems in my motherhood crown was rocking my babies to sleep each night. There is nothing more peaceful and delicious than smelling that freshly-bathed aroma while they rested their chubby cheeks on my chest and gazed up with droopy eyelids in one last attempt to stay awake. I *loved* that look. It reminded me that these little ones just wanted assurance that Mama was there – that they were safe – before letting go and sleeping peacefully, like only a baby can.

It was actually a privilege each night to lull them into the best sleep that they'll ever have in their lives. A sleep that is Ambien-free, stress-free, nightmare-free, worry-free, and carefree. In a few short years, they will be bogged down with homework, drama with friends, heartaches, jobs, bills, household chores, and babies of their own that will need their help to fall asleep at night. And in that moment of rocking their own freshly-bathed cherubs to sleep, they will remember me, just as your babies will remember you. And all our sleepless nights will finally be worth their weight in gold.

Something happens to your baby when he turns one. It may be chemical, it may be hormonal, it may be possession... but whatever it is, it has the power to change your once precious little lamb into a general from the Third Reich.

How do I know this devastation to be true? Simple. I have a one-year-old. And for 364 days, he was my shining joy, my prize, my little baby love. At day 365, the sweetness melted away, and it was replaced by ear-piercing screams and aggression to the fullest degree. He'd punch, pinch, kick, jab, slap, bite, and claw. It's as if my baby had taken on the soul of a wild jaguar and was circling his prey (*me*) before finally going in for the kill.

When I went to the store, I'd see the stares. I saw other people eyeing my bruises and noticing my scratched skin. They couldn't ignore the drops of blood crusted around my previously bleeding nose nor the lump already forming on my skull where I was head-butted just minutes before. I knew what they were wondering as they eyed my husband with disdain. Little did they know that the real culprit was the angelic little cherub in the cart, chattering away and waving "bye-bye" at passersby, smiling a toothy grin, soaking up all the "Aws" he could get. Yes. My abuser was thirty-two-inches-tall, had six teeth, and couldn't walk independently.

It was the perfect cover.

Prior to turning one, Wyatt followed me from room to room, cooing at my feet as he investigated the floor, contents of cupboards, and whatever else happened to be within reach. His gentle exploration was always accompanied by sing-song tones and baby gurgles—the sounds that could make your ovaries ache with the sheer cuteness of it all.

And then there was his first birthday—it was the single moment, the terrifying fulcrum of change. From that point on, I lived on pins and needles as I wrangled my little terror from room to room, him flailing and throwing himself back from my arms, me desperately trying to keep my child from requiring a cranial operation before he turned two.

If he wanted up, it's only until I'd pick him up and he realized that he actually wanted down. If he wanted in a cupboard, it's only to chuck the cupboard's entire content across the room, followed by finger pinches in the drawer, climbing into the dishwasher, putting toy cars in the toilet, unrolling all of the toilet paper, growling at the vacuum cleaner, chewing on the computer cable, putting Cheerios down his diaper, biting the dog, pulling all things off the table via the corner of the table cloth, eating the puppy food, screaming because he was angry, screaming because he was tired, screaming because he was hungry, because he was teething, because he was happy or he was itchy or sick or because the dog wouldn't play with him or because he was trying to make me lose my mind!

Gone are the days of watching my baby sleep peacefully in my arms. Gone are the cuddles and the precious baby coos. My child's soothing baby chatter began to take on a harsh sound as he tried his tongue at new consonants. Then he just sounded German—a short, mean German baby—raising his hand to smite me down like a true tyrant.

I'd actually flinch. I'd flinch and shudder when he'd raise his hand. I learned that a finger to the eye hurts for hours and a slap to the nose will bring me to my knees. But when I tell him "No!" in my firmest of tones, he'd reply with shrieks of laughter, finding my attempt at control simply hilarious. One-year-old feels too young to start a strict disciplinary regime, but apparently, my life depended on it. Desperate times called for desperate measures. However, let me tell you, friends, that Little Man was good. After he'd smack me repeatedly, I'd put him down and give him a light tap on the hand as I mustered a firm "No, no!" And then he'd produce the lip. That bottom portion of his mouth that would cause him to look like the saddest most misunderstood baby ever to have lived. And it's only seconds before the gut- wrenching tears would stream from his horrified eyes, and I'd be forced to blow in his face to help him catch his breath. How could I? Worst Mama of the Year awards flashed through my mind. Subsequently, like any mother wanting to comfort her sweet little angel, I'd pick him up and pull him to my chest, whispering gentle shushes in his ear.

At which point he'd immediately stop crying and begin to giggle as he'd pinch my neck skin. It turned into some sort of twisted game, and I was forced to play because I'm the mama and the trainer of the children. It's up to me to show him that there is a gentler way. A peaceful way. A way that doesn't end in bloodshed (quite specifically, *mine!*).

Yes. My sweet baby had turned into a German tyrant. And I love him to pieces. So, here's hoping that the *terrible twos* are a step in the right direction!

Nonetheless, before having children, I had ideas of what motherhood would look like. I would do the right things, say the right things, and I would always know what the best thing for my children would be.

Life didn't go as planned. When I wasn't able to conceive and we chose to foster Cameron and Taylor, I missed the baby stage entirely. We got our two beautiful children, but we lacked that crucial bonding time in the beginning of their lives. I didn't get to rock them to sleep, cuddle them in my arms, give them their first baths, or watch their first steps. No, when we adopted our older two, they were already little people. There was the occasional butt wiping and helping them undo the buttons on the tough shirts, but overall, they came pre-grown.

And then, when my husband and I found out that the kids' bio mom was pregnant with Isaac, we were hesitant to bring him into our home. After all, we had gone from no kids to two kids overnight, and the thought of adding a baby to the mix just a few months later, a baby that we knew was going to be born addicted to drugs, well... that just sounded like lunacy.

But since we were already crazy, lunacy sounded like a fantastic way to round out our family. We brought Isaac home from the hospital, and he was with us through all of his baby stages. We did get to give him his first bath, and we cuddled him in our arms, rocked him to sleep, and saw his first steps.

But even though I was there for it all, Isaac was *Pat's baby*. My husband was the mother and the father for that first year. He stayed home with Isaac because his job allowed him to. He did most of the feedings, most of the baths, most of the cuddles. By the time I got home, helped Cameron and Taylor with homework, cooked dinner, and cleaned up the house, I got to spend a couple of hours with Isaac, half of which he slept through. I felt similar to a well-liked babysitter, not like a full-fledged mama.

Perhaps losing Isaac made conceiving Wyatt all the more precious. This was the first time I would know what it was like to have a baby grow inside of me. To watch my belly change shape with each roll and kick. To feel my body physically respond to the life inside of me. This was my chance to truly bond with a child in a way that I hadn't been able to before.

But even though I was given such an amazing blessing, a difficult pregnancy often hampered those "good feelings" I was hoping for. I held on to the day of delivery, knowing that his arrival was going to be the best moment ever– the moment I would be able to push him into this world and hold him close to my chest for those first few precious minutes of his life. I could hardly wait.

Well, we all know how that turned out! I was completely aware that those special moments to bond were quickly slipping through my fingers. I felt cheated. This was finally my chance to bond with a child, and all I had to show for it was a whole lot of sickness and very few "good feelings." But nursing—that was going to be my way to attach with my new son. That would be the way I would finally get to connect with him!

Except guess what? Breastfeeding completely sucked! For six weeks, all I did was cry. All he did was cry. We cried and I was in pain and I was constantly worried about my milk supply and my pump and my nipples and my engorgement. I couldn't leave the house. I couldn't feel happy. I couldn't figure out what I was doing wrong. No one had prepared me for it to suck so badly.

Then, after a good two months of our nursing schedule and all of its horribleness, something amazing happened. Nursing stopped being wretched. I stopped feeling constant pain. My nipples stopped feeling like they were being ripped from my body by a tiny beaver. I stopped shooting milk across the room because of engorgement. All of a sudden, what had been so hard for so long began to feel easy. Natural. *Connected.*

Pretty soon I found myself enjoying that alone time with my baby and not dreading it. Those moments were ours and no one else's. So many people were all about public nursing and fighting tooth and nail for that "right." But to be honest, I wanted our moments to be private. I loved to stare into his eyes and rub his tiny fingers as he fed – to caress his cheek and hear him giggle, producing little milk bubbles in the corners of his mouth as he did. I loved to watch him fall asleep against my chest and to be the one who could comfort him better than anyone else. *I liked being his one and only, if even just for a time.*

It was my plan to nurse him until he was one year old. When he turned one, I knew that he could drink whole milk and that he would have several teeth; he was going to be turning into a toddler, and it was my choice to pull the boob-plug on him at that time.

And then his first birthday came and went. Little man hated cow's milk with a passion, even with breast milk, almond milk, or chocolate milk mixed in. The doctor said to give it a few weeks, but that I could always keep nursing in the meantime. I jumped at the opportunity in a way that I never thought I would.

When I was younger, before having these little people in my life, remember those preconceived notions I said that I had? Yeah, I thought people who nursed past one year were kind of... *icky.* Now, after knowing how sweet those times of being near my little one was, knowing that in a few short months he would no longer be a baby, that he wouldn't need me in the same way anymore... Friends, I struggled letting go of those moments. It was not icky. It was not inappropriate. What it was, I quickly found, was grief.

Pat and I had decided that we weren't going to try for more children. We had two older kids, a toddler on the weekends, and a full-time baby. Quite frankly, we didn't have the car space! Whereas a lot of mamas can stop nursing at a year and feel like they're regaining their booby freedom, I felt that I was saying good-bye to the one pleasant bonding experience I've been able to have with just the one child I was able to have it with. Other mothers would start planning for their next child, and instead, I was saying good-bye to babies forever, saying good-bye to an entire stage in my life. The stage that I wanted for so long was over in an instant.

Point your fingers, tell me I'm being crazy, look at me with judgment if you must. But I'm guessing that I'm not the only mama out there that has grieved the ending of their baby era. I'm aware that I could've kept nursing if I'd wanted to, but I do feel that it was time. At thirteen and a half months, it was time for him, and it was time for me. "You'll know when it's right," is the phrase I'd heard over and over. And it's true.

I know that I'll always be his mama. And I know that my kids will always need me and love me. But with a fond farewell and tears in my eyes, I said a sorrowful good-bye to breastfeeding.

Wyatt loved Isaac. They shared a special bond. Close in age, similar in height, they shared their toys, fought over snacks, and enjoyed snuggling together in a chair while looking at the pictures in a train book. And when Isaac was all of a sudden gone, Wyatt couldn't forget that he was missing such a special person in his life.

Once he could start making words, Wyatt would walk to all the pictures of Isaac in our house, point, and say "Izey!" with a look of glee on his face. And once he realized that pushing the home button on my iPhone brought up Isaac's picture from our last weekend with him, Wyatt would push it over and over and over, just to say Isaac's name with the same amount of happiness and surprise each time.

As we neared Wyatt's second birthday, six months after our last moments with Isaac, there were times when Wyatt didn't seem to remember his name without prompting. And as he grows bigger, Wyatt now wears many of the outfits that were worn by Isaac just a few months prior. Despite the pain I feel when I relive those moments, I religiously show Wyatt his brother's pictures. I show him the videos, and we look through the scrapbooks.

Wyatt doesn't seem to mind when I cry, and I find great comfort as the recognition brightens his face with each picture. There are still some songs that I can't sing to Wyatt... still some books I can't make it through. There are even some outfits that I will never be able to put Wyatt in. But I've learned to make peace with those things.

Instead of keeping those memories of Isaac held hostage in my mind, creating an emotional shrine to be relived each and every day, I chose to allow myself a few items, a few memories that would be special. They would be just mine and Isaac's. It was my way to keep Wyatt's memory of Isaac alive without sending me into a daily tailspin of tears and panic attacks.

My husband, being a wonderful provider for our family, has given me the ability to work part-time for our church. It's the best job in the world. I love what I do, and I love that I can do most of it in the presence of my children. Because spending my day-to-day moments with Wyatt helps my heart heal. It gives me a sense of peace that is a struggle to find amidst anxiety.

Wyatt has taught me to love again. After a loss so great, I feared that my heart would never be whole enough to love fully, to love in the same way. But Wyatt challenges me daily, with his hugs, his new words, and his smile, to not remain in the place of grief. He reminds me to get up each day and love all over again. Even when it's hard, even when I'm tired, even when all my kids are cranky, and I miss Isaac terribly.

Because in that sadness, I found joy. I am *proud* of myself for making it through all the difficulties of this motherhood thing, knowing that by grace, I'll also make it through the challenges that lie ahead. Despite the RAD, the behaviors, the loss, and the wretched labor, I have survived. My striving for sanity is a daily one, and quite often, it leads me down a road that I never would've chosen—a road that has been filled with more pain than any sane person would seek of their own free will. But our family has learned how to love, and so I count it all blessed.

Four sets of little hands will grasp mine and Pat's as we walk together into our next stage of life. So much thanks for this time. So much love for them all. So much still left to come. Still, I rise. Still, I love. Because sometimes Hope means learning how to love from the very ones you're supposed to teach love to. I may be raising my children, but it is, in fact, my children who have raised me.

AUTHOR'S NOTE

If you've been touched by our story—if any part of our lives has resonated with yours—then this is what I ask of you.

Fight. Fight for the children that are in your local towns. The ones that are being abused, neglected, exposed to drugs and domestic violence. These children, they don't have a voice. When they cry out, no one is there to listen. But in each city of each state, there are untold amounts of these young ones who have very bleak futures because our child welfare system cannot possibly take them all.

So, what can you do? First of all, you can assess your own talents and giftings. What is God calling you to do? Maybe you are willing to be a foster parent. Perhaps you have the space to take on sibling groups in order to keep these children together during an incredibly traumatic time of life. Maybe you are capable of taking on the babies that are born addicted to drugs or with fetal alcohol syndrome. Or you may have the desire to take on older children when their behavior has turned others away—these are the ones that were left for too long without help.

But they are not too far gone.

Perhaps you are part of a church or a charitable organization that can wrap around current foster and adoptive families. You can be a shoulder to cry on, a prayer warrior, a babysitter, a chauffeur, a cook, or a laundry doer! I promise, whatever you can do to help, it will not go unnoticed or unappreciated. You may be the difference for a parent's sanity in that particular day.

Advocate. If there is a word that I can stress the most, it is this. So much of our child welfare system is left up to local government. Very little of it is controlled federally. So, if you have a political bone in your body, or if you're willing to learn, then research your local legislation and statistics regarding foster care, funding for child abuse investigations, and what your county actually defines as "child abuse".

If you take the time to seek out this information, you will be amazed at what actually qualifies as abuse and what is just acceptable. Research trauma in children who are exposed do drugs and alcohol and perpetual neglect – bring these to your local state representatives. Share the information on social media . Go to your town meetings and refuse to be silenced.

Because once we stop speaking, the children stop hoping.

There will be no one left to inspire change. No one will advocate for them. And the cycle will continue for generations to come. It is no longer an option to turn our heads to the children of our nation. If it takes a village, then we are all responsible to do our parts.

What will you do?

CPSIA information can be obtained
at www.ICGtesting.com
Printed in the USA
LVOW10s1436230517

535498LV00019B/801/P